Gentle Galilean Glories:
The Tender Teachings of Jesus

Dwayne Cole

Parson's Porch Books
www.parsonsporchbooks.com

Gentle Galilean Glories: The Tender Teachings of Jesus
ISBN: Softcover 978-1-949888-69-0
Copyright © 2019 by Dwayne Cole

All rights reserved. No part of this book may be reproduced or transmitted in any form or by any means, electronic or mechanical, including photocopying, recording, or by any information storage and retrieval system, without permission in writing from the publisher.

Gentle Galilean Glories

Contents

Preface 7
Introduction 13
Chapter One 25
   God as Creative-Relational Loving Kindness
Chapter Two 31
   Jesus Self-Actualized
   The Creative Relational Loving Kindness of God
Chapter Three 39
   Gentle Galilean Glories of Jesus
Chapter Four 51
   Glory of God In The Gentle Teachings Of Jesus: A Vision of Reality
Chapter Five 66
   Jesus' Gentle Teachings
Chapter Six 75
   Gentle Teaching: Agape
Chapter Seven 81
   Gentle Teaching: Peace
Chapter Eight 87
   Gentle Parables
Chapter Nine 93
   Gentle Actions Of Jesus
Chapter Ten 99
   Gentle Invitations
Chapter Eleven 106
   The Place Of Miracles In Jesus' Gentle Teachings
Chapter Twelve 113
   Cross And Resurrection
Chapter Thirteen 120
   Is there Love On a Cosmic Level?
Chapter Fourteen 123
   Spirit
Chapter Fifteen 128
   Trinity---The Way God Relates To Us

Chapter Sixteen 135
  The Role Of The Church In Jesus' Gentle TeachingsWhat Makes A Church Effective?
Chapter Seventeen 139
  Worship In The Gentle Teachings Of Jesus
Chapter Eighteen 147
  The Place Of Prayer In Jesus' Gentle Teachings
Chapter Nineteen 159
  The Place Of Prayers In Healing
Chapter Twenty 163
  The Place Of Forgiveness In Healing
Chapter Twenty-One 168
  The Role of Ethics in Theology
Chapter Twenty-Two 171
  Saving The Environment
Conclusion 178
  An Unrealized Dream
Glossary Of Terms 181
Appendix A 182
  Jesus And God Consciousness
Appendix B 185
  New Testament Churches Living The Gentle Teachings
Appendix C 188
  The Influence Of Psychology And Consciousness In Interpreting The Gentle Teachings Of Jesus
Appendix D 193
  The Search For The Historical Jesus
Appendix E 196
  My Process Hermeneutic: The Gentle Teachings of Jesus
Appendix F 199
  Kindness As A Trinitarian Metaphor
Bibliography 202

Preface

"Words lead to deeds…. They prepare the soul, make it ready, and move it to tenderness." Saint Teresa.

God's *"tenderness is directed towards each actual occasion, as it arises."* Alfred North Whitehead, *Process and Reality*, p. 105.

    In the words above Saint Teresa and Alfred North Whitehead captured the attraction of the tender teachings of Jesus as an expression of God's tenderness. Jesus' words acted tenderness and his deeds spoke tenderness. In a sense this book on the gentle life and tender teachings of Jesus is an exposition of these two quotes. It is prayerfully presented as a step in rekindling the vision of Jesus' transforming gentle teachings.

    To rekindle the flame of faith and re-energize the vision of world transformation we must have a clear vision of how God relates to the world and to all people. It requires thinking Christians who recover the role of theology as transformation. Theology is simply God (θεος) words (λογος) that help us to understand the meaning of God and how God relates to the world in transforming loving kindness And it is precisely to this age of radical evil, of terrorist attacks, ethnic cleansings, mass starvation, epidemic diseases, and gun violence in our schools that Jesus' gentle teachings bring a renewed vision of how God is in our lives and in our world in saving ways that give courageous hope.[1]

---

[1] There is no denying the need for Jesus' tender teachings today. Ours is an age of unspeakable violence. The terrible fact is that more people were killed by violent means in the twentieth century---roughly 185 million—than in all previous centuries combined. Pope John Paul II described our century as the "culture of death." Some biblical scholars writing in this time of violence have sought to turn Jesus into a zealot who sought the radical overthrow of ruling powers. This book, *Gentle Galilean Glories: The Tender Teachings of Jesus,* offers a different perspective and balance to this tendency. Christians around the world are increasingly becoming victims of violence. The Center for the study of global Christianity in the United States estimates that 100,000 Christians are targeted and die because of their faith every year, eleven every hour. Pakistani churches are burned and worshippers regularly slaughtered. Nigeria and Egypt have recently seen the worst anti-Christian violence than has been seen in the last seven centuries. Persecution is increasing in China and North Korea. Among the worst places that Christians are persecuted are Somalia, Iraq, Iran, Syria, Afghanistan, Saudi Arabia, and Yemen. According to the Pew Research Center, Christians are the

Jesus' tender teachings actualize God's aims and purposes for all creation. They transport us back to beginning times and enable us to glance forward to end times. Jesus learned to incorporate each moment of his life in an experience of God's life and his consciousness of God's presence linked the past action of God in the prophets to his ministry that created a vision for the future. That union was a fusion of human and divine loving kindness. Thus in Jesus' words and actions we see and feel God acting. Past, present, and future become a unity bound up in love. Loving kindness is a uniting force. Staying power resides in these tender teachings. **Simple acts of loving kindness to our self, our family, and to all living things are the most hopeful and powerful transformers in the world.**

The words and actions of Jesus open a window on gentle Galilean glories; and, if we take time to look and listen, we see and hear Jesus saying to his followers, "Consider the birds of the sky. They don't plant or harvest. They don't store grain in barns. Yet, God takes care of them." Then using these beautiful biophilic (love of life) nature images, Jesus says to those who have left all to follow him, "God will take care of you."[2]

Jesus followed the saying about birds with another gentle biophilic saying, "Consider how the flowers of the field grow. They don't work hard for their clothes. But I tell you that not even Solomon with all of his wealth was as well clothed. Look at their beauty. God gives beauty to everything that grows."[3]

> Seeing and hearing birds, the brain makes melodic music.
> Seeing and smelling flowers, the soul is enraptured.
> Considering God's care for us…
> We believe and trust.

---

most persecuted religious group in the world. My book, *The Book of Revelation: Jesus' Kindness Transforms Suffering,* addresses how kindness overcomes violence and gives a new vision of hope.

[2] biophilic is the transliteration of two Greek words I find in the New Testament, βιος-life , φιλια-love. Could also use ζωη-life, φιλια-love, for βιος and ζωη are synonymous in New Testament. Biophilia is a theory popularized by E.O. Wilson, Professor of Science at Harvard University, that we as humans have an innate love of life, of all of nature, as a result of our evolutionary history. Humans prefer to live in natural environs, near mountains, streams, or lakes. This theory has had great impact in many fields, most notably among environmentalists and architecture. Frank Lloyd Wright's house, Falling Waters, is a prime example of biophilic design. I have found Wilson's biophilic theory helpful in understanding Jesus' teachings and why they have had appeal through the centuries. Since Wilson's term, biophilia, is a known theory, I will use it instead of zoephilia that I have coined to express the same truth.

[3] Matthew 6:25-34.

The Greek verb Jesus used in these nature images, εμβλεψατε, translated as "consider" can also be translated as "an entreaty or plea to look at intently," "see into," or "contemplate" these gentle teachings. When I take time to hold these gentle words in my hands and heart, to taste and see their goodness and beauty, I find my search for meaning, the central search for every person, being fulfilled; and I am most fully alive, for to see is to take part in the abundant life Jesus offers.[4]

In these gentle teachings of Jesus, εμβλεψατε is joined with τρεφει, translated as "take care" or "feed". As used by Jesus it means God your Father who cares for the birds and flowers will take care of you. Even though Jesus used the name, Father, he balanced this masculine image with the verb, τρεφει, which carries the meaning of being fed at the breast, as a mother nurtures her child. Thus, the meaning is your God who is like a kind Father and a nurturing Mother will take care of you.[5]

The Greek word, τρεφει, is used in the same saying with psyche, the Greek word for life or soul. I have joined them to form the word, psychetrophic; and I have given it the meaning, feeding or nourishing the soul. Translators and commentators of the Gospels have missed the importance of finding these two Greek words in Jesus' Gentle Galilean Glories given by a peripatetic teacher, one teaching while walking in nature, along the Sea of Galilee among the beauty of flowers and birds. It is correct to say, "God will take care of you as God cares for the birds and the flowers, by providing you with physical food." God's good creation does provide food, but we have to plant, cultivate, and gather the food. Jesus certainly wanted all to have adequate food. The one miracle found in all four Gospels is the feeding of the hungry crowds. But Jesus also saw that one does not live by physical bread alone. He sought to give both physical and spiritual food. As one must work for physical food, so we are to seek spiritual food. Thus, the deeper meaning of these biophilic and psychetrophic teachings is that God will nourish our souls as we practice the presence of God, as we fill our minds with beauty, truth, goodness, and love.[6]

The foundation stone of these gentle teachings can be found in the wisdom of Job in the Old Testament. Jesus knew his sacred scriptures and they shine through his gentle teachings. In Job we find these gems: "When times get bad, people cry out for help. They cry for relief from being kicked around, but never give God a thought when things go well. Then God sets

---

[4] John 10:10.

[5] In my prayers in worship I often teach this gender sensitive way of referring to God with this sentence: "Loving God: we are grateful that we have come to know you to be **like** a kind Father and nurturing Mother."

[6] See the devotional classic, *Practicing the Presence of God* by Brother Lawrence.

out the entire creation as a classroom and puts spontaneous songs in their hearts, using birds to teach wisdom" (Based on Job 35:9ff.). "If you want to learn go and ask the birds and flowers. They can tell you what God has done. Every living creature is in God's hands."[7]

Perhaps the Song of Solomon also provided inspiration for Jesus: "For lo, the winter is past, the rain is over and gone; the flowers appear on the earth; the time of the singing of birds is come, and the voice of the turtledove is heard."[8]

Another foundation stone for understanding Jesus' gentle teachings is what has been called the Great Commandment of Jesus. In an old but new commandment, Jesus summed up the Old Testament relationship of God and persons and persons with each other in two sentences: "love God with all your heart, soul, strength, and mind; and love your neighbor as you love yourself." This commandment was taken from Jesus' sacred Scriptures, the Old Testament, with one new word: Jesus added "mind".

We once interpreted this as a head and heart commandment. Keeping a balance of head and heart in worship and service has always been difficult. New brain and body research is giving us deeper insights. Diane Ackerman wrote: "People think of the mind as being located in the head, but the latest findings in physiology suggest that the mind doesn't really dwell in the brain alone but travels the whole body on caravans of enzymes, busily making sense of the compound wonders we catalogue as touch, taste, smell, hearing, vision."[9] The list of senses is growing every day, with new ones like hunger, thirst, empty stomach, and low blood sugar levels. We might add worship, prayer, and faith to this list, if we want to understand Jesus' gentle teachings.

We now have new insights into the implication of Jesus adding to this commandment that we should love God and each other with our minds, bringing all of our expanded senses to this amazing commandment. Jesus certainly used all the senses in his gentle teachings as a peripatetic teacher. In the springtime parts of Galilee were like a beautiful garden filled with fragrant flowers, insects, and birds. Walking with his disciples while teaching about the glory of God realities,[10] Jesus' parables are filled with illustrations from

---

[7] Base on Job 12:17ff.
[8] Song of Solomon 2:11-12.
[9] Diane Ackerman. *A Natural History of the Senses*. New York: Random House, 1990, p. xix.
[10] Glory of God is one of the phrases I use for the Kingdom of God in the teachings of Jesus. The word, Kingdom, has negative connotations for many today. It implies ruling with coercise power. The gentle teachings of Jesus reveal more the persuasive luring influence of God in our lives. See chapter four for Kingdom of God.

nature as can be seen in the sayings above about birds and flowers and in his many parables like the sower of seeds.

To harness the beauty and goodness of nature for our physical, psychological, social, and spiritual health, we need the gentle agapetrophic (agape and troph are used separately in Jesus' gentle teachings. I have joined them and given them the meaning ---love nurturing) teachings of Jesus. Loving kindness has the power to re-awaken wonder and restore the psyche, and a restored psyche leads to restored physical health (somatrophic, body nurturing). To see, in the sense as used above leads to faith, and to experience fuller transformation to wholeness. The goal of this book is to see in the gentle Galilean glories of Jesus a path to truth, beauty, goodness, adventure, peace, and kindness that transforms. I invite you to see with eyes of faith, take the pulse of the universe, and find that all is well. Will you taste and see these biophilic and psychetrophic teachings?[11]

---

[11] The quotes at the beginning of many of the following chapters that are not cited as Scripture or other authors should be seen as my quotes that have evolved from my lifetime of living with the gentle teachings of Jesus.

Introduction

When one tugs at the love words in the gentle teachings of Jesus, one finds them attached to the heart of God.

The Greek word, αγαπη, in noun and verb form, is the most common Greek word in the New Testament for love, occurring two hundred and fifty-eight times.[12] Agape has become an English word and is recognized by most Christians. Agape is self-giving love--the kind of love Jesus self-actualized in his gentle Galilean glories. It is love at whatever the cost---the greatest expression being Jesus' sacrificial service and death on the cross. Agape is gift love that calls for a response; however, it is not something we earn or merit by our being faithful.

Jesus gave concreteness to love in his gentle teachings and actions. The agape commandment is the heart beat of all Jesus' gentle Galilean glories and the grammar of his theology. Theology is simply words about God (Θεος, God, and λογος, word) that help us to understand the meaning of God and how God relates to the world in transforming love. This relational view of theology affirms that we write about God from our personal experience and the way we view the world.

In his book, *Modes of Thought*, Whitehead wrote, "The character of the lecturer arises from the molding it receives from the social circumstances of his whole life. These social circumstances depend on the historic epoch, and this epoch is derivative from the evolution of life on this planet. Life on this planet depends on the order observed throughout the spatio-temporal stellar system, as disclosed in our experience."[13]

Recognizing that all things are inter-connected, I am sharing this personal information in this introductory chapter for two reasons. First, it is a personal example of the way the gentle teachings of Jesus slowly but surely transform our lives. Second, as Whitehead affirmed, we write from our personal experience and the way we view the world. I like to know the background of writers when I am reading their book. So, let me briefly tell you how I came to focus on the gentle teachings of Jesus based on agape.

I was raised on a farm in a large loving family of thirteen children with a kind father and gentle mother. As the eighth child with six brothers and six sisters, I grew up knowing the love and support of both older and younger brothers and sisters. My mother wanted to be a school teacher, but she did not have the opportunity of going to college to earn a degree. Thus, she could not teach in the little red school house we attended. Yet, she had

---

[12] See chapter six of this book for a fuller treatment of agape.
[13] Alfred North Whitehead, *Modes of Thought*, New York: The Free Press, 1968, p. 87.

her own school, her own classroom, in our home. The Bible was the main book. One of my fondest memories is of her reading the Bible to us at night.

From birth to age eighteen I was part of a family oriented rural Church that nurtured me in the Christian faith. Our social life centered in the activities of that Church. We had Bible study for all ages for an hour before Sunday morning worship and we had one-hour church training sessions that focused on our Christian beliefs and practices before Sunday evening worship. We seldom missed any of those and other activities that consisted of many social events.

While studying to be a public school music teacher in college, I felt called to become a minister, and I changed my major focus of study to religion. I served as pastor of a mission Church with about 100 members while a senior in college and for a year after graduation, saving money to go to seminary. I also taught high school English and French during that year (1963-64).[14]

During my time at seminary (1964-73) I served two different Churches as pastor and developed a deeper interest in New Testament studies, focusing on the four Gospels, Matthew, Mark, Luke, and John, also the Epistles of John, and Revelation. After receiving the Master of Divinity degree (a three-year graduate level program) and a Master of Theology degree (one-year program with written thesis), I entered the Ph.D. program, majoring in New Testament studies with an emphasis in Greek. In the next four years of graduate study I translated much of the Greek New Testament into English and held each word in my hand, parsing the verbs and declining the nouns. The Greek words for love and gentleness were especially meaningful to me, and these words became the grammar of my theology. My mentor and doctoral supervisor for my Greek studies was Dr. Frank Stagg, who was a gentle but tough teacher who lived and breathed the Greek New Testament. After completing my graduate studies, I served two churches from 1973-85 as Senior Minister and taught college and seminary level courses as an adjunct professor.

From 1965-85, I attended annual Southern Baptist Conventions (representing 13 million members) that dealt with serious theological and social issues. These fundamentalist debates on the Bible's authority and inspiration became more heated in the decade of the 80's, and I found myself asking, "What do the gentle teachings of Jesus have to say about these issues?" It seemed to me that many of the church leaders had skipped over the gentle teachings of Jesus, grounded in inclusive love (agape) and wrapped

---

[14] I was a member of the Southern Baptist denomination and they did not require college and seminary training before ordination. Therefore, I could be ordained and serve as minister as a senior in college. I became a Cumberland Presbyterian minister of word and sacrament in 1992.

in kindness, for the legalism of Paul and the ways of Caesar---the ways of power, politics, and big business models. In the local churches I sensed that members were ceasing to think theologically, i.e., to think seriously about important matters, and were therefore becoming fragmented over social concerns rather than finding solutions through the eyes and heart of agape.

By 1985, at the age of 45, experiencing drastic changes in the religious denomination that had nurtured me and some mid-life crisis due to serving as a minister in churches with multiple staffs for 25 years, I decided that I no longer wanted to be a Southern Baptist minister.[15] I felt it was almost impossible to be the senior minister of a Church and meet all the daily needs of 1200 members not including extended family and circle of friends, so I resigned from my Church, identifying with Einstein's remark, I am a religious unbeliever.

For the next seven years, I built houses as a general contractor.[16] While building I continued in Church, helping my wife, a children's Bible curriculum specialist at the Baptist Sunday School Board in Nashville, Tennessee, teach little children in Sunday School. I made well over a million dollars in five years and lost it all in one year due to my lack of money management skills and I would like to think it was also due to the national building collapse, one of the largest in our nation's history. The Savings and Loans Bank where I financed my homes failed and went into receivership. Resolution Trust, formed by the federal government to rescue failed Savings and Loans, stepped in and called my loans. Like about half of my building associates whose loans were also called, my houses were sold on the court house steps at a fraction of their worth, and I was sent a bill for the balance. For example, a house that cost me $600,000 dollars to build was sold for $300,000. I was responsible for the difference. I had a total of four houses that went into receivership and sold at a great loss. My attorney friends from the churches I served advised me to declare bankruptcy at the end of that decade of the eighties.

I found myself broken and hurting, like many of my business friends. We rode the upswing cycle of building in Nashville, Tennessee and got

---

[15] This is not intended as a judgment of Southern Baptist. I am grateful for the nurturing I received and the nurturing of my family who are mainly still affiliated with Southern Baptist Churches. Baptists continue to do wonderful work. I was moving and growing in other directions.

[16] Not as big a change as it seems. I studied for the license like it was a graduate level course. On the farm we built many of our buildings. I took high school shop for four years learning about tools and construction. In the Churches I served we were always building sanctuaries and educational buildings. The Church I served in Virginia built a beautiful new sanctuary in the shape of a Greek cross and the one in Brentwood, Tennessee built a large multi –purpose family life center. In these projects I worked with banks on loans and architects with building plans.

trapped when the bubble burst. Some of my building friends turned to alcohol and their families crumbled and fell apart.

I still had my loving family and my wife, Beth, had a good job at the Baptist Sunday School Board. Beth and I met in a Greek class at the seminary and we were married at the end of that first year. She was my rock and stabilizing force during this difficult stretch. My church friends were supportive and gave me renovation jobs, and life moved on. Beth and I focused on getting our daughter and son through Georgetown University and into graduate schools where our daughter received an M.D. degree in family medicine from the University of Colorado, at Denver and our son received a Ph. D. in economics at Berkeley. Their stability and maturity were a source of strength for me.

During my time of brokenness, I **returned** to the gentle teachings of Jesus and began putting my thoughts in writing. I had been introduced to process philosophy in the mid 1970's by Lewis S. Ford while I was serving as a minister and teaching as an adjunct instructor at Old Dominion University in Virginia. Like many who were raised in a conservative background, I found process invigorating and helpful in envisioning God and the world in new ways. I was especially fortunate to be able to engage in dialogue with Dr. Ford about a groundbreaking book he was writing in which he sought to relate process philosophy to biblical thought. Reading and discussing this book, *Lure of God*, opened my eyes to new ways to interpret the biblical message.[17]

I used this time in my life to read more widely in process philosophy and process theology and found new ways to understand the gentle teachings of Jesus. My first realization was how far I had strayed from those gentle teachings. For seven years I had lived in the rough construction world where some sub-contractors actually shot a general contractor, and I was a general contractor. Perhaps, I was not tough enough and business smart enough to be a general contractor, for I do believe that many sub-contractors, employees, and some clients took advantage of my more gentle nature. I gained a greater appreciation for those who earn a living in the competitive business environment. I also realized that my training was in ecclesiology not economics.

Back in my more familiar settings, teaching little children in church was healing for me. I would come in to the fellowship meals on Wednesday night hurting and tired from doing more hands on home renovations; and the little children would run to greet me, throwing themselves into my arms and hugging me. My heart was warmed, and my soul was healing, especially as I heard them sing, "Jesus loves me, this I know, for the Bible tells me so."

---

[17] This book was groundbreaking in the way it linked biblical thought, especially the Old Testament, to process philosophy. It opened the door to writing process theology with enriched meaning.

When I heard them sing "love" I heard agape, and all the rich meanings of this word that I had learned in my Greek studies came flooding back into my soul. **I have shared my experience as a testimony that kindness works transforming miracles.**

President, George H. Bush, began his term in 1988 by saying, "I would like to see a kinder gentler nation." I think this desire came out of his classical education where he was trained to be a servant of the people. This statement also fueled my desire to write more on the gentle teachings of Jesus. Then a strange thing happened. The cartoonist interpreted President Bush's statement as a sign of weakness and the media had a field day portraying him as wimpy. The media did not understand that true gentleness and meekness implies real strength.

Was President Bush's strong action in the war in the Gulf partly an attempt to shake that image of weakness? What would have happened if the churches had picked up his plea for a kinder gentler nation? I was at a national church meeting in Atlanta in 1991 and heard President Bush speak about his decision to enter the war and he wept---and for me this was a sign of great compassion and strength. Surely Jesus was weeping that the churches had not joined in sounding the call for gentleness.[18]

For the next few years I wrote more on Jesus' "Gentle Galilean Glories." In 1994, I was called to be the pastor of a small Cumberland Presbyterian Church. The connection was made by Jim Guenther, a deacon in the Baptist Church where Beth and I were members and teaching children. I had given up on being a minister, but I had not given up on the need for church community and fellowship. Jim Guenther's associate in his law firm was Jamie Jordan who was an elder in the Mt. Sharon Cumberland Presbyterian Church. Mt. Sharon was looking for a minister and Jim told Jamie to call me, saying, "I would probably preach for them until they found a minister." After preaching every Sunday for six months, one of the longest trial sermons on record, they asked me to become their full-time minister. I preached the gentle agape of Jesus in that little Church (95 active members, quite a change from the last Baptist Church I served that had 1200 members) and saw love transform lives. My life continued to be transformed in this special relationship for the next three years with those Christians who I would call the "salt of the earth," to use a biblical concept.

Attending the General Assembly of the Cumberland Presbyterian Church each year, I heard the call for elder training and church member spiritual growth. Beth and I developed a Spiritual Growth Center focused on

---

[18] This example should not be seen as an endorsement of one political party. I voted for George H. W. Bush, but usually vote democratic. However, I feel that ministers should teach Christian principles and let church members use those teachings to determine the best candidate.

the Christian practices of love and gentleness and put it in practice when I served the First Cumberland Presbyterian Church of Chattanooga (900 members) from 1998-2002. We continued to develop materials for spiritual growth when I served the Lawrenceburg Cumberland Presbyterian Church from 2002-2005, and I continued to preach and write, publishing sermons and Sunday School lessons on the gentle teachings of Jesus that supported spiritual growth and transformation.[19]

Let me explain why I also call these teachings "Gentle Galilean Glories." Why Galilee? Galilee was Jesus' home. According to Mark, followed by Matthew and Luke, Jesus performed the majority of his ministry in Galilee. The Gospel of John focused more on Judea and Jerusalem.

Why Glories? Jesus' gentle Galilean ministry as the self-actualization of the λογος (word, meaning) and σοφια (wisdom), was the guiding light of all who come into the world. His gentle ministry was like the glorious rays of sunlight falling on lives that had been lived in dark times.[20]

I cannot separate my personal faith from my writing. So I want to share with you my personal faith, more specifically, how and why I believe in Jesus and his love for me. You might see some of your own faith story in the heartbeat of my experience. It is hard for me to assess where my faith in Jesus started. No doubt, my parents were a bridge to my faith in God and my belief in the love of God revealed in Jesus for me.

However, my life was so tied to our family farm and God's good earth that it is as though I sprang from the soil, the streams, and the trees that made up our farm in North West Georgia. With my fingers and toes literally in the soil of God's good earth, my biophilic faith in the goodness of the world grew. Thus, in one sense my experiential faith in the world preceded my faith in God. If my faith in God expressed in creeds and dogmas, my faith in people, and even my faith in the church were taken away, I believe that I would still have faith in the awe-inspiring beauty and goodness of the natural world. If asked today where I am from, I do not answer, Georgia, I say that I am from the earth. Yet, for me, it is not an either or. The natural world opens windows into the religious world, and the outer world connects to the inner world.

The closer I am to nature, the closer I am to God revealed in Jesus; and it is hard for me to separate these streams of my faith. I truly see God in

---

[19] During this time from 1993 to 2005 I also taught in the Program of Alternate Studies, sponsored and supervised by the Memphis Theological Seminary, an ecumenical seminary of the Cumberland Presbyterian Church. This book on the tender teachings of Jesus continued to grow during those years of teaching new ministers.

[20] Matthew 4:12-17; Luke 1:78-79, 4:14-15.

all that I see around me. I feel God in the pulse of every new morning; and, indeed, in the pulse of the universe. I live and draw my energy from this faith in the world. I am an avid fly fisherman, not so much to catch trout or salmon, but to go out into nature and let nature become my eyes and ears through which I take the pulse of the universe and measure the health of my soul. Standing in a stream and seeing a rainbow trout leap out of the water after taking a dry fly I have patiently tied is awe inspiring, and in that moment, I know that all is well with my world and my soul. Now living in Alaska, the Last Frontier, I have daily opportunity to feel the pulse beat of the universe. For example, one snowy morning when I took my grandchildren to school, I witnessed a five-year-old student coming to school on her skis, being pulled by her father on his fat steel-studded snow tire bike.

As I write and ponder these words, I sit at my desk with a view of the snow-capped Chugach Mountains, like a pair of binoculars with legs, I survey the rising expanse, and bio-philic consciousness oozes through the green leaved tree limbs that try to shield the awe-inspiring view from my tingling awareness. As a product of evolution something within me connects with the trees, the snowcapped mountains, the mother bird whose wings look like scissors cutting across the blue cloth sky coming to feed her baby birds now nesting in the tree outside my condo, and I am one with all creation, yet different.

My interest in science, biology, physics, the genome project, and all endeavors to understand the world and our place in it, also feeds my active faith. For me, God is truly in all things and in God revealed in Jesus all things hold together.[21] My concept of the world is best described as an energy event----the world is held together by divine love energies. Our love energies make a difference in how the world is shaped and moves forward toward completion. It makes sense to me that God called forth the world using the grammar of evolutionary energy. My faith perspective leads me to say that God's spiritual presence is in all things, creating, shaping, and evolving at all times, luring rebirth (palingenesis) and cosmic genesis.[22]

Creative evolution is the best way I know to describe my faith perspective or my worldview. It is exciting to begin each new day with the realization that my life is a part of this palingenesis/cosmogenesis and is moving forward in harmony with God's creative work. I see this harmony between science and faith at its best. God is the source of all truth and truth is the goal of both science and faith.[23]

---

[21] Colossians 1:15-23.
[22] Titus 3:5ff.
[23] Many of these insights came from reading Teilhard de Chardin's writings. For me Chardin was a natural lead into Process Philosophy. See Appendix for a brief article defining Process Philosophy.

I need to point out for you one important distinction here. I am not speaking of pantheism, the belief that all things are God. I am saying that God is in all things, pan (all)-en (in) theism (God). God's spiritual presence is in all things luring, creating, shaping, and evolving toward completion. God's loving kindness embraces and enfolds all of creation. I think this is the meaning of the mythic statement in Genesis, God looked at everything God had made, and God was very pleased (1:31).

A minister spent several hours a week teaching a first-grade religion class. In one class he was teaching the children about different ways creation pleases God. He told them that trees make God happy by being trees. Dogs make God happy by being dogs. Cats make God happy by being cats. Clams make God happy by being the best clams possible. Then he asked the big question: "How could the boys and girls make God happy?" There was silence as the boys and girls thought about the question. Finally, Jennie jumped up, almost singing the answer: "I know! I know! We make God happy by being as people-ly as possible," she grinned. Everybody clapped.

"Being as people-ly as possible!" Not a bad answer. "Maker of heaven and earth," gently lure us with your loving aims so we can become as people-ly as possible." The temptation of humans has always been in two directions: (1) to be less than human, i.e., animalistic, and (2) to be more than human, i.e., to be God. We are made to be human and that should be the goal of life. In all my life time of reading the Bible, theology, philosophy, psychology, and science, the gentle teachings of Jesus are the best model, the ideal model, for life transformation and world transformation.

This is my faith that holds me strong in times of tragedy and testing. Most Christians can point to an event in their past which spoke to them in an unusual way about God. One such revelatory event happened in my life when I was a senior in high school. Wendell was my best friend from the time we entered the first grade in school. We did all the things boys typically did growing up in the rural South in the post-depression decades of the forties and fifties. On the school grounds we played marbles and the daring game of follow the leader which took us on adventures through the surrounding woods. In high school we played baseball and football. Wendell was a big guard in football, and he was good enough to consider a college scholarship and a pro career. I was a skinny right end who is lucky to be alive after four years of being tackled. After canning his opposing guard, Wendell would often block for me on short pass plays. In fact, he could be one of the reasons I survived.

Then it happened. Just two weeks before graduation from high school, Wendell was killed when two cars collided head-on at a curve in the road. His older brother who was driving while intoxicated was injured, but fully recovered, at least physically. The two people in the other car who were outstanding citizens and active church members were both also killed instantly, as was Wendell. I was stunned and filled with grief.

At Wendell's funeral service the minister said that this tragedy was God's will. He said, "We may not understand it, but we must not question it. We can only accept it as God's will." Without knowing why at the time, this answer disturbed me.

I remember going home from the funeral and climbing on the old Allis Chalmers farm tractor to plow. I wanted to be alone with my thoughts undisturbed. Soon a thunderstorm began to form, and the sky darkened, as though nature was in sympathy with my mood. Lightning flashed and thunder rolled. I cried out, shaking my fists at the heavens, "Why, O God, did Wendell die?" No answer came. The clouds were not rolled back, and there was no voice from heaven. But the storm passed on. The gentle rain came and washed away my tears. As the tractor rumbled on, I had a deep feeling of God's presence. A rainbow appeared on the horizon, and I found strength and hope to go on.

Feeling somewhat better I took the tractor back to the shed to get some dry clothes. As I switched off the engine, I heard a whining noise. At first, I thought it was just the ringing of the tractor motor still reverberating through my eardrums, but there it was again. A soft whining and a few little yelps could be heard from the far corner of the shed. As I approached the sounds, I realized that it was my beagle, another of my best friends; and she was giving birth to four little pups.

> Trembling,
> I watched in awe and wonder.
> I picked one up and
>
> held it close to my heart.
> It too was trembling
> and still frightened by birth.
>
> I gently stroked the new born pup
> held it like a cup
> sipping a gentle kiss until it was calm.
>
> Stroking with sweet balm.
> Mother looked on with caressing eyes and tender concern.

In the midst of the tragedy of death, I was witnessing new birth and new beginnings. This episode would always have meaning for me, and its impact would grow through the years. All endings hold the possibilities of new beginnings. In process theology this is an ongoing ever changing and enriching experience. Yet, there are significant times when the shaking of the foundations leads us to build new stronger foundations and thereon to erect greater edifices. These are self-created acts under the inspiration of God's luring and transforming love.

As a farm boy with my fingers and toes literally in the soil, I was much more at peace with the storm, the rain, the rainbow of promise and security, and the birth of little beagle puppies. These bathed my soul with comfort and peace, revealing God's care for me.

The minister's suggestion that God takes the life of a young man in a cruel car accident was strange to my thinking. This kind of thinking did not resonate with my soul, but I simply did not have the words to express my feelings. Later my language and linguistics studies would reveal to me that there are non-verbal, pre-reflective emotions, feelings, and thoughts that are virtually impossible to express in a one-to-one correlation to words and phrases.

I have also come to see that faith is best defined as the embodiment of these feelings or moods of existence rather than codified beliefs or tenets. Doctrines and creeds written by persons of another age may or may not come to correspond with one's inner feelings and emotions. However, this sense of inner resonance and harmony needs to happen for them to become one's personal and private beliefs.

We need to develop a core belief or faith system if we are to deal with the growing complexity of life. My faith is Jesus centered. My faith in the world is in harmony with my faith in the gentle teachings of Jesus. In the New Testament we see the birth of new beginnings and possibilities in Jesus who is revealed as the personal plan and goal of creation. In Colossians, Paul wrote, Christ is the visible likeness of the invisible God. He is the first-born Son, superior to all created things. For through him God created everything in heaven and on earth. . . God created the whole universe through him and for him. Christ existed before all things, and in unison with him all things have their proper place (1:15-17). In the following chapters on Jesus, I will suggest that you can change the title Christ with Jesus who incarnated the λογος (word, meaning) and σοφια (wisdom), the creative principles of God, without any loss of meaning. The title, Christ, Messiah, is a stumbling block in some religions, especially Judaism and Islam, whereas the title, Jesus, has wide-spread acceptance. Therefore, throughout this book I will use the title Jesus rather than Christ except in some scripture quotes.

Jesus, who was born as a human being like us, grew spiritually until he became totally God-conscious and self-actualized the creative principles or logos and Sophia in his life and teachings.[24] By embodying the creative

---

[24] The importance of seeing Jesus as a human like us will become more evident in the later chapters on Jesus.

wisdom of God that guided the evolving universe, Jesus who was fully human opens the way for us to see all persons like Moses, Confucius, Mohammed, Buddha, Martin Luther King, Jr., Mother Teresa, and others who respond to God's call to self-actualize the novel love aims of God for their lives and inspire others to do the same.

Galatians 4:4-5 expresses the humanness of Jesus in these words: "In the fullness of time Jesus was born of woman, born under the law, so that we might become the children of God." Jesus fulfills the plan of the ages. To believe this mystery of Jesus' faithfulness is to have faith. What do we need more than this optimistic faith? As a senior in high school who had lost a best friend in a cruel accident, I needed that faith---faith that life is not meaningless; it has purpose and direction. This faith in Jesus provides for me a center that holds.

The next chapter will seek to show how God relates to us and the world in this centering, transforming process. This chapter will lay the groundwork for understanding Jesus' gentle Galilean glories.

Chapter One

God as Creative-Relational Loving Kindness

*What God likes best
is showing kindness,
justice, and mercy
to everyone on earth.*[25]

God is love.[26]

In the love of God is the preservation of the world.

A pastor, like a filibustering senator on "Cruz" control, once preached a 60 hour and 31-minute sermon. If I were asked to preach the shortest sermon, I would stand and say these three words, "God is love," and sit down. When speaking of God, sometimes fewer words are better. Human words are often inadequate to express the mystery of the divine. Yet, all theistic religions, those affirming faith in God, have attempted to understand the nature of God and how God relates to the world. If God is like a mystery locked in a biblical safe, then the key to the safe is found in these three words: God is love.

From a Christian perspective, two other terms have been helpful in seeking to develop a doctrine of God: transcendence and immanence. In one sense God transcends all human thoughts. The biblical writers recognized this. Isaiah wrote that God's thoughts are not our thoughts and our ways are not God's ways. Expressing his thoughts about God, Paul wrote, "We see in a mirror dimly." [27]

Transcendence for some equates to absence. For example, the Deist saw God as One who created the world, wound it up like a clock, and then basically left the world to run on its own, governed by natural laws. In this view, only occasionally does God intervene. While many would not say they are Deist, they live daily as if this were their world view. For some, God's

---

[25] Jeremiah 9:24, CEV.

[26] I John 4:16

[27] 1 Corinthians 13:12.

transcendence equates to mystery that leads to awe and wonder. For others the practice of mysticism reveals some things about this transcendent God.

When transcendence is dominant God can seem remote, separated from human concerns and human suffering. Soon after the New Testament was written in Greek, Christians became more influenced by Greek culture and Greek ways. This process of Hellenization brought Greek philosophical thought into Christian theology. Greek mythology saw the god's separate from the life of mere humans. This view virtually left God as separate from the world and passionless, for to be in the world and suffer with the world is to show weakness. To have perfect power is to be beyond suffering, to be totally unaffected by the world and therefore unchangeable. Thus, traditional theology came to say that nothing humans can do can change God in any way.

My theology unfolding from the gentle teachings of Jesus sees the wonder of God immanent in all creatures and all of nature. From the New Testament, we know God revealed in Jesus as a uniquely personal and relational God, best described as creative-responsive love.[28] For me, creative-responsive love captures the truth of transcendence and immanence in more personal and relational ways. As the creative impulse and adventurous energy that gives value to all possibilities, God transcends creation. Yet God is immanent in the coming into being of all things. God calls all things into existence, through eons of time. In Jesus' gentle teachings and his unique response to God's call, we see God present in the world and acting for the world in saving ways.

> The biblical image of faith in the time of Jesus was of a child wrapped in the folds of a mother's garment where there is security, comfort, and nurturing, and hope.

As Christians we live and move and have our being in the circle of God's love. God is in us and for us, in the world and for the world. Love does not define God; God exists before human love and God revealed in the gentle teachings of Jesus defines love. Jesus was responsive to God's love aims and purposes for his life and became more God conscious with each self-actualization. In this sense it is appropriate to say that Jesus was divine, but only in the sense that each of us can also become more conscious of

---

[28] I first encountered this phrase, "God as Creative Responsive Love," in *Process Theology: An Introductory Exposition*, by John B. Cobb, Jr. and David Ray Griffin. I saw it as the best description of God as revealed in the Bible. Once you see it and think about it you can't forget it. I have added kindness to the word, love, to expand its reach and place more emphasis on kind actions.

God's presence in us. Jesus' God consciousness enabled him to be more conscious of the needs of others, and thus more fully divine and human.

Jesus spoke to God as a child would speak to a parent, confidently and securely. Jesus saw God like a kind father and nurturing mother.

Psalm 131 says, "I have learned to feel safe and satisfied, just like a child on its mother's lap. People of Israel, you must trust the Lord now and forever."

God's love involves God as immanent in the world. Responsive love is suffering love. God suffers with the world. We know from personal experience that love is a sympathetic response from one person to another. True love feels what the other person is feeling, rejoicing in their joys and hurting with their pains. We would doubt that a husband loves his wife if he were not aware of her feelings and if his feelings did not reflect her feelings.

As we experience God revealed in the prophets and in Jesus, we find God rejoicing with us in our times of joy and weeping with us in our times of sorrow. This is responsiveness that is worthy of worship, prayer, and service. Our love of others is based on this responsive love we see in God. Our theology should reflect the awe and wonder of God being in the world, in us, and for us, holding us close as a mother holds her child on her lap.

The world does not exist apart from God. God the Gardener loves natural beauty and has a desire to create order out of chaos. The Gardner hovers over every blade of grass and whispers, "Awake. Grow. Grow beautiful and green." Meadows grow, giving way to gurgling streams, water plants, butterflies, hummingbirds, flitting from red, orange, and yellow flowers. Beautiful gardens answer the call and over eons of time, all nature is lured toward ever enriching possibilities until conditions are right for life forms to emerge. Over billions of years God called forth a world able to support human beings. Humans are a new song that nature hums, the music swells with each new stanza, giving purpose and meaning. Humans moved from being gatherers in the garden to being gardeners, ever singing nature's love songs.

God did not create the world and then abandon creation as the Deists once thought. God is in the creative evolutionary process, placing novel love aims and goals within all parts of creation. God is supremely socially related with the purpose of sharing goodness and love with all of creation. God, all nature, and humans are interconnected. As God is immanent in the world, I am in nature and nature is in me. As I write these words, I am looking at the snow-capped Chugach Mountains of Alaska. I am in the mountains and the mountains are in me, singing their song, filling every part of my body and spirit with a wealth of beauty.

The individual as a deciding entity who sings the biophilic song of nature is not lost in this creative evolutionary process for all of life is socially related. Each entity, the interconnected process that make up the world of rocks, plants, trees, animals, and persons, receives possibilities from the past, and is partially self-created in an act of concrescence. Concrescence is the act of becoming by unifying possibilities from the past into the self-actualizing entity or person. Humans are partially created by their heredity and environment, what is given to them from the past, and the lure of the future (God); but humans exercise personal choice in the final act of becoming, psychologically speaking, this is self-actualization.

The God we meet in the beauty of nature and on the pages of the Bible is in us and for us. The goodness and beauty of creation reflects the goodness and love of God. God is present in creation. The call of God toward goodness is a call to all people. Some in freedom respond, others deny the call. The Bible is a record of human response to God's call; it tells both the rejection and response to accept and move forward in a creative advance with God. Some men and women responded in beautiful and marvelous ways in the Old Testament and New Testament times, as people have in all cultures. For Christians, Jesus is the supreme example. To affirm this does not lessen the role of Mohammed for Islam or Buddha for Buddhism and other important religious teachers. When any one relates to the God of creative possibilities, creative transformation occurs, bringing harmony and peace. Gentle teachings that are present in all religions offer a pathway to peace in our global age.

God's love is persuasive and luring, not coercive and demanding. This concept found in Plato, came to fruition in Jesus' gentle teachings, and was developed into a philosophy of organisms by Alfred North Whitehead.[29] Relational love does not seek to control with coercion. Relational power is greatest in its ability to influence others. If we love someone we do not seek to control or pressure them with promises and threats. Instead we try to persuade them with luring love to actualize the possibilities for good. The gentle Galilean glories of Jesus define power in terms of love. This is also a good theology for parenting.

Does this emphasis on God's persuasive power rather than coercive power make God weak? Does this question have merit? Are humans more at home with coercive power than luring and persuasive power?

People who want to have coercive power for themselves and for God often ask, "If God is All-powerful, why doesn't God change things?" One businessman expressed the feeling like this: "If I were God, I would show people who is boss." This man could very well have been the father of a little boy in the cartoons, down on his knees by the bedside, saying his prayers, and almost out of patience with God: "Aunt Stella isn't married yet. Uncle Hubert hasn't got a job. Daddy's hair is still falling out. I'm tired of

---

[29] See Appendix for a summary statement of Process Philosophy.

saying prayers for this family without getting results." We all know of the silence of the sky. The Book of Job turns on it. If God is Almighty as the Apostle's Creed says, why doesn't God rid the world of all its evil?

Well, in a theology based on love, love is a qualifier for the term, "Almighty." The Creed says, "I believe in God the Father Almighty."[30] The history of the church might have been different if the Creed had read, "I believe in God the Father and Mother, nurturer of all."

Traditionally "Father" as qualifier has been interpreted as divine self-limitation. A parent is somewhat limited by parenthood. A parent must withhold power and wait with patience for a child to grow. In this view God is able to act with coercive power but chooses not to do so. Because our Parent God allowed humans to evolve with the freedom to choose, even to say yes or no, God's power is limited. Thus, you might call this self-limitation.

Continuing this traditional view, God has allowed us to be in the world with freedom to make our own decisions and take the consequences of our actions. God, like a human parent, lays out a place in a shop area for children to learn to work and gain responsibility. A parent does not rush in and stop everything when children make mistakes, even if they ruin a good piece of wood. How else would they learn responsibility this argument goes, even responsibility for mistakes? God, like a father and mother, is good and patient with us in the same way.

This view of divine omnipotence has appeal but needs to be seriously reviewed. If God could control every event in life, but chooses not to do so, then God is ultimately responsible for such horrendous acts as the Holocaust! Also, if God grants us the freedom to choose, then that freedom could be revoked. There are times when I feel a little intervention would be good. A good parent would intervene if he or she saw their children about to cause serious harm to themselves or others. Not to do so would be criminal.

The basis issue is not the quantity of power God has, but the nature of divine power. The phrase, "I believe in God the Father Almighty," invites us to see a different kind of power, a power qualified by a parent's love, a persuasive and luring power that sets novel aims and gently lures us toward fulfilling those aims. This parental image of God, while often overlooked, is a common view of the Bible and is seen most clearly in the gentle teachings of Jesus in the Gospels.

Parents do have some coercive power over their children and can force them when small to stay in a certain place or eat a food they do not like, but when they have to resort to this coercive power they have basically failed as parents and are virtually impotent!

---

[30] See the chapter on Father/Son for a fuller discussion and reinterpretation of the term, Father.

Is this gentle relational love weak? Or is gentle love the one force that slowly but surely transforms our lives, our communities, and our world? The latter is a key concept in this agape theology of gentle teachings, both philosophically and theologically. God's love expressed in Trinitarian relationships and bound up in community relationships is the most powerful force in the world!

God's power is best expressed as a power-field of love energies. These love energies are first seen and experienced in the triune relationships of God who relates to us as Father (the term Mother, Parent, Lover, etc. may also be used), Son (the terms λογος, word, σοφια, wisdom, savior, lover, etc. may also be used), and Holy Spirit (παρακλησις, helper, friend etc. may also be used). This relational triune God calls all persons into this power field of love energies that transform persons and God's own self. God is first and foremost transformed by the experience of Jesus' life, suffering, death, and resurrection. Through Jesus' deep socially developed God-consciousness, God is revealed to us in new and transforming ways. This is God's own self-revelation. In these triune relationships God wills to be in us and for us, in the world and for the world.

The gentle Galilean glories of Jesus become the touch stone for understanding the triune God. These gentle teachings when energized by the Spirit become a transforming power-field that can change and transform lives.

Since the cross as the symbol of sacrificial love stands at the center of Jesus' life experience, the cross becomes the heart of the triune God and the best route for understanding God's own being as self-giving love before it becomes a symbol of salvation. When one experiences this reality of love, omnipotence comes to mean God's vulnerable love seen in the crucifixion of Jesus and the vindication of the resurrection of Jesus. Can there be a more powerful and persuasive love than this?

The next few chapters will show how Jesus responded to God's call and self-actualized the love aims and purposes of God in his own being, making it possible for God to come to us in Jesus, to be with us and for us in new transforming and saving ways.

Chapter Two

Jesus Self-Actualized
The Creative Relational Loving Kindness of God[31]

God's love and kindness will shine upon us like the sun that rises in the sky. On us who live in the dark shadow of death, this light will shine to guide us into a life of peace (Luke 1:78-79, CEV).

When one tugs at a single kind love word of Jesus, one finds it is attached to the heart of God.

The Gospel narratives about Jesus' birth are confined to the first two chapters of Matthew and Luke. These two separate accounts have been merged in the popular mind into a single Christmas story. Actually, Matthew and Luke record different facts in different order of events. It is not our purpose to sort out the different events or to tell one continuous story of Jesus' birth. In the telling and re-telling of the birth narratives, they have taken on some mythic qualities. Since we are seeking to show the humanness of Jesus, this chapter moves behind the mythic additions to see Jesus in his own time and culture.

Our purpose is to highlight the tender, gentle elements in the story of Jesus' birth, life, death, and resurrection. Our guiding light is the spirit of Luke 1:78-79, God's love and kindness will shine upon us like the sun that rises in the sky. On us who live in the dark shadow of death, this light will shine to guide us into a life of peace. Paul expressed the coming of Jesus in similar terms: When the kindness and love of God our Savior was revealed, he saved us (Titus 3:4).

In order to fully understand how truly gentle Jesus was we must first briefly capsule the period and environment of his life. One cannot

---

[31] The main sources for this chapter are the four Gospels of the New Testament. Non canonical sources like the Gospel of Thomas and archaeological findings like the Dead Sea Scrolls, though important, have not added significant information about Jesus.

understand the character of Jesus' life with seeing the social circumstances in which he lived and his broader historic epoch.[32]

The Jewish People

The Jewish nation in Jesus' time was a small weak nation in a remote and infertile land with only a few exceptions. Since the return from the Babylonian exile (586-538 B.C.), the Jewish people had very little political independence. They were dominated by a long succession of foreign powers from the Persians to the Romans. Yet Israel's faith in God was like a vital nerve center that sustained her in these perilous times. And in one sense Israel had the greatest significance of all religions. Judaism in time became a major world religion, not in numbers with only about fourteen million Jews worldwide today. Judaism's significance is seen in the fact that Judaism started a monotheistic revolution that changed the Western world. This monotheistic Movement gave birth to Christianity with 2.2 billion members, almost one-third of the world's population and Islam with over one billion members, roughly one-fifth of the world's population.

The spread of the Greek culture throughout the Near East following the conquest of Alexander the Great was the continuation of a life-long struggle for Israel to maintain a distinctive and vital faith. It was during this struggle between Judaism and Hellenism that the Jewish sects and parties emerged.

The Pharisees first appeared under the rule of John Hyrcanus (135-105 B.C.). The name "Pharisee" is generally interpreted as "the separate ones." They had the reputation of excelling the rest of the nation in the observance of the law. This group gave birth to many of the oral laws and traditions that governed the daily life of the average Jew in Jesus' time. Jesus had to justify His gentle words and actions to the Pharisees.[33] The Sadducees held what little political authority the Jews possessed. The Saducean high priests were the connecting link with the foreign powers. They were a small group, more political than religious, and exercised a widespread influence. They were even harsher than the Pharisees in their dealings with Jesus.

A third major Jewish sect, the Essenes, outdid the Pharisees in piety by withdrawing into small communities where they lived simple and abstentious lives. The wilderness west of the Dead Sea was a favorite location

---

[32] See Alfred North Whitehead. *Modes of Thought*. P. 87 for the way these circumstances shape one's life and message.

[33] For an excellent book on the Jewish sects in the time of Jesus see Joachim Jeremias, *Jerusalem in the Time of Jesus*. Also see Amy-Jill Levine, *The Misunderstood Jew: The Church and the Scandal of the Jewish Jesus*.

for their communities. The Dead Sea Scrolls discovered in the middle of the twentieth century have shed light on the Essenes and shown possible connections with John the Baptist and thereby Jesus. This connection is minor and could be explained by the syncretistic nature of Jewish life in the first century rather than a direct link.

The party of the Zealots made up a fourth group among the Jews. It was founded by Judas the Galilean who stirred up a rebellion against the Romans in A.D. 6 (Acts 5:37). The Zealots were opposed to paying tribute to pagan emperors, for God was the only true King. They usually concealed daggers and were ready to destroy the hated Romans when the opportunity was presented to them. At least one of Jesus' disciples was a Zealot. There have been periodic attempts to tag Jesus with the "zealot" name, most recently Reza Aslan.[34] Aslan's central thesis seems to be that since Jesus grew up in Galilee where the zealot spirit was rampant, he was shaped by this spirit. Aslan places a lot of weight on the one passage in Luke 22:35-38 where Jesus asked his disciples as tensions increased with the ruling authorities to sell some of their clothes and buy a sword if they did not have one. When the disciples said that they already had two swords, Jesus replied, "It is enough." This could be translated, "It is enough about that!" It was common advice to take a sword on dangerous trips in the time of Jesus. This advice is found only in Luke and v. 37 places it in the context of a quote from Isaiah 53:12, a suffering servant song. The spirit of the suffering servant who willingly gives life would certainly give a new slant to this advice of buying a sword. Jesus' response after the remark about already having two swords would seem to support this interpretation. In frustration about the disciples not understanding his role, Jesus says, in effect, "that is enough about swords." The one clear principle from Jesus' life and teachings is that one has the right to give life but never to take life. History shows many examples of men and women who rose above the spirit of their times and became shapers of events not followers---Abraham Lincoln, Gandhi, Martin Luther King, Jr., and Mother Teresa to name a few.

The Herodians are mentioned in the New Testament as enemies of Jesus, both in Galilee (Mark 3:6) and in Jerusalem (Matthew 22:16; Mark 12:13). The term apparently denotes an attitude rather than a political party or religious sect. It seems to refer to the Jews who supported the Herodian rule and the Romans.

The vast majority of Palestinian Jews were unaffiliated with any of these groups. These multitudes were known as people of the land, "Am-haaretz." The Pharisees felt that these common people from the country were ignorant of or indifferent to the Mosaic law; thus, they were considered immoral and irreligious.

---

[34] Reza Aslan, *Zealot: The Life and Times of Jesus of Nazareth*.

Without excluding the others, it was more self-exclusion. Basically, it was this group of common people who were recipients of Jesus' gentle, Galilean glories. Though the Pharisees saw them as worthless outcasts, Jesus saw them with compassion because they were helpless like "sheep without a shepherd."[35]

Jewish Worship

The focal point of Jewish worship in each village or town was the synagogue, where the Scriptures were read and explained each Sabbath and the people prayed to the one who in their faith was the only God. The ruler of the synagogue selected readers and preachers, which accounts for the times Jesus addressed synagogue audiences.

Although the synagogue was the focal point of the religious community, the Temple in Jerusalem was the focal point of national life and worship. Whereas the synagogue was principally a school for religious instruction, the Temple was a place of sacrifices. The one Temple symbolized their belief in one God and the unity of their faith. Most Jews longed to visit the Temple at least once in their lifetime.

The priestly taxes necessary to take care of the elaborate cultic system combined with the Roman taxes amounted to about 35-40 per cent of the total income of the nation. This was an impossible economic system by the time of Jesus. This unhappy situation was ripe for fanatical false messiahs who constantly deluded followers and created scenes of violence. Jesus would steadfastly resist the pressures of the crowds to be a political messiah.[36]

The Birth of Jesus

The simplicity and gentleness of the birth narratives of Jesus are all the more striking against the Jewish background given above. The nativity scene evokes the best feelings in our human nature: the devout mother and father, the child in a bare manger, the shepherds and wise men who come to worship him, and the angels who bridge the lowly earthly scene with the heavenly spheres, a bridging which the life, death, and resurrection of Jesus would make complete.

What is striking in these accounts, especially Luke, and for the sake of simplicity we will mainly follow Luke's story line, is the simple but noble Jewish piety that was the cradle for the birth and infancy of Jesus. The Lukan

---

[35] Matthew 9:36.
[36] John 6:15.

Canticles are marked by profound motives of humility, gentleness, loyalty, and obedience to the divine will.[37] The note of joy and gladness is sounded throughout. Mary's song of praise moves between lowliness and exaltation: My heart praises the Lord; my soul is glad because of God my savior, for God has remembered me, God's lowly gentle servant. Then comes the exaltation: God has lifted up the lowly.[38]

The circumstances surrounding the birth of Jesus defy all that the world would have expected of so great a prophetic teacher. Jesus lay cradled in a lowly manger! Hollywood would no doubt have had God in flowing royal robes walking down the golden staircase of heaven with a blond haired, blue-eyed baby wrapped in diamond encrusted blankets.

It is almost unbelievable! The human Jesus was born in a remote nation in the humblest of circumstances and was cradled in a manger, perhaps a feed trough.[39] So, Jesus was born in humble circumstances, surrounded by gentle Mary and Joseph, lowly shepherds, and glorious angelic choruses. The Gospels make it clear that God took the initiative and came near to people. In Luke's words, God came in tenderness and the bright light of heaven shone upon all who walked in darkness.[40] Jesus would respond to the call of God and reveal gentle Galilean glories.

Infancy Narratives

Luke's Gospel is the only one which has anything to say about Jesus' early years. After the shepherds visit, the story continues with the circumcision of the child on the eighth day of his life, in fulfillment of the law the child was formally given the Greek name Jesus which is the same as Joshua in Hebrew.[41] It was a common name meaning "he saves" or in its full form, "Jehovah saves." The presentation of Jesus in the Temple places us once again in the very heart of Jewish piety and worship. In keeping with the Mosaic law, Mary observed the purification rites by presenting an offering of a pair of doves or two young pigeons while at the same time presenting the child to God.[42] The offering indicates that Mary and Joseph were poor. According to Leviticus 12, the offering called for a lamb but mothers who were poor could substitute the less expensive offering.

---

[37] Luke 1:14-17, 32-33, 35, 46-55, 68-79; 2:14, 29-32, 34-35.
[38] Luke 1:4648, 52.
[39] It is important to see that the birth of Jesus did not violate our understanding of human nature.
[40] Luke 1:78.
[41] Luke 2:21; cf. Genesis 17:9-14; Leviticus 12:3.
[42] Leviticus 12:1-4, 6; Luke 2:22-24.

In the Temple, Joseph and Mary encountered a good, God-fearing man named Simeon who was waiting for Israel to be saved. When Simeon took Jesus in his arms to bless him--an appropriate symbol for the one who would later take children in his arms and bless them--Simeon burst forth in praise to God: Now Lord, you have kept your promise, and you may let your servant go in peace. With my own eyes I have seen your salvation, which you have prepared in the presence of all peoples: a light to reveal your will to the Gentiles and bring glory to your people Israel.[43]

There was also in the Temple an elderly prophetess, a widow named Anna (Hannah in Hebrew). Anna worshipped God day and night, fasting and praying, never leaving the Temple. She too recognized who the baby was and with thanksgiving to God "spoke about the child to all who were waiting for God to set Jerusalem free."[44]

Having completed the requirements of the law, Joseph, Mary, and Jesus returned to their home town of Nazareth in Galilee. In Galilee Jesus grew and became strong, increasing in favor (graciousness) with God and with humans.[45]

These birth and infancy narratives are stamped throughout with the mark of Jewish piety. We meet Judaism at its best as the cradle of Jesus. We see humble, lowly, gentle servants of God who have spent their whole lifetime glorifying God and waiting patiently for God's deliverance and salvation.

These accounts make it clear that God comes to waiting people, taking the initiative and drawing near to them. In kindness God came to lift up the lowly and gentle servants.[46] The heart throb of tenderness and gentleness beats throughout. Not only is God kind and gentle, Joseph is gentle and considerate of Mary. Joseph was a bridge for Jesus' understanding of one who would become a heavenly Father to him.

Also, we have seen that the lowly are exalted or glorified. Heavenly glories shine throughout these narratives and will continue to shine through Jesus' gentle Galilean glories. When reading these Gospel accounts of the birth of Jesus we need to remember that they were written 80-90 years after the birth of Jesus, and while they are historical, they have naturally taken on some legendary and mythic qualities.

The only other glimpse of Jesus the Gospels give us of his early years was his visit to the Temple at the age of twelve. On this visit Mary and Joseph

---

[43] Luke 2:29-32.
[44] Luke 2:36-38.
[45] Luke 2:52.
[46] Titus 3:4; Luke 1:48, 52.

miss Jesus and began to look for him. They find him in the Temple asking serious questions and saying, I must be about My Father's business.[47]

This seems to be a very significant time in Jesus' self-actualization. The kindness, gentleness, and love of God that had been prefigured in Mary and Joseph and his faith community were now affirmed as being rooted in God. While this was a significant insight or rite of passage for Jesus, he went back to Galilee with Joseph and Mary where he continued to grow in body and in wisdom, gaining favor with God and humans. The Greek word translated as "favor" here is a form of χαρις. It is usually translated in the New Testament as grace. It can also be translated as kindness.[48] It describes the qualities of grace and kindness that make a person attractive or favorable. It also describes the attitude of goodwill, respect, or approval of others toward a gracious and kind person.

Jesus returned home to Galilee. Home for Jesus included four brothers: James, Joses (or Joseph), Judas, and Simon. He also had sisters, but we are not told how many nor are we told their names. Clearly Jesus grew up in a large household which was no doubt lively.

How much formal education Jesus received is not known. Joseph would have started Jesus' education in the home as the Jewish law commanded. Every pious Jewish father, and we are told that Joseph was devout,[49] taught his son the Shema: Israel, remember this! The Lord--and the Lord alone--is our God. Love the Lord your God with all your heart, with all your soul, and with all your strength. Never forget these commandments that I am giving you today. Teach them to your children.[50] Jesus made this the first commandment of all of his teachings.[51] It is interesting that Jesus added "with all your mind" to his presentation of the great commandment. We know that Jesus had an active and perceptive mind.

In addition to learning from Joseph at home, Jesus probably attended the synagogue school in Nazareth. How much, if any, formal education he had, of course, is not known. A popular view today is to see

---

[47] Luke 2:49.

[48] The American Bible Society's Contemporary English Version often translates χαρις as kindness. See pages 54ff. below for a treatment of χαρις. I have checked the usage of this word from Plato up through the time of Jesus and found that they are justified in translating χαρις as kindness. See my Book, *Jesus' Kindness Transforms Suffering: Essays and Sermons Inspired by the Book of Revelation*, where I used kindness as my hermeneutic for interpreting John's message to the suffering followers of Jesus in the seven Churches.

[49] Matthew 1:19.
[50] Deuteronomy 6:4-7.
[51] Mark 12:28-30.

Jesus as a simple uneducated carpenter. The Gospels themselves point in the other direction. In the Gospel of Mark, the verb, "teach" occurs seventeen times, and in all but one of these Jesus is the subject. Jesus is very often called teacher by his disciples and his opponents. The fact that Jesus was called teacher by his opponents would seem to indicate that they recognized his qualification to teach. According to Luke, Jesus read the Scripture lesson in the synagogue at Nazareth.[52] In his teaching he assumed that his hearers had heard their scriptures read and some probably had read some biblical scrolls. He would often ask, "Have you not read…?"[53] Jesus had an almost encyclopedic knowledge of his Holy Scriptures and with penetration and independence he combined and interpreted them in a unique way. Jesus read and spoke Aramaic. He knew Hebrew well enough to read it in the synagogue. He, of economic necessity, had a carpenter's command of common Greek, which was becoming the common language of his day. Jesus' study of the Old Testament Scriptures helped to shape his understanding of his ministry and message. This was especially true of the Suffering Servant passages of Isaiah.

---

[52] Luke 4:16-20.
[53] Mark 2:25, 12:10; Matthew 12:5; 19:4; 21:16, 42.

Chapter Three

Gentle Galilean Glories of Jesus

God's love and kindness will shine upon us like the sun that rises in the sky. On us who live in the dark shadow of death, this light will shine to guide us into a life of peace (Luke 1:78-79, CEV).

The goal of the Christian should be to live in harmony with the gentle teachings of Jesus.

Serving for almost fifty years as a parish minister, I learned a lot about the need for gentleness in our human relationships. We all fight hard battles and need at least a bushel of kindness a day. Every person and every family needs gentleness to survive. Simple acts of kindness to oneself, one's family, and to all living things are the most powerful transformers in the world.

My own father and mother were examples of gentleness for me and my six brothers and six sisters. My father often prayed public prayers in our little country Church, and one of his favorite expressions was "Kind Father." He started his prayers with this address and repeated it several times throughout the prayer. He said it so many times that I was embarrassed about it. Of course, it doesn't take much to embarrass an adolescent when it comes to his or her parents.

Today I treasure this memory and it has helped me to be a kinder person. My mother and father taught me by word and example that God is kind. They were gentle and loving parents and they made it easy for all thirteen of us to believe in a gentle and loving God. For their children, parents truly are the first bridge to the love of God.

My theology springs from this source and holds up the gentle Galilean glories of Jesus as the guiding light for our lives, our Churches, and our world. What do we mean by "Gentle Galilean Glories?"

Why Galilee?

Galilee was Jesus' place. It was his home, his country, and the home of his gospel. According to Mark, the first written Gospel, Jesus preached in Galilee, and he called his disciples in Galilee. Jesus performed the majority of his ministry in Galilee.

We are not trying to say Galilee was the scene of all Jesus' ministry. We are simply using this as the framework, as Mark did, and as Matthew and

Luke basically did, as Jesus' home. The Gospel of John takes a different view. John presents the ministry of Jesus as shifting back and forth between Galilee and Judea during the first six chapters of his Gospel, and from chapter seven onward the scene shifts wholly to Judea and Jerusalem.

The weight of evidence does mark Galilee as the place Jesus came to perform his gentle ministry and where he told his followers that he was coming at the end time. The risen Jesus commissioned the women to go tell Peter and the other disciples, "I am going to Galilee ahead of you, there you will see me."[54]

Why Galilean Glories?

As Jesus was exalted and glorified, Galilee as Jesus' home had the opportunity to be glorified: "And you, Capernaum (Jesus' headquarters in Galilee), will you be lifted up to the skies?"[55]

Matthew gives further significance to Galilee as the place of Jesus' ministry by pointing out that it is the fulfillment of Scripture: "When Jesus heard that John had been put in prison, he went away to Galilee. He did not stay in Nazareth, but went to live in Capernaum, a town by the lake Galilee, in the territory of Zebulun and Naphtali, on the road to the sea, on the other side of the Jordan, Galilee, the land of the Gentiles! 'The people who live in darkness will see a great light. On those who live in the dark land of death the light will shine.'"[56] So, Jesus fulfills the Old Testament prophecy by appearing in Galilee. His gentle Galilean ministry as the actualization of the logos and Sophia (word, meaning, wisdom), the guiding light of all who come into the world, will be like the gentle rays of sunlight falling on lives that have been lived in dark times.

There were about two million people living in Palestine in the time of Jesus, some Jews, but mostly Gentiles. This was the place for Jesus to come first to the lost sheep of the house of Israel and then to reach out as the light to the Gentiles---the whole world.

Important roads of commerce and trade came through Galilee, and there was a military station and customs post in Capernaum. Travel and commerce brought a spirit of openness and receptivity to new ideas, while at the same time allowing these ideas to spread rapidly.

In contrast to the bleak gray of much of Palestine, Galilee, especially the plain of Gennesaret, was a very fertile, magnificent garden, inspiring Jesus' bio-philic teachings. Jesus preached gentle Galilean glories in this delightful countryside. The flowers of the fields, birds of the air, farmers

---

[54] Mark 16:7.
[55] Luke 10:15.
[56] Matthew 4:12-17; Isaiah 9:1-2.

sowing seed, and fishermen casting their nets all came into Jesus' teachings and parables. This earthly beauty gave Jesus a vision of heavenly glory. This vision is what we are referring to as "Gentle Galilean Glories" that came in Jesus to shine on the highways and byways of Galilee with tenderness and gentleness, transforming lives.

Let me hasten to say that Galilee was not all sweetness and light, neither was the rugged carpenter from Nazareth. Not for a minute do I imply that with this theme of gentle teachings. Personally speaking, I had to learn to balance gentleness and toughness in my own life. I grew up on a working farm and life was sometimes rough as a cob. I played football for four years of high school, playing both offensive and defensive right end for the whole game. I worked in a wire mill on the "graveyard" shift to help pay my way through college. In that mill I received a real lesson about toughness and heard plenty of "gutter" language that was more suitable for the halls of hell than the halos of heaven. At least this experience prepared me for unruly deacon and elder meetings in the church more than seminary did. Building houses for seven years and going through great success and failure also revealed a tough side of life to me. However, my basic nature still tilts toward tenderness due to my family background and the gentle teachings of Jesus seem to reveal the same about Jesus.

Even so, the people of Capernaum, who had the opportunity to be exalted to heavenly glories, could just as easily fall to Hades, warned Jesus. Jesus' reproach upon the unrepentant citizens in Capernaum, Chorazin, and Bethsaida was quite severe, saying that they had seen his tender ministry of miracles and were still unrepentant.[57] Jesus added this scathing remark: "If the miracles which were performed in you had been performed in Sodom, it would still be in existence today! You can be sure that on the Judgment Day God will show more mercy to Sodom than to you."

Yet, these harsh reproaches issued in some of the most compassionate invitations ever given to anyone: "Come to me, all of you who are tired from carrying heavy loads, and I will give you rest. Take my yoke and put it on you and learn from me. Because I am gentle and humble in spirit; and you will find rest."[58]

The Zealot movement began in Galilee. The Zealots in the time of Jesus were a fanatical group of men who were zealous for the Jewish law and opposed the Roman presence with violence. They had taken a vow to kill any Roman when given the opportunity. The Zealot would take the life of an

---

[57] This mythic-poetic three-tiered universe with heaven above earth and Hades below was the common world view of Jesus' day. We bring a different scientific world view to the scriptures today but the spiritual truths remain. The Bible is a book of faith not science.

[58] Matthew 11:28-29. A latter chapter will be devoted to gentle invitations.

Israelite, if necessary, out of his zeal for the law of God. Jesus called Simon the Zealot to be one of his disciples (Luke 6:15; Acts 1:13) and that is a little like calling a terrorist today. The seeds for class warfare were sown early and reap an ever-increasing crop.

This background makes Jesus' "Gentle Galilean Glories" all the more amazing with transforming power. Simon the Zealot was slowly transformed by Jesus' gentle teachings. And the Gentle Galilean Glories of Jesus are a vision of world peace for every age.

So why do we speak of Galilean Glories? In Galilee Jesus became totally God-conscious, self-actualizing the glory of God in his life; and, thus, became a bridge between earthly and heavenly glories. The depth of his relationship to God was the uniqueness of his life and ministry. Jesus revealed this relationship by addressing God as "MY Father." (The importance of this relationship will be dealt with in a later chapter). The disciples are drawn into this dialogue between Jesus who was like a Son and God who was like a Father, and thereby are drawn into a heavenly activity and glory. John described this as the glory of Jesus: "The word, the creative principle or wisdom of God, was self-actualized in Jesus; and Jesus, full of grace and truth, lived among us. We saw his glory, the glory which he received as the Father's Son" (Based on John 1:14).

Jesus' prayer in John, chapter seventeen, reveals even more the depth of this glory: "Father, the hour has come. Give glory to Your Son, so that the Son may give glory to you." This prayer should be called the "Lord's Prayer" and the one we call the "Lord's Prayer" should be called the disciple's prayer. The disciples were the recipients of this glory: "I give them the same glory you gave me, so that they may be one, just as you and I are one" (John 17:22). The disciples in turn are to reflect this glory to the world: "My glory is shown through them" (John 17:10). As one who embodied this glory, Jesus became a heavenly messenger who acts out of his oneness with God. How does this fit with Jesus' lowly ministry in Galilee as seen in Mark? We might speak of this as a lowliness hidden in glory.

It is probably accurate to say that lowliness and glory, humiliation and exaltation, are not separated in Jesus' life and ministry like two stages on a journey---his lowliness seen in Galilee and his exaltation in Jerusalem. They are rather united with each other at all times in Jesus' life. If, indeed, the Temple visit at the age of twelve is an indication, Jesus was aware at that point of his unity with God. His response to his mother was, "I must be about my Father's business" (Luke 2:49). We have to remember that the Gospels were written from the end backward to the beginning. That is, they were written about forty to fifty years after the crucifixion and resurrection of Jesus. As happens with any important person, in the writing they take on mythic and legendary characteristics. The Temple visit is an example. Luke the Gospel writer is known as a historian and gave attention to detail, and this can be seen in the story, giving it an historical kernel.

At least from the time of his baptism onward, Jesus' union with God is a growing reality: "As soon as Jesus came up out of the water, he saw heaven opening and the Spirit coming down on him like a dove. And a voice came from heaven, "You are my Son. I am pleased with you'" (Mark 1:10-11).

The earthly Jesus who goes forth into a world of suffering and death does not lose his sense of oneness with God. Instead, he dies with this awareness on his lips: "Father, in your hands I place my spirit!" (Luke 23:46). Jesus' total commitment to God's aims is his glory, and this glory shone on the face of Jesus all through his gentle Galilean ministry. The Gospel of John seems to have substituted the "glory of God" for Mark, Matthew, and Luke's use of the "Kingdom of God."[59]

Why not Jerusalem glories? We must ask, "If Galilee was so important, why did Jesus leave Galilee and journey toward Jerusalem?" Jerusalem was the holy center of the land and of the people of Israel. Jesus must pursue Jerusalem, even if he could only weep over her. He would seek to cleanse the Temple and make it a House of Prayer for all nations. The uniqueness of the self-actualization of God's purposes in Jesus for Israel and for all people, is seen in Jesus' journey to the cross.

The authorities take Jesus prisoner and hand him over to Pilate to be crucified. At his death the veil of the Temple was rent, and the curtain is made null and void.

The resurrected Jesus directs his disciples back to Galilee, the place where he first came and the place where he will come again to commission them.[60] In Galilee the exalted and glorified Jesus bridged his earthly ministry with the ongoing Galilean Christian community built on Gentle Galilean Glories. It is this significance given to the Galilean ministry that we are seeking to recover. I am not saying that all the gentle teachings of Jesus occurred in Galilee. I am using Galilee in the broader sense, as a theological concept, as the home and place of Jesus and as an umbrella concept for his gentle teachings that slowly transform our lives and our world.

Why Gentle Galilean Glories?

We have asked why Galilee: Why Glories? Now we ask why Gentle? Does the New Testament verify that Jesus was gentle? The Greek New Testament does not have just one term for gentle. Several Greek words are used by different writers to describe gentleness in its various aspects. The

---

[59] This will be further developed in chapter 4 of this book.
[60] Matthew 28:16-20. See later chapter on resurrection in this book.

same is true of other concepts like love (αγαπη, ερος, φιλια). The Greek terms that best denote the gentle attitude are πραυς and πραυτης.

Jesus' Words of Gentleness

Πραυς, Πραυτης (gentle, gentleness)

In reference to persons, πραυς and πραυτης, the noun and adjective form, are best translated as gentle and gentleness. The two terms are used about 15 times in the Greek New Testament and may also be translated as meek, humble, friendly, or pleasant, in both adjective and noun forms. As used in these different forms the words imply gentleness as opposed to rough, harsh, or violent. Gentleness is a synonym of ελεος, mercy. It is an active attitude not passive submission, a sign of strength not weakness.

Among the Greeks, a gentle and friendly attitude toward family and friends was highly prized. It was the quality of a great soul like Socrates. However, it was alright to be harsh to one's enemies. For Plato πραυς was the mark of the ideal kingdom. For Aristotle it was a mean between anger which had a positive value and indifference.

In its Hebrew form, πραυς is used twelve times in the Old Testament. It is used only once in the Pentateuch, the first five books of the Old Testament, but it is a significant summary description of the great leader, Moses---"Moses was a humble (gentle) man, more humble than anyone else on earth."[61] Linking this word with Moses demonstrates its strength. One would never describe Moses who confronted Pharaoh as weak. Linking πραυς with Moses gives the word courage and boldness.

In the Old Testament gentleness is rooted in God. The inheritance of the land promised to Abraham and his descendants comes to the gentle who wait---"The humble will possess the land and enjoy prosperity and peace."[62]

These eschatological overtones are expressed as a messianic prophecy in Zechariah 9:9, "Rejoice, rejoice, people of Zion! Shout for joy, you people of Jerusalem! Look, your king is coming to you! He comes triumphant and victorious, but gentle and riding on a donkey."

In the New Testament, the mission of Jesus is the fulfillment of gentleness. In fact, it is the self-designation of Jesus in Matthew 11:28-30-- "Come to me, all of you who are tired from carrying heavy loads, and I will give your rest. Take my yoke and put it on you, and learn from me, because I am gentle and humble in spirit; and you will find rest. For the yoke I will give you is easy and the load I will put on you is light." In interpreting the

---

[61] Numbers 12:3.
[62] Psalm 37:9-11.

New Testament, the titles and descriptions that Jesus applies to himself should carry the greatest weight. Jesus did not hesitate to say, "I am gentle."

In fulfillment of eschatological hope, Jesus said, "Blessed are the gentle, they will receive what God has promised!"[63] As a further fulfillment of prophecy,[64] Jesus entered Jerusalem on what we call Palm Sunday as king---"Now this occurred to fulfill what was spoken by the prophet: 'Tell the daughter of Zion your King is now coming to you, Gentle, and riding on a donkey, Yea, on the colt of a beast of burden.'"[65]

This self-designation of Jesus as gentle is all the more significant when set against the Zealot and political messianic expectations of the first century in Galilee. The Gospel of John tells us that after the feeding of the five thousand these feelings were so strong that the crowd came and sought to force Jesus to become their king.[66]

That Jesus was πραυς, tender of heart, is also supported by the Letters of Paul in the New Testament and in non-biblical sources like the Gospel of Thomas, the Sibylline Oracles, and Pistis Sophia. In Second Corinthians chapter ten, verse one, Paul wrote, "Jesus himself was humble and gentle." Colossians 3:12 grounds kindness in the being of God, "You are God's people so be gentle, kind, humble, and meek." Titus 3:4 also describes God as kind.

ταπεινος, ταπεινοω, ταπεινωσις

This group of Greek words occurs thirty-four times in the New Testament, and they are usually translated "lowly", but they carry the connotation of gentle or gentleness. Here we will be concerned for the one occurrence that refers to Jesus. Again it is significant in that it is a self-designation, like πραυς. Jesus said of himself, "I am gentle (πραυς) and lowly (ταπεινοω) of heart (Matthew 11:29). Other occurrences of ταπεινος will find their way into our study at later stages.

χρηστος

Jesus used χρηστος twice, once to describe the nature of God as kind to the ungrateful and wicked (Luke 6:35) and once as a self-designation, describing himself as one who is kind or merciful in what he requires of those who come to him.[67]

---

[63] Matthew 5:5.
[64] Zechariah 9:9, quoted above.
[65] Matthew 21:4-5. Williams translation.
[66] John 6:14-15.
[67] Matthew 11:30.

It is important to see how χρηστος was used in the Septuagint in reference to God. A key passage is found in Exodus 34:6, "I am who I am, and I am kind and patient with my people, I show great love and I can be trusted." Here kindness takes on the quality of good character. God can be trusted to act with loving kindness toward the people of God, and this is the basis of the covenant God forms with the people of God. Even when Israel failed God, God continued to be kind and forgiving. In this context kindness takes on the qualities of patience and forgiveness.

Paul understood kindness in this way as well. In Romans 2:4 he writes about the "fullness of the χρηστητος, kindness, of God and God's patience, μακροθυμιας. In Romans 11:22 Paul speaks of the kindness of God being shown for the ones who have fallen away from God. In these uses of kindness Paul is true to the Old Testament understanding of the gracious action of God and he sees this fulfilled in the actions of Jesus. In Galatians 5:22-23 Paul listed kindness as one of the fruits of the Spirit that should be growing in the life of Christians.

1 Peter 2:2-3, shows the saving action of kindness. "Like new born infants, long for the pure spiritual milk, so that by it you may grow into salvation. If indeed you have tasted that the Lord is good and kind, χρηστος.

The crowing verse on kindness in the New Testament for Christians is Ephesians 4:32---"Be kind and merciful, and forgive others, just as God forgave you because of Christ." This key verse links kindness with forgiveness and anchors these qualities in God's own actions with the gentle ministry of Jesus.

ελεος

Ελεος occurs three times in Matthew and is usually translated as mercy. The Good News Bible translates it as kindness, its original Old Testament meaning. This can be seen in Matthew 9:9-11, which reports Jesus' call of Matthew to discipleship. After Jesus called Matthew, he was having a meal in Matthew's house with other tax collectors and outcasts. Some Pharisees saw this and asked, Jesus' disciples, "Why does Jesus eat with such people?" Jesus heard them and answered, "People who are well do not need a doctor, but only those who are sick. Go and find out what is meant by the scripture that says, 'It is kindness that I want, not animal sacrifices.' I have not come to call respectable people, but outcasts." This and the other two passages in Matthew that use ελεος (12:7; 23:23) characterize Jesus' ministry as merciful kindness toward the outcasts and demand the same for the disciples who would follow Jesus.

Ελεος, mercy, occurs six times in Luke. Five of these are in the birth announcements of John and Jesus and refer to the wonderful kindness and tender mercy God is showing toward the people of God.⁶⁸ Luke 1:78 is most relevant to the theme of "Gentle Galilean Glories:" "Our God is merciful and tender. God will cause the bright dawn of salvation to rise on us and to shine from heaven on all those who live in the dark shadow of death, to guide our path to peace."

σπλαγχνον, σπλανγχνιζομαι

In Luke 1:78, ελεος is combined with σπλαγχνον and is translated as "tender mercy." The verb form, σπλαγχνιζομαι, occurs twelve times in Matthew, Mark, and Luke, the Synoptic Gospels, and is usually translated as "having compassion." Ten of these represent Jesus as one in whom divine compassion is present. Jesus is moved with compassion toward a man with a dreaded skin disease,⁶⁹ the crowd of people who were like sheep without a shepherd,⁷⁰ and the hungry crowd.⁷¹

Jesus also had compassion on the widow of Nain and raised her dead son back to life⁷², and with compassion he restored sight to two blind men.⁷³ The verb, having compassion, also had a central place in three of Jesus' most significant parables: the unforgiving servant who had been forgiven with compassion,⁷⁴ the good Samaritan whose heart was filled with compassion when he saw the wounded man lying by the roadside,⁷⁵ and the parable of the prodigal son, better called the waiting father, for it is the father who saw the son a long way off and had compassion and ran to meet him.⁷⁶

In all of these teachings of Jesus that use σπλαγχνον and σπλαγχνιζομαιi, Jesus' human emotions are described in the strongest terms possible in order to stress the tender compassion with which God claims persons in saving grace. This was also true of all the other Greek words we have studied.

---

[68] Luke 1:50, 54, 58, 72, 78.
[69] Mark 1:41.
[70] Mark 6:34; Matthew 14:14.
[71] Mark 8:2; Matthew 15:32.
[72] Luke 7:11-17.
[73] Matthew 20:29-34.
[74] Matthew 18:21-35, See verse 34.
[75] Luke 10:25-37, see v. 33. Also the whole act of the Samaritan was summarized as an act of kindness, see v. 37.
[76] Luke 15:11-32, see v. 20.

χαρις

The χαρις word group appears about 175 times in the New Testament, with the majority occurring in the Epistles of Paul. Most English versions of the Bible translate χαρις as grace or gracious. However, the *Contemporary English Version* of the American Bible Society almost always translates χαρις as kindness. A survey of the history of the term from its early Greek origins to the time of the New Testament justifies this use of kindness. In both the Old Testament and the New Testament, the Hebrew and Greek words usually translated as grace implies a kind turning of one person to another in an act of assistance. God's covenant grace also implies kindness.

Perhaps the most significant uses of χαρις come in the Book of Revelation. At a time when the followers of Jesus are being persecuted and dying for their faith, John holds up a vision of the kind Jesus. The book starts with this prayer: "I pray that you will be blessed with kindness and peace from God, who is and was and is coming. May you receive kindness and peace from Jesus, the faithful witness."[77] Revelation ends with this prayer: "I pray that Jesus will come soon and be kind to all of you."[78] Summary: Yes, Jesus was gentle, lowly, and kind. The word clusters we have examined leave no room for doubt. What struck me was how Jesus described himself as being gentle. The parables and gentle invitations of Jesus examined in later chapters will further illustrate this quality of kindness. Thus, we are on solid ground when we speak of "Gentle, Galilean Glories." The glory of God shines in the words and deeds of Jesus. The disciples and the crowds who followed Jesus saw the glory of God shining through his gentle Galilean glories. Can there be any doubt that Jesus lived and taught gentle, Galilean glories?

Summary Remarks about the Importance of Gentle Teachings

It is my conviction that "gentle bio-philic teachings ring true in all cultures" and can be a unifying theme for dialogue between most religions of the world, offering a path to peace. Following the amazing discoveries of the genome project, the mapping of the human chromosomes, biologists speak of the genetic unity of all living things, believing that all organisms descended from the same ancestral life forms. Thus far the genome project has shown that the common ancestor of all living things was similar to single-celled microbes with the simplest molecular composition that go back several

---

[77] Based on Revelation 1:4-5 from the Greek New Testament.
[78] Based on Revelation 22:20-21, from the Greek New Testament. For a fuller treatment of this use of χαρις as kindness in Revelation see my book, *The Book of Revelation: Jesus' Kindness Transforms Suffering*.

billion years. Thus all living things share a molecular history and are interrelated, interconnected.

This dialogue must take place if we are to have reconciliation between the world religions and find a route to peace. The greatest challenge to theistic religions is the pervasive reality of evil and the misery it leaves in its wake. This unifying theme of gentleness is one possible solution to this problem, especially the growing divide between Christianity and Islam.[79]

"Loving-kindness" is a major theme in Judaism. The Psalms of the Old Testament are full of this concept that is key to understanding God and God's people. Since Judaism gave birth to Christianity and Islam, the two largest religions in the world, this unifying theme is something all three religions hold in common. "Metta" is a strong concept in Buddhism and carries the meaning of loving kindness or unconditional love. Buddha said, "My religion is kindness." He sought love without attachment. In much Buddhist thought love when practiced moves from self to friend, to enemy, and to all beings everywhere. "Karuna" or compassion that leads one to assist others is also key. Meaningful dialogue could be held around the theme of gentle teachings that could transform the relationships of these major religions.

Also, the longer I have lived with the New Testament the more I have become convinced that a major thrust of these sacred scriptures is to show the humanity of Jesus. We have focused on this purpose without violating any natural biological processes, and this makes Jesus' sacrificial death on the cross more meaningful with more transforming power. This approach also opens the door to see that other major religious leaders like Moses, Confucius, Mohammed, Buddha, Gandhi, and Martin Luther King, Jr. can also self-actualize creative love aims and purposes that transform lives and our world.

One may not be able to write a biographical account of the life of Jesus. My graduate study in New Testament led me on a search for the historical Jesus and I read all the major sources and many lives of Jesus, some in French and German. I have tried to keep up with the new search for the historical Jesus and the Jesus seminars.[80] However, I do believe you can locate in the Gospels the authentic gentle teachings of Jesus. Whether they all come from Jesus, some come from the Gospel writers, or some from the early Church community, really do not matter in one sense. They are all inspired by Jesus gentle ministry and remain insightful, challenging teachings than can change and transform lives and offer a path to peace.

---

[79] Surely the solution is not to ban all Muslims from our shores. Many ethnic groups have their terrorist elements. Dialogue based on kindness seems to be a more promising road to peace.

[80] See Appendix for a brief article on the search for the historical Jesus.

Jesus' Galilean vision of reality has flickered through many cultures since the time of Jesus, but it has never been fully realized. Yet Jesus' vision still holds the promise of creative advance and world transformation.

Chapter Four

Glory of God in The Gentle Teachings of Jesus: A Vision of Reality

Look deep into the gentle teachings of Jesus and you will find a source of inspiration, a vision for your life.

Every great movement has a theme or watchword. The Civil Rights movement and the life of Dr. Martin Luther King Jr. is a good example. Dr. King was a martyr of the civil rights movement and a great American who was shot by a sniper's bullet in Memphis in 1968 at age 39. His words and actions proclaimed a social justice that our nation could not ignore. In 1964 he was awarded the Nobel Peace Prize for his principles of nonviolence which were based on the teachings of Jesus and the example of Gandhi, the sage of India. Dr. King's movement was inspired and continues to be fueled by his "I have a dream" speech given on the steps of the Lincoln Memorial in 1963, in which he said, "I have a dream that one day this nation will rise up and live out the true meaning of its creed: 'We hold these truths to be self-evident; that all men are created equal.'" Then in a powerful voice he challenged our nation to "let freedom ring" until we are all "Free at last! Free at last! Thank God Almighty, we are free at last." Yes, every great movement has its visionary leader and theme.

According to the Gospel of Mark, the world-transforming theme of Jesus set out in his first sermon was: "The right time has come, and the Kingdom of God is near! Turn away from your sins and believe the Good News!"[81] Almost all New Testament scholars and New Testament theologians accept that the "Kingdom of God" is a major theme of Jesus. However, many today shy away from the term, "kingdom," because of its association with male dominance and power. We need to pay attention to meaning attributed to words and realize that abusive words often are the prelude to abusive action. The word, Kingdom, has become an abusive term for many. In my linguistic studies as a New Testament Greek major, I was also required to learn to read Hebrew, German, and French. These language studies have led me to see that words do not have meaning, they have usage. As Jesus used the term, Kingdom of God, it has a very rich meaning as long

---

[81]Mark 1:15, Good News Bible, TEV.

as it is seen in the context of Jesus' gentle teachings, but it has lost that rich meaning today for many.

This loss of meaning is due to the gap between the centuries. Words do not have meaning, they have usage; and that usage changes with the passing of time and changing cultures. Jesus' culture was patriarchal and monarchal, ruled by men and kings. Women were kept in submission by most. However, Jesus elevated the role of women, and we could not say after studying the gentle teachings of Jesus that his use of Kingdom of God was demeaning. This was not always true for Paul and the early church. In fact, the church is often the slowest to recognize abuse and to change. Instead of challenging abusive actions, the church often hides its head in the sand like an ostrich. The church needs to be more like a crustacean that sheds its theological skin every few years in order to grow a new one that is freeing.

When interpreting the Bible, one needs to acknowledge the gap between the centuries and ask two questions: "What it meant" and "What it means." Using this realistic hermeneutical principle made popular by Krister Stendahl, let us first ask what the kingdom of God meant in the New Testament.[82] In answering this question we use all the tools of biblical exegesis available to us, so it is not a simple question. University and seminary trained theologians are best equipped to answer this question, but it is a helpful question to ask for anyone reading the Bible. The second question we ask is what does the phrase Kingdom of God as used by Jesus mean today. Again, those who are skillfully trained as Bible scholars, theologians, and history are best able to see how meaning has changed across the centuries in the theology and creeds of the church, but they may not be best able to say what it means today and translate it into meaningful words and actions for today. Poets, musicians, and artists, with tender patience, can bring skills to capture the meaning for today. Lay persons skilled in the hard knocks of life can also offer deep insight into how scripture can meet daily needs of hurting people. Thus, lay people need to be involved in doing theology today.

It is a difficult thing to translate and interpret the phrase, "The Kingdom of God." In word and action Jesus proclaimed the βασιλεια (Greek word usually translated as Kingdom) of God in his Gentle Galilean Glories. Some interpreters of the New Testament simply Anglicize this Greek word and use the word Basileia for kingdom. If Galilee was his place, the theme, βασιλεια (Kingdom) of God, was his message. His last message before his ascension was about the βασιλεια of God. Luke tells us in the Book of Acts: For forty days after his death he appeared to them many times in ways that proved beyond a doubt that he was alive. They saw him, and he talked with them about the βασιλεια of God (Good News Bible, Acts 1:3). In between

---

[82] I used Stendahl's realistic hermeneutical theory in my Ph. D. dissertation, "Baptism and the Lord's Supper in the Gospel of John: a Hermeneutical Inquiry."

these bookend actions, the Gospels tell of Jesus speaking about the Kingdom of God and its equivalent, the Kingdom of Heaven, almost one hundred times. It is, indeed, one of his key watchwords.

A careful reading of the Gospels reveals a variety of meanings for these many uses of the phrase, Kingdom of God, revealing great freedom to use different words. The most notable change is the way Matthew prefers to use Kingdom of Heaven instead of Kingdom of God because of his Jewish audience. For Matthew and his audience, the name of God was so holy that one did not use the name often. Matthew was more comfortable with Kingdom of Heaven.

It is generally accepted by New Testament scholars today that Mark was the first Gospel written. Matthew and Luke used about 90% of Mark in writing their Gospel, adding from their own special sources. They also both quoted from a common source know as Q (Quelle, German word for source).

When reading these first three Gospels, laid alongside of each other in parallel columns,[83] one can see a variety of words suitable for giving the meaning of kingdom in the teachings of Jesus: heaven, glory, agape, good news and many other words and phrases. This variety could be put in the following formulas:

>   Jesus + agape (inclusive love) = Kingdom of God
>   Jesus + Good News = Kingdom of God
>   Jesus + glory = Kingdom of God
>   Jesus + gentle teachings = Kingdom of God

What we learn from these formulas and others linked in similar fashion is that the New Testament writers felt free to use different words to express Jesus' Good News about God. I believe the phrase, "Jesus' Gentle Galilean Glories," wrapped in love, expresses best what Jesus meant by the Kingdom of God.

Let us now test these words, agape, glory, good news, appointed time, gentle teachings, and see if they are true to the way Jesus used the phrase Kingdom of God and faithfully reinterpret the way it has been used in the teachings and creeds of the church since the time of Jesus. The headings below reflect the ways the kingdom of God in the teachings of Jesus have been understood by New Testament scholars through the ages.

---

[83] See *Gospel Parallels*, Thomas Nelson Publishers.

Time Is Fulfilled

Jesus' vision of reality is grounded in the Old Testament, where phrases like "His kingdom" and "Thy kingdom" appear often. They have been interpreted by many theologians to refer to God ruling in sovereign, kingly power. Yet, God's nurturing of Israel as a vineyard gives us more the picture of God as a Gardner, a Mr. Green Jeans, or Mother Nature who patiently and lovingly nurtures the vines to bear fruit. An example of the many uses of vineyard in the Old Testament and God as the vineyard keeper is Isaiah 4:7, where the prophet speaks for God saying, "Israel is the vineyard, and Judah is the garden I tended with care." Much of the Old Testament supports the view of God as creative responsive love. So, one could faithfully use "agape of God" for "Kingdom of God."

Jesus' understanding of the Kingdom of God as a vision of reality is patient and luring, similar to the prophet Habakkuk and to Daniel. Habakkuk wrote, "For the vision is yet for the appointed time; it hastens toward the goal, and it will not fail. Though it tarries, wait for it; for it will certainly come, it will not delay" (2:3).

In the Greek translation (Septuagint) the word for "appointed time" is Kairos. The vision of the appointed time when God will come near to God's people is also in Daniel with the same use of Kairós.[84] Here one could use "Kairós of God" or "appointed time" for Kingdom of God.

Jesus picked up on this familiar vision of the end time and dared to say that the awaited time was now taking place in his ministry: The time is fulfilled, and the appointed, awaited time (Kingdom) of God is near! By linking the Kingdom of God with the vision of the appointed and awaited time in Habakkuk and Daniel, Jesus gave a new vision of reality. God has now come near to people in the everyday compassionate ministry of Jesus in Galilee. In this vision of reality, the power of God's love is brought near to weak and struggling humans. As such it is a transforming and redeeming vision, gathering up broken individuals in the Galilean villages and country side and enlivening them with God's love aims and love energies. This agape of God equals the Kingdom of God.

Kingdom of God (Glory of God) Is Present

The Jews had long awaited the coming of God's glory. According to Mark, Jesus said in his first recorded sermon that the Good News of God was already at hand. Some translations say that the Kingdom of God is "near," meaning that it is coming in the near future. The confusion comes over how to translate *hggiken* in Mark 1:15, which can be translated as "near"

---

[84] Daniel 8:17, 10:14; 11:27, 35.

or "at hand," meaning "has arrived." For Jesus the glory and love of God was a present reality. When he read from the scroll of Isaiah in the synagogue of Nazareth about agape activity of God, saying---The Spirit of the Lord is upon me, because God has chosen me to bring good news to the poor. God has sent me to proclaim liberty to the captives and recovery of sight to the blind, to set free the oppressed and announce that the time has come when the Lord will save his people---He closed the scroll and said, This passage of scripture has come true today, as you heard it read (Luke 4:16-20).

Jesus no doubt understood that it is easier to project our hopes into the future than to claim them as present realities. So, he kept driving home the point that Good News realities are present now in his compassionate healing and helping ministry. Since Jesus did not fit their Messianic expectations, some of the Jewish people, especially the leaders, tried to label Jesus' activity as demonic. Once when Jesus had cast out an evil spirit from a man's life, someone in the crowd said, he casts out demons by Beelzebul, the ruler of the demons (Luke 11:15). Others in the crowd, seeking to test Jesus, cried out, Show us a sign from heaven (v. 16). In other words, "Jesus, are your actions a sign of God's saving presence?" Jesus answered,

"If I cast out demons by the finger of God then the glory (kingdom) of God has come upon you" (v. 20). In this verse one can faithfully translate kingdom as glory, agape, or good news. The aorist tense of the Greek verb, *ephthasen*, definitely described the agape of God as already present. The similar saying in Matthew 12:28 is further support for the presence of the agape glory of God in the healing ministry of Jesus: No, it is not Beelzebul, but God's Spirit, who gives me the power to drive out demons, which proves that the glory of God's Spirit (Kingdom) has already come upon you. Here one can translate kingdom as the Spirit of God has come upon you.

In sayings like these it is clear that the miraculous love energies of God are present in Jesus' ministry. The powerful love energies of God that permeated creation and were now present in Jesus' compassionate ministry were at work in overcoming the reign of evil. Perhaps one reason the crowds had trouble accepting that the love energies of God were present in Jesus' ministry was that they had a different view of power. They wanted a military king like King David, who would come riding on a great white horse and overthrow the Romans. They wanted a show of force and coercion. Jesus taught the persuasive power of love.

Many of the parables of Jesus, especially the ones concerning growth, imply that the glory of God is already present, even though the consummation is in the future. The parables of the farmer sowing seed and the housewife putting leaven in bread demonstrate that the Garden (kingdom) of God is already present, but its fruit is not fully mature. A future harvest is still awaited.

Kingdom of God (Glory of God) Is Future

Paradoxically the glory of God is both present and future. It is present wherever God rules, but God's rule is limited in the present, waiting on willing hands and devoted hearts. Jesus brought the glory of God near in his gentle Galilean ministry, and he will bring it to completion at the end time when he will rule for ever and ever.[85]

Jesus spoke of a future glory, but never gave a calendar date. In Mark 9:1, Jesus said, I tell you, there are some here who will not die until they have seen the agape of God come with amazing energy. In interpreting this verse we might place the emphasis on seeing, meaning that the agape of God has already come but some have not yet seen it. The emphasis could also be on energy, stressing that the agape energies are present but will come in greater glory. Perhaps, it is Jesus' prayer that these will see and experience the luring energy of the agape of God that comes through sacrificial service before they die. The glory that has already come for some does lie as possibilities to be actualized in the immediate future for others. In speaking of future glory Jesus sees God as the creative agency of future actuality, luring the world forward in creative advance.

At the institution of the Lord's Supper, Jesus spoke of this future glory: I tell you that from now on I will not drink this wine until the glory of God comes (Luke 22:18). This Lukan reading, which is also found in Matthew and Mark, anticipates a future consummation, while not denying it is already present.

The parable of the fig tree, using bio-philic language, also speaks of a future coming: Think of the fig tree and all the other trees. When you see their leaves beginning to appear, you know that summer is near. In the same way, when you see these things happening, you will know that the Garden of God is about to come to fruition (Luke 21:29-32). The phrase, when you see these things happening, refers to the natural phenomenon that will precede the coming of the glory of God.

Kingdom of God (Glory of God) Is Present and Future

In the bio-philic teaching of Jesus, then, the glory of God is both present and future. As present it is incomplete but growing and developing like a beautiful garden. It is growing like the grain of mustard seed that has sprouted into a bush.[86] It is expanding in the world like the leaven in the dough (Matthew 13:33). Under the persuasive creative energy of God's love aims and love energies it is growing and moving toward the Omega Point of

---

[85] Revelation 11:15
[86] Matthew 13:31-32.

all creation. Under the impulse of God's divine love energy, the calling forward, the glory grows from within. Jesus' Gentle Galilean Glories brought the agape glory of God near, so near that it possessed the hearts of many making them the children of God. Jesus' powerful love energies cast out malign spirits and brought healing and wholeness.

Thus, for Jesus the agape of God was his world transforming vision of reality. In his vision past and future meet, creating a dynamic present. Drawing on the powerful force of memory (the past---Habakkuk's and Daniel's visions) and anticipating God's redemptive future when all things would be unified (the future---his vision of reality and the locus of divine creativity), Jesus created a dynamic present in which the lure of God's novel love aims and love energies were powerfully felt (his present and our present). Seen in the light of this vision of reality that shone on the face of Jesus as he carried out his gentle Galilean ministry our lives take on new meaning and purpose.

Without a vision people perish. Hope in a meaningful future is essential for individuals as well as for societies. Jesus was a visionary. All great leaders are visionaries. Martin Luther King Jr. had a dream, a vision for America's black people and for all Americans. Gandhi had a vision for India's poor masses that brought renewed hope to the hopeless. President Bill Clinton said, at a crucial time in his run for the presidency, "I still believe in a place called Hope," and this visionary concept helped to propel him to victory.

A true visionary knows of heavenly glories and earthly realities. Jesus' gentle Galilean ministry bridged the two. What is seen in Jesus' gentle ministry is transformed into a reality in heaven and heaven's glory reciprocally flows back into Jesus' gentle teachings. He saw the world as it was and as it could be. Both perspectives are necessary for a true picture of reality---a vision of reality must capture both dimensions. Vision implies heavenly glory and reality gives it earthly grounding. A vision of reality is needed today as we live under the ever-present threat of nuclear holocaust.

Our everyday life is mundane without the inspiration of a vision. The world cannot become what it should without the creative transforming energy of agape realities. Jesus' depth and height of vision took in both realities. It looks both backward and forward; it takes us back to the Alpha of creation and forward to the Omega of final reconciliation when all things are one in God. In this sense Jesus' vision is a cosmic vision of reality which is all-inclusive.

While the agape of God proclaimed by Jesus spoke primarily of the rule of God, it implied a realm, a religious community, the church. However, the agape glory (kingdom) of God in its present reality is not to be equated with the church. It is a much larger reality that is cosmic in nature; yet, it does include the church. The church is identified with the agape of God wherever and whenever it is living the energy of God's love aims and purposes experienced in the gentle Galilean glories of Jesus.

The church can never grasp the full meaning of the agape glory of God, any more than it can grasp God; Christians can only be grasped by God and God's agape realities. Jesus' proclamation of the Good News called for repentance and belief. The church has been guilty on the one hand of relegating the agape teachings to the past of the historical Jesus and on the other hand of projecting them into the future of the cosmic Christ coming on the clouds of heaven. In both cases they lose their creative transforming power in God's dynamic present and in what could be our energized present. We need to repent, to turn, back to these Gospel truths and believe them with heart, mind, and soul. Such sincere belief will fuel the church with a renewed vision of glory of God realities. Without such a vision the church will surely perish.

On Seeing and Living the Glory of God

We have talked about seeing the glory of God, sensing its luring power, and entering the power field of these love energies. How do we see this vision of reality? Do you remember seeing 3-D movies where you wear special glasses that make the images on the screen seem to leap out at you? Viewers duck to avoid oncoming objects and yell as they follow sleds down a steep slope at bread-neck speeds. In one movie house the action of a herd of water buffalo stampeding through a river was so real that those sitting on the front row got water splashed in their faces. That is, they did until the usher discovered a gang of small boys hiding under the front seats shooting their water guns every time the stampede scene occurred!

The secret of 3-D movies, and there is a growing number of these today, is the way the special glasses you are given unifies two different images projected onto the screen. Now the movie producers are able to create the same effect on the screen and enable us to see two different perspectives without our having to wear the special glasses.

Seeing the world from two different perspectives is what Jesus asked his followers to do. Jesus embodied the logos, creative principle, and in so doing he brought heaven's perspective to bear on earthly realities. Those who heard Jesus teach lived in the hard knock world of political domination and economic hardships. Jesus spoke of a world of love, joy, and peace---a world of happiness and fulfillment. In this new heavenly world lions can lie down with lambs in perfect harmony. Jesus called this experience the βασιλεια of God (βασιλεια is the Greek word for kingdom that we have translated as Good News, glory, agape, Spiritual presence, and the sum of Jesus' gentle teachings).

Some who heard Jesus wanted the glory to come mainly in terms of earthly realities. Jesus saw the "big picture." He saw the glory of God in terms of heaven's realities being lived out on earth. The parables of Jesus are "earthly bio-philic stories with heavenly meaning." The Lord's Prayer also shows this big picture view of reality: "Thy Kingdom come. Thy will be done on earth as it is in heaven." This model prayer is spoken in Hebrew parallelism. The first phrase is a statement of fact, and the second phrase interprets the first. The first phrase, the statement of fact, could be translated as "Let your glory come." And "Thy will be done on earth as it is in heaven" is its interpretation. Thus, the glory of God is a time when God's will is done on earth as it is in heaven. This is a good principle of biblical interpretation to remember when you are studying the Hebrew Scriptures like the Psalms. Yet, it is a difficult task to hold these two perspectives in balance. As in 3-D vision, it requires the blending of two views, heavenly realities and earthly realities.

How does one receive this agape reality? Jesus' first sermon announced the Good News and marked the way to receive it. Listen to the heart of the sermon recorded for us in Mark 1:14-15---Jesus proclaimed the good news of God, saying, 'The time is fulfilled, and the agape of God has come near. Repent, and believe in the good news.

We have demonstrated that Jesus' believed the agape of God was already present in his life and teachings, and it was present as good news. In one parable Jesus described the good news as "treasure" and in another as "a pearl of great price." Listen to his words: The Good News of Heaven is like treasure hidden in a field, which someone found and hid; then in his joy he goes and sells all that he has and buys that field. Again, the agape glory of God is like a merchant in search of fine pearls; on finding one pearl of great value, he went and sold all that he had and bought it.[87]

These twin parables make use of a favorite theme in storytelling. Treasure! Stories of treasure-trove delight young and old to this day. Who has not thrilled to the tale of Long John Silver? Beyond doubt the treasure is the focus in both parables. The Gospel, the good news, is like treasure. Every word in the parable's points in this direction.

In Palestine, long subject to invasions, the discovery of treasure hidden in fields was a common experience. Somebody buried the treasure at the time of an invasion, was killed or exiled; and then, the plow of some laborer uncovered it. Treasure! The Gospel is like treasure from heaven.

It is a treasure that is found in Jesus! His birth is a gift from heaven. His life is a portrait of God. His loving deeds reveal the heart of God as love.

---

[87] Matthew 13:44-46.

It is a treasure that is found in Jesus! His death is the work of evil, and yet the revelation of the power of sacrificial love. While sin was doing its worst, Jesus was doing his very best. His death was the ultimate gift of love.

It is a treasure that is found in Jesus! His resurrection was the victory over sin and death. The empty tomb is like the mouth of God shouting to one and all "He is risen. He is risen indeed!

What a treasure we have in the Gospel of unconditional love! When the great joy of finding this treasure sweeps us away, no price is too great to pay to receive it. The twin parables move in with great force and say, complete surrender is the price we pay. To enter the glory of God we must be willing to give up everything else for the privilege of receiving it.

This is the meaning of repentance. Upon hearing the good news, we are to turn from our old ways to the ways of God. We cannot be filled with the glory of God unless we lay all else aside. These parables call for complete commitment to the will of God.

There is an excitement and joy that permeates these glorious parables. This is especially true about the treasure that is found. When the plowman found the treasure, Jesus said, in joy he goes, and sells, and buys the land (Matthew 13:44).

We have lost this sense of Joy and enthusiasm for the agape of God today. We handle the treasure of the Gospel with a familiarity that borders on casualness and complacency. We take this Good News so for granted that the brightness, spontaneity, and joy are all but lost.

Emerson wrote, "Though we travel the world over to find the beautiful we must carry it with us, or we find it not." There is a little ditty that goes like this: "Pussy cat, pussy cat, where have you been? I've been to London to see the Queen. Pussy cat, pussy cat, what did you there? I frightened a mouse under her chair!" So often we come to church wanting to find something beautiful and to take something away, but what do we bring to the worship experience? Do we come in a spirit of prayer and expectation? Do we put out heart and soul enthusiastically into the worship service? Do we sing with joy, pray with fervor, and commit our all?

When we come to worship the door of opportunity is opened to us. The treasure of the Gospel is here to be found. The opportunity of a new life, the very life of God, is laid on the altar like a pearl of great price. All we have to do is receive the treasure

In the Sermon on the Mount, Jesus asked his followers to see the treasure all around them in the birds of the air and the flowers of the field. Then Jesus used these beautiful bio-philic gifts to speak of God's love and care for them. These lovely images from nature invite us to open our eyes and see. The Greek verb, εμβλεψατε, translated as "consider" also can be translated as "an entreaty or plea to look at intently," "see into," or "contemplate" these gentle teachings.

When I take time to hold these gentle words in my hands and heart, to taste and see their goodness and beauty, I find my search for meaning, the central search for every person, being fulfilled; and I am most fully alive, for to see is to take part in the abundant life Jesus offers.

In these gentle teachings from the Sermon on the Mount, εμβλεψατε is joined with τρεφει, translated as "take care" or "feed". As used by Jesus it means God our Heavenly Father will take care of you. Even though Jesus used the name, Father, he balanced this with the verb, τρεφει, which carries the meaning of being feed at the breast, as a mother nurtures her child. Thus, the meaning is your God who is like a Father and a Mother will take care of you.

> When I wake in the night with fear
> for the safety of my grandchildren,
> I consider the birds of the air
> and the flowers of the fields…
> I gather the peace of the gentle teachings
> and rest in the gentle care of God.

Those who are happiest in life are seeking to live these gentle teachings in their family life and in their everyday work. The example of Mr. Archie Roach comes to my mind. Mr. Roach was a retired farmer when I came to know him. He was also chairman of our stewardship drive every year at our Church in Chesapeake, Virginia. Mr. Roach had a favorite saying, "We should give until it hurts." Then he would add, "In fact, we haven't really given until we give sacrificially---we must give until it hurts." Mr. Roach knew what it means to seek the glory of God first in life.

We cannot buy and trade our faith on margin like we do stocks. In order to gain this treasure, we have to lay everything on the line now. The man who found the treasure and the pearl went and sold all he had and bought them. Buying stock on margin is a risky business. You may or may not gain on your investment. You buy a lottery ticket hoping to win millions. The odds are about one in fifty million that you will win. Finding this treasure is a sure thing. All you have to do is believe and trust God's love to transform you into a child of God. Then the treasure of the Gospel is yours.

In simple fact, we must put everything into this faith transaction in order to get anything from it. Jesus said that we must lose our life for the Gospel's sake in order to find it. To give anything less than our all is to get nothing but the shame of hypocrisy and disillusionment.

When we lose ourselves into these agape realities, we become a totally new person, and we are given a new name by God. D. J. Butler has written a little song that tells this story:

I will change your name,
You shall no longer be called
Wounded, outcast, lonely or afraid.
I will change your name,
Your new name shall be
Confidence, joyfulness, overcoming one,
Faithfulness, friend of God, one who seeks My face.

This is what it means to enter the glory of God. You are a new person, with a new name and a new vision of reality!

Glory of God and Jesus' Birth

Agape energy must be interpreted in light of the birth of Jesus and growth in his God-consciousness. According to the Gospel of John the Word that was in the beginning, the Word that created all things, became flesh and dwelt in our midst.[88] We might interpret this as God seeking to influence the world by calling Jesus to live God's love aims and purposes in the world. The self-actualization of God into the world through the gentle teachings of Jesus brought the birth of new possibilities for all created things. The divine power of transformation is demonstrated as creative persuasive love rather than coercive power. Jesus demonstrated the power of persuasion as opposed to controlling power as the most effective power of reality.

Jesus' God-consciousness evokes the best from us. The stories of Mary and Joseph, the baby Jesus in a stable manger, the shepherds, Simeon, and Anna are couched in tender words that warm our hearts and evoke the best from us. And we should not miss the fact that these are the powerless people of the world. Jesus came into Caesar's world, but these are not Caesar's stories, and these are not Caesar's ways. These are stories of the lowly people of the world being lifted to heaven's glory and of lives being transformed by angelic visitations. And the Gospel writers will not let us forget that it is the creative transformation of God's love that is at work in these lowly events.

Glory of God and Jesus' Gentle Galilean Ministry

Jesus' Gentle Galilean ministry dwelt on the tender ways of life that slowly operate by the persuasive power of love rather than coercion. Jesus' power is seen precisely in the absence of force and coercion, and in the motivating power of love. Jesus' parabolic teaching as can be seen in the Parable of the Good Samaritan focused on the broken and bruised ones in

---

[88] John 1:1-14.

the world. The powerless receive the power of God. Jesus' teaching often focused on the widows and children, both who were powerless in the first century. The fragile child is lifted up as the symbol of the essence of the glory of God.

The vision of reality that is expressed in these tender sayings and actions of Jesus needs to fuel the Christian vision today. The Church and its steeple stand more as symbols of power and influence today than as beacons that call the needy to the source of lifesaving. The church is too enamored with political power that borders on demagoguery. Only Jesus' vision of reality can shake us out of our complacency and open us to creative transformation.

Glory of God and The Suffering Death of Jesus

Good News as persuasive love rather than coercive force is most clearly seen in the Gethsemane prayer and arrest of Jesus. When the soldiers came to arrest Jesus, Peter and the other disciples wanted to draw their swords and fight, in fact we are told that one of the disciples drew his sword and cut off the ear of the High Priest's servant.[89] Jesus had to tell them to put up their swords. His glory would not be founded on violent overthrow of political systems but on the power of sacrificial love. Jesus was willing to die for the principle he had made central to his Gentle Galilean ministry: If you want to save your own life, you will lose it; but if you lose your life for me and for the gospel, you will save it. Jesus followed this central saying with a warning: Do you gain anything if you win the whole world but lose your life?[90]

There is no symbol of powerlessness greater than death by crucifixion. The victim is bound to an old rugged cross with nails driven through the hands and feet. A crown of thorns is shoved on the brow causing blood to trickle down the face. The broken and bruised individual hangs in the blistering sun with no clothes for protection. Parched and dried by the sun the victim is not even able to get a drink of cool water. As a mockery vinegar is placed on the dry cracked tongue. Finally, a spear is thrust in the side as a final act of cruelty. Can any individual be so powerless as a crucified one? Yet Jesus said, if I be lifted up, I will draw all persons to me! Jesus' agape ways are not the ways of the world. And the Scriptures say of Jesus' ways: There is no greater love than this: that a person would lay down life for another.[91]

---

[89] Luke 22:49-50.
[90] Mark 8:35-36.
[91] For a fuller discussion of the cross and resurrection, see chapter 12 later in this book.

Glory of God and The Resurrection of Jesus

Jesus' gentle teachings and his sacrificial gift on the cross are wrapped in his agape of God theme, and it is in light of those gentle teachings and sacrifice that we must understand the resurrection of Jesus. Jesus lived life out among the hurting people, and he spoke to them of the birds of the air and the flowers of the field saying, God cares for them, how much more will God care for you. In these bio-philic nature teachings, Jesus was trying to help people have a better life here and in the hereafter. He loved and cared for people, and he touched their lives in healing ways. The transforming healing power of Jesus' gentle teachings open the possibility for us to see the transforming nature of God at work in the resurrection of Jesus!

Jesus' resurrection was the vindication of the kindness that has always been at the heart of God. Jesus' resurrection continued his theme of strengthening and encouraging others for the living of life, here and now. Jesus called and taught his disciples so they could continue his gentle teachings based on the love commandment and extend them into the world. Jesus' resurrection makes love energies more real and possible on a continuing basis.

Glory of God and The Church

The church should be about what Jesus was about, i.e., teach and preach what Jesus taught and preached. Jesus came preaching: The glory of God is near! Turn away from your sins and believe the Good News![92] Not only did Jesus preach agape, he commissioned the disciples to do the same: Go and preach, "The glory of Heaven is near."[93]

Our challenge is to participate now in agape activity, and here are a few simple guidelines for the Church in living agape realities.

> 1). The church does not generate this activity; it receives it as a gift of grace and mercy or what the Psalms would call, lovingkindness.
>
> 2). The gift of God's rule is cause for the church to celebrate in joy and thanksgiving with all of God's children everywhere, without any exclusions based on gender, sexual orientation, race, religion, or economic status.
>
> 3). Jesus is the supreme revelation of God's rule in human history. The proclaimer of God's love became the proclaimed. Jesus told parables about the glory of God, but to experience Jesus, who

---

[92] Mark 1:15.
[93] Matthew 10:7; see also Luke 10:1-12.

became totally God conscious, was to experience the rule of God. Jesus' life, death, and resurrection are at the heart of agape.

4). Jesus' invitation to enter the glory of God is a call to radical change. This is a call to ongoing repentance and conversion. It is also a call to covenant and communal living.

5). Agape creates its own energy field. We are drawn into this field by the power of the Holy Spirit. To live and walk in the power of the Spirit is to participate in God's New Age.[94]

6). In its worship and corporate intercessory prayers, the Church is drawn into this power field and becomes a partner with God in bringing about glory of God realities.

7). The Good News of agape is freeing and liberating. It relates to all of life and all conditions of life. Society and the church often bind and oppress rather than liberate.

How do the gentle Galilean glories of Jesus transform our lives? Jesus lived the creative love of God in his words and actions. Jesus' words acted God's new reign of love and his actions spoke God's love. When we receive Jesus' gentle teachings, believe them in our hearts, speak them in our words, and live them in our actions, we are open to God's creative responsive love. When we believe that Jesus was totally God-conscious, one with God, we are more open to God's aims and purposes for our lives and are more likely to respond to God's creative love more fully and positively.

Wherever authentic gentle teachings of Jesus are lived and spoken, Jesus is embodied, and the glory of God is present and the self-actualization of the creative love of God occurs anew. The church exists to extend the gentle teachings of Jesus revealing the love of God in a broken world. As we are transformed by God's love present in Jesus, we make that love available for all other persons and things, we become as one in cosmic community. Where the gentle teachings of Jesus are faithfully taught and lived, there the gifts of love, joy, and peace are given. Is there anything our broken world needs more than this transformation?

God is in all acts of transformation, in our transformation and world transformation, feeling our joys and sorrows, our fears and hopes, taking them all into the divine life, and God is enriched in the process, for giving and receiving love is always energizing, enriching, and transforming!

---

[94] See Galatians 5:16-26 and 1 Corinthians 4:20.

Chapter Five

Jesus' Gentle Teachings Father/Son

The words of the father and mother lead to the deeds of the son and daughter. Gentle words prepare children, make them ready for life, move them to tender words and actions.

The description of deities as "Father" can be found in many religions. In the environment of Israel, our concern here, the Babylonian moon-god, Sin, was called the father of gods and men. The Stoics spoke of their god as father of the universe. In the Old Testament, God was called the "Father" of Israel from the exile onwards (Jer. 3:19; 31:9). Prior to the exile God was called "Father" of the kings (2 Samuel 7:14). The decline of the monarchy may have supplied the impetus for broadening the concept to take in the whole nation of Israel.

While at times God's fatherly and motherly care reached great depths of meaning for Israel, as can be seen in Hosea 11:1-4, "When Israel was a child, I loved her/him, and I called my children out of Egypt. But as the saying goes, 'The more they were called, the more they rebelled.' They never stopped offering incense and sacrifices to the idols of Baal. I took Israel by the arm and taught my children to walk. But they would not admit that I was the one who had healed them. I led them with kindness and with love, not with ropes. I held them close to me: I bent down to feed them." Here God is imaged as a mother bending down to feed her child at her breast.

Yet, it remained for Jesus to move this parental goodness and care into the center of his understanding of God. In chapter one, we suggested that if one is not comfortable using the term, Father, for God that it is okay to substitute Mother or Parent, using the biblical example of Hosea. Hosea also showed great kindness in going out and finding Gomer and restoring her in their family. The story of Hosea and Gomer is like a parable showing that God still loves and cares for people in spite of what they might do or in the case of Gomer it might be more accurate to say, what is done to them.

If you grew up with an abusive father and mother, or if you were abandoned by one or both parents, you may not be able to use any of these terms for God. Some under these conditions are able to find an adoptive mother and father who are very loving, and they are able to use these terms again for God. Still others may discover that even though our human parents fail us, God will always be with us, in us and for us in loving and caring ways; and they are comfortable using these terms for God.

Since the relationship of Jesus as Son with God as Father stressed filial relationship and obedience, not biological or sexual significance, nothing would be lost in finding a substitution for this Father/Son analogy.

Perhaps the best solution is for us to find a balance of terms, using the different terms where appropriate, and there are places to use mother for God, as in the example of Hosea. We should always use Bible translations that are gender sensitive in choice of language and be gender sensitive in our choice of words and actions, for words do become the grammar of our theology. Abusive words often precede abusive action. If I am using the term, "Father," for God I usually add that God is like a father or God is like a mother. For God to call forth creation out of chaos, a creation that was conducive for the evolution of humans as male and female, shows that God understands human sexuality; but God is neither male nor female.

To speak of God who is like a Father/Mother is to speak of Jesus as like a Son of God. In the New Testament this is always a mutual relationship. Historically the starting point of this relationship is with God; it is not circular in this sense. The infinite reality that sustains the whole of life is the reality of God. Living in the faith community of Israel, Jesus affirmed this. However, the historical understanding of God was given a quite new and distinctive understanding through the historical ministry of Jesus and his biophilic gentle teachings. In this sense, faith in God as One who is like a Father is one with faith in Jesus as one who is like a Son of God who reveals to us that we are all daughters and sons of God.

The term, Son of God, was present in Jewish thought prior to Jesus. It was used to describe the nation of Israel as a whole as can be seen in the phrase, "Israel is my first-born son," in Exodus 4:22. Surely the meaning here is that Israel is like a son or daughter of God. In Psalm 2:7 it is said of the anointed King David, "You are my son, because today I have become your father." Some apocalyptic writings like Enoch 105:3 and IV Ezra 7:28-29 use the title Son of God for the promised Messiah. All of these references stress the filial obedience that should be present between a son/daughter and a parent and not biological relationship. So, we could say that Jesus became like a son of God in the sense that he discovered this relationship in his sacred Scriptures and self-actualized the concept in his own relationship with God.

In mediating this relational role, Jesus is a bridge, not only for our understanding of God, but also for our understanding of existence. Jesus' gentle ministry in Galilee is rooted in God who was experienced to be like a kind father and gentle mother. Jesus' gentle ministry moves us to be kind and tender-hearted to one another, and forgiving of one another, as God has forgiven us,[95] realizing that all of us are daughters and sons of God, in the one family of God[96]

What did Jesus do to this belief of the prophets, psalmists, and sages, this belief in God as Father, to give it such power, influence, and wide use in the New Testament? The use of the name "Father" for God by Jesus is found four times in Mark, fifteen times in Luke, forty-two times in Matthew, and one hundred and seven times in John.

The use of the name "Father" in the other books of the New Testament are three times in Acts, thirty-nine times in the Pauline Epistles, three times in the Pastoral Epistles, two times in Hebrews, three times in James, three times in I Peter, one time in II Peter, sixteen times in I and II John, one time in Jude, and four times in Revelation.

The writings of John have by far the greatest use with one hundred and twenty-seven. Matthew has the next highest with forty-two, seventeen of these occurrences are in the three chapters of the Sermon on the Mount. So, basically it has been the writings of John and the Sermon on the Mount, especially the Lord's Prayer, that have had the greatest influence in making the name, Father, familiar to Christians. The comparatively high use in the Epistles of Paul is less significant when we take into account their size in comparison with I and II John and the Sermon on the Mount.

You may ask why there are so many uses of the term, Father, for God in the Bible and so few places where God is seen more like a mother. All literature is shaped by its environment and culture. In the time of Jesus daily life was patriarchal and all the New Testament writers were men. This accounts for the heavy use of male terms. The unique thing about Jesus' gentle teachings and actions is that they were so inclusive and elevated the role of women.

In showing his great love for Jerusalem, Jesus said, "Jerusalem, Jerusalem! How often I wanted to gather your people as a hen gathers her chicks under her wings."[97] Many of Jesus' gentle teachings and miracles were with women like the woman with a long term illness reported in Luke 13:10-17, the widow of Nain,[98] the widow's offering that is held up as the true example of sacrificial giving,[99] and many other stories that elevate the dignity and personhood of women. Women also played a prominent role in Jesus' gentle ministry, most notably his Mother, Mary, and his friends, Mary and Martha who are featured in three major Gospel stories.

---

[95] Ephesians 4:32.
[96] John 1:12.
[97] Matthew 23:37-38; Luke 13:34-35.
[98] Luke 7:12.
[99] Mark 12:41-44; Luke 21:1-4.

Luke also reports that there were many women who benefited from Jesus' compassion and care and who in turn ministered to him and along with him, even travelling with Jesus as disciples and evangelists.[100] Jesus' gentle words and actions modeled a decisive move toward the formation of a new community based on inclusive and nonrestrictive agape. It remains for the community Jesus called forth to continue to live this love and break down all barriers.

Jesus' Use of Father in Mark

    Jesus' first use of the address, Father, comes, according to Mark, after Peter's confession of Jesus as the Messiah at Caesarea Philippi: If a person is ashamed of me and of my teaching in this godless and wicked day, then the Son of Man will be ashamed of him when He comes in the glory of his Father with the holy angels (Mark 8:38). Jesus openly addressed God as Father from this point on.
    Jesus had spoken of his Father; now he speaks to the disciples about their Father: And when you stand and pray, forgive anything you may have against anyone, so that your Father in heaven will forgive the wrongs you have done. Some manuscripts add the reverse thought. If you do not forgive others, your Father in heaven will not forgive the wrongs you have done.[101] Jesus drew the disciples into his relationship with the Father: my Father is your Father.
    Jesus also spoke of "the Father" in a general way, perhaps implying the Father of all. When asked about the end time he replied: No one knows, however, when that day or hour will come--neither the angels in heaven, not the Son, only the Father knows.[102] This is the first time the title "Son" has been used in Mark in the "Father-Son" relationship. Sonship has been implied in the other uses. Some New Testament scholars believe that this use of the title, Son of God, is the creation of the early church. Yet, just why the church would insert "the Son" into such a hard to understand saying leads one to think that it came from Jesus. This would support the change that came in some manuscripts when "not the Son" was dropped. Luke using the same source as Matthew in writing his Gospel dropped the verse entirely. Is it not hard to understand why the Church would create a saying of Jesus which would cause so much embarrassment and would later seek to erase it from the record?

---

[100] Luke 8:1-3, there were more than twelve disciples, this number is symbolic for the twelve tribes of Israel, showing how Jesus fulfills the purpose of God's people.
[101] Mark 11:25-26.
[102] Mark 13:32.

Mark has one other use of "Father" and it is an address to God in prayer.[103] This will be dealt with later in a section on Jesus' use of the title "Father" in his prayers. All the uses of "Father" for God in Mark come after Peter's confession of Jesus as Messiah. When the four occurrences are looked at together (the fifth occurrence in Mark 11:26 is not included on textual considerations; it is not in the oldest and best manuscripts we now have of Mark), there seems to be a progression of revelation on the part of Jesus; and Mark as the first and earliest Gospel reflects this developing concept.

Jesus was very conscious of false messianic expectations that were rampant in Galilee, the home of the Zealots. Thus, he questioned the disciples about the popular opinions of his ministry; Who do men say that I am?[104] The various answers given by the disciples indicated much speculation as well as confusion: Some say you are John the Baptist; and others say you are Elijah; but still others say you are one of the prophets.[105]

More importantly, Jesus wanted to know what his disciples thought so he asked, but who do you say that I am? Peter answered, you are the Messiah! Immediately, Jesus warned them to tell no one about him.[106] Jesus wanted to continue to teach his disciples about the nature of his sacrificial suffering servant role. As a part of this teaching he reveals his relationship to God in filial terms as Father and Son. The revelation is first "my Father," then "your Father," and finally "the Father of all."

Jesus' concern for the growing messianic expectations was real. After the feeding of the five thousand, the crowd from Galilee tried to seize Jesus and force him to become king (John 5:15). This struggle virtually ended the Galilean ministry. Jesus could no longer openly teach the crowds without inciting them and possibly starting a riot.

Jesus' Use of Father in Matthew

In Matthew Jesus refers to God as Father forty-two times. In eight cases Matthew uses Father in material that is common with Luke and not found in Mark, often called Q from the German word Quelle, meaning source. Almost half of Matthew's occurrences are found in the Sermon on the Mount. The remaining instances in Matthew conform to the pattern seen in Mark: they come after Peter's confession and are in Jesus' prayers or in discourses with the disciples.

---

[103] Mark 14:36.
[104] Mark 8:27.
[105] Mark 8:28.
[106] Mark 8:30.

Jesus' Use of Father in Luke

In Luke Jesus refers to God fifteen times as Father. Nine of these uses are in the Q source and six are in the material unique to Luke, sometimes called L. Luke conforms to the pattern seen in Mark and Matthew: with one exception they come after Peter's confession and are in Jesus' prayers or in discourses with the disciples.

Jesus' Use of Father in John

The Gospel of John presents Jesus using the name, Father, for God one hundred and seven times. In fact, it is the Gospel of John which has made "Father" the natural name of God among Christians. So, apparently, like Matthew, John has brought into the foreground something which was far more important to Jesus--something which was the very essence of the Gospel.

The writer of the Gospel of John showed the greatest freedom in his use of the gospel stories about Jesus and the traditions that circulated in oral form. For example, there is no commission to baptize and no institution of the Lord's Supper in the Gospel of John, probably due to the fact that there was a growing conflict between Christians and Jews over the cleansing rites of Jews and baptism among Christians. Also, the Lord's Supper was becoming like a medicine of immortality as can be seen in Ignatius. So John shifts the emphasis from water to Spirit and from bread and cup in the Upper Room to gifts of love, joy, and peace, joined with prayers for unity.[107] In chapter four where we find Jesus' long discourse with the woman of Samaria, long discourses is a feature of the Fourth Gospel as opposed to the first three, we find another shift in the use of the term, Father. After using the term, Father, a few times in the conversation, the woman reveals more of her background and needs. She probably had an abusive relationship with several men for she had lived with five husbands and was currently living with a man who was not her husband.[108] This does not necessarily mean that she was a sinful woman. Levirate laws of that time required that if a married man died, his next oldest brother was required to take his wife as his own. Did this happen to the woman of Samaria five times, until there was no one to take care of her? In a patriarchal society there were very few ways a woman could care for herself.

---

[107] See my Ph. D. dissertation, "Baptism and the Lord's Supper in the Gospel of John: A Hermeneutical Inquiry.

[108] John 4:18.

At the end of their conversation, Jesus shifts from using the address, Father, perhaps seeing the woman wince at the mention of this male term, to saying that God is Spirit and is to be worshipped in Spirit.[109] Jesus may have realized that this abused woman could not relate to God as Father so he refers to God as Spirit.

Father as an Address to God in Jesus' Prayers

The Gospels are unanimous in their witness that Jesus always addressed God as "Abba", "Father", in his prayers. The only exception is Jesus' cry from the cross: Eloi, Eloi, lema sabachthani, which means, My God, my God, why did you abandon me?[110] Jesus addressed God as Abba, Father, in prayer sixteen times.[111]

Joachim Jeremias has made an extensive study of Jesus' use of "Abba" (Aramaic form of Father) as an address to God, and he could not find a single example of God being addressed as Abba in Judaism, but Jesus always addressed God in this way in his prayers. Jeremias admits that it is only Mark who has handed on Abba as an address to God, and Mark also follows Abba, the Aramaic term, with the Greek ο πατηρ. "Αββα ο πατηρ" as an address to God became widespread in the early church as can be seen by its use in the Greek text of a general Epistle like Galatians 4:6 and in the Greek text of a wide-flung church like Rome as seen in Romans 8:15. In these text the phrase, Αββα ο πατηρ, is found along side of "Spirit" as a calling out of the Spirit, "Abba, Father."

It is the unusual character of this address, Αββα ο πατηρ, joining the Aramaic and Greek terms for father in one address, and the remarkable variation of the structure of the Greek forms, πατηρ μου, translated as "my father," as personal address, and ο πατηρ, translated as vocative, and sometimes both ways in the same verse or passage that has led Jeremias to say that Jesus always addressed God as Abba in his prayers.[112] The only exception is the cry from the cross mentioned above. In the Judaism of Jesus' day, abba was a child's word, used in everyday talk. The Jews would have

---

[109] John 4:24.

[110] Mark 15:34, the first phrase of this verse is in Aramaic, a language spoken in Palestine at the time of Jesus, and the last phrase is a quote from Psalm 22:2. The quote provided the structure and choice of words.

[111] Mark 14:36; Matthew 6:9; 11:25f., 26:42; Luke 10:21; 11:2; 23:34, 46; John 11:41; 12:27f.; 17:1, 5,11, 21, 24f..

[112] For a fuller discussion of the use of Abba as an address to God, see Joachim Jeremias, *New Testament Theology*. New York: Charles Scribner's Sons, 1971. , pp. 61-68. See also, Jeremias, *The Prayers of Jesus*.

considered it disrespectful and therefore unthinkable to address God with this familiar word.[113]

The complete novelty and uniqueness of abba as an address to God in Jesus' prayers supports its authenticity. It would have been almost unthinkable for the disciples and the Gospel writers to have created this message. Clearly, Jesus spoke to God as a child would speak to his father: "Confidently and securely, and yet at the same time reverently and obediently" (Ibid.). This awareness, more than any- thing else, shaped Jesus' message and ministry, especially his gentle Galilean glories.

The question must now be asked, why was there an increase in the use of the title "Father" for God on the part of Jesus from Mark (4), to Luke (15), to Matthew (42), and finally to John (107). It is almost universally agreed that Mark was the first Gospel writer and John the last. Is Mark reflecting the historical situation accurately, and therefore each of the other Gospel writers increasingly expanded the usage?

I believe that Jesus passed through a religious experience comparable to what is called "stages of faith" or "passage" today. His understanding of God as Father was the core of that experience. That awareness was awakening at the age of twelve when Jesus said to his earthly parents, I must be in my Father's house,[114] and it was fully realized when he was baptized by John: You are my dear Son. I am pleased with you.[115] In this vision and voice from heaven Jesus received his mission and message.

Jesus' realization of God being like a father was such a deeply personal religious experience that he only spoke of it to a few chosen disciples. However, that which was the supreme reality of his life shone through his words and actions in such a way that those who saw him saw God in loving ways like a child would see a caring father and mother. In Jesus as one who was like a son of God, people saw the light of the glory of God. For Jesus God revealed like a father or mother was the supreme reality of his life; and his mission and message would make this intimate relationship known to his disciples and through them to the world.

The increase in usage of the name, Father, was due to Matthew and John's tendency to add to and expand the usage. In so doing they were endeavoring to bring into the foreground even more something they saw to be at the very center of Jesus' understanding of God and his relationship to God.

Another way to interpret this phenomenon is that Mark suppressed the usage. If he was writing for a Galilean Christian community instead of a

---

[113] Ibid., p. 67.
[114] Luke 2:49.
[115] Mark 1:11.

Roman community as is supposed by some, there would be a reluctance to highlight Jesus' usage of the term, Abba, Father, for it would be a stumbling block in a Palestinian Jewish setting. This would especially explain why he reported only one occurrence of Jesus addressing God as Abba, Father, in his prayers.[116] As we saw above there are no examples in Palestinian Judaism of "Abba" as an address to God in prayer. This everyday usage of Abba in conversation would not have been appropriate for an address to God. So, just as Jesus suppressed its usage in public and reserved its use in prayers and discourses with his disciples for fear of exciting uncontrollable messianic hopes, Mark suppressed it for a somewhat similar reason--it would be a stumbling block in his community.

Luke follows the lead of Mark and is perhaps more historical in doing so. Matthew and John writing for different audiences, and for John a later time, saw no reason to suppress the usage so they brought to the foreground what was central to the Gospel message.

No matter which direction one takes in interpreting the evidence, it is firmly established that Jesus himself made his intimate relationship with God central to his teaching, and we need to find some name for God that is meaningful in our personal relationship with God. For Jesus being like a son of God was not a divine title to be claimed, but a relationship to be shared. It is the controlling motif in understanding the gentle, Galilean glories that shone in the face of Jesus.

It is important to say in conclusion that Jesus used the name, "Abba, Father," for God and "Son of God" as a personal self-designation to show the relational way he had come to know God's love in his own life and ministry. Whatever name we use for God, it should not be used to show gender or gender preference in titles for God and should communicate a loving caring relationship. Jesus clearly elevated the role of women in this gentle actions and teachings. These concepts will be discussed further in the chapter on the Trinity.

---

[116] Mark 14:36. Garden of Gethsemane prayer.

Chapter Six

Gentle Teaching: Agape

Study Jesus' gentle love words. They will never fail you.

The gentle teachings of Jesus affirm that God is in the world and for the world, in us and for us, and that God's actions are best described as creative relational love. On the deepest level, we have learned that love involves a sympathetic response to the loved one. Sympathetic love cries with the hurting and rejoices with the one feeling joy. Jesus whole gentle Galilean ministry reveals this truth.

Love is hard to define. Part of the difficulty is that in English one word, love, is used to carry all the multifaceted aspects of this rich concept. If our understanding of love is shallow, and we say God is love, then our understanding of God is shallow. In this sense, it is best to say that love does not define God; God defines love. God revealed in Jesus' gentle teachings is the best starting point for defining love and understanding love actions. Thus, this whole book about Jesus' gentle teachings and actions is about giving content to love and therefore defining love. Jesus is a love-event. His actions speak love, and his speech acts love.

The Greek language uses many words in its attempt to speechify love. The three most common love words in Greek are ερος, φιλια, and αγαπη. Eros is love elicited by a lovely object or person. It is rooted in the desire to possess the lovely and attractive. Our English word erotic gives a bad connotation to ερος. This is not necessarily so in Greek. Plato and other Greek writers praise ερος as the creative driving power of the soul which strives for the highest divine gifts. Sensual love is one of these gifts, and ερος as sensual love can be beautiful and good. Unfortunately, ερος is not found in the New Testament. Its message would be enriched by a thorough discussion of sensual love, and this is one place that Christians can learn from other world religions, especially Buddhism.

Φιλος is love mutually expressed between persons. It usually connotes fraternal love, family love, brotherly love, and societal love. Φιλος is used twenty-nine times in the New Testament. The verb form, φιλεω, is used twenty-five times in the New Testament, and thirteen of these are in the Gospel of John. In John 5:20 it is used to express the Father's (God's) love for the Son (Jesus), perhaps in keeping with the filial aspect of this relationship.

Agape in noun and verb form is the most common Greek word in the New Testament for love, occurring two hundred and fifty-eight times.

While ερος never occurs in the New Testament, there is hardly any evidence of the use of agape in Greek literature. Agape as a noun is used one hundred and sixteen times in the New Testament, but only twice in the Synoptic Gospels and seven times in the Gospel of John. It is used twenty-one times in the Epistles of John, and most of the other occurrences are in Paul. The verb, agape, is used one hundred and forty-two times in the New Testament: Twenty-six in the Synoptic Gospels, seventy-three in the writings of John, and again most of the others are in Paul.

Agape is self-giving love--the kind of love Jesus incarnated in his gentle Galilean ministry. It is love at whatever the cost. It is volitional and loves the unlovely as well as the lovely. If ερος is sensual love and φιλος is social love, agape is sacrificial love--the greatest expression being Jesus' death on the cross for all.

In the New Testament love is more an action verb than a static noun. The verb is much more frequent than the noun, especially in the teachings of Jesus. In Paul and the early church love becomes a noun, perhaps because a noun is more controllable. Love verbs as used by Jesus are full of energy and slippery. The sayings of Jesus account for ten percent of the love language in the New Testament. One might think this is a small percentage. However, it was Jesus' great commandment on loving God and neighbor that accounts for its widespread use in the rest of the New Testament. Also, Jesus acted love more than he spoke love.

Jesus and Love

In an old but new commandment, Jesus summed up the Old Testament relationship of God and persons and persons with each other in two sentences: love God with all your heart, soul, strength, and mind; and love your neighbor as you love yourself. Both of these commands are well known sayings from Jesus' sacred Scriptures, the Old Testament. In making them a part of his teachings, Jesus is standing in the moral tradition of Israel on the one hand and going beyond Israel on the other hand in making them a summary of all his teachings and as the norm of all right relationships with God and others.

In this command which is to be volitional and expressed in concrete actions, Jesus is placing himself and his followers under the total control of God, as a slave places himself under the lordship of the master. To fulfill the Great Commandment, as it is called, is to be bound to God and one another with cords of love.

What is the relationship between these two commands? Is love of God and love of neighbor the same thing? No, God is the source of all love, and therefore God's love makes possible all other love. God as creative responsive love interacts reciprocally with people and calls out love for the neighbor. God is unchanging in loving purpose and character but changing in experience and relationship. God's love is distinct from human love in all its aspects, including love of neighbor. In Jesus' teaching God's love takes precedence. Our love enriches God as it does neighbor and self. Love of God is not merged with love of neighbor. Neither does one love another person as a means of loving God. This would not be true love of the other person.

What then is the meaning of Jesus' double commandment? Jesus has clearly linked them together. Could it be that the love of God energizes us and frees us to love others, even our enemies? In fact, the love of enemies is included in the commandment to love our neighbor. The spontaneous and unmotivated love of neighbor is marked as being even more unmotivated in the love of one's enemies. The Christian's love of enemies is a correlative to God's love of the sinner. Christian love for enemies shows itself as spontaneous agape.

The Great Commandment of Jesus frees neighborly love from the narrow restriction to fellow Israelites and concentrates it upon the helpless and needy ones without any restrictions of race, sex, different sexual orientations, economics, or status in life. The Gospel of Luke follows the love commandment with the parable of the Good Samaritan.

Unlike Matthew and Mark, who report Jesus as saying the love commandment, Luke places it in the mouth of the teacher of the law who was trying to trap Jesus. So, Jesus asked the lawyer how he interpreted the scriptures. The man answered, "Love the Lord your God with all your heart, with all your soul, with all your strength, and with all your mind; and love your neighbor as you love yourself." You are right, Jesus replied, "Do this and you will live." The lawyer then asked, "Who is my neighbor?"[117] Jesus answered by giving the parable of the Good Samaritan.

Parable of the Good Samaritan: "There was once a man who was going down from Jerusalem to Jericho when robbers attacked him, stripped him, and beat him up, leaving him half dead. It so happened that a priest was going down that road; but when he saw the man, he walked on by on the other side. In the same way a Levite also came there, went over and looked at the man, and then walked on by on the other side. But a Samaritan who was traveling that way came upon the man, and when he saw him, his heart was filled with pity (σπλαγχνιζομαι). He went over to him, poured oil and wine on his wounds and bandaged them; then he put the man on his own animal and took him to an inn, where he took care of him. The next day he took out two silver coins and gave them to the innkeeper. 'Take care of him,' he told the innkeeper, 'and when I come back this way, I will pay you whatever else you spend on him,'"[118]

---

[117] Luke 10:27-29.
[118] Luke 20:30-35.

After telling the parable, Jesus asked the lawyer, "In your opinion, which one of these three acted like a neighbor toward the man attacked by the robbers?" The teacher of the law answered, "The one who was kind (ελεος) to him." Jesus replied, "You go, then, and do the same."[119]

This parable contains two of the key words in Jesus' gentle Galilean teachings: σπλαγχνιζομαι (compassion) and ελεος (merciful kindness). The parable is a picture of Jesus' gentle actions throughout Galilee on behalf of the lowly ones and the outcasts. The truth of the parable is this: As God is loving, kind, merciful, and compassionate, so you should be the same.

Actually, the Synoptic Gospels are more concerned with love actions than love words. Mark, as well as Matthew and Luke, brackets his Gospel with the saying about the "Beloved Son" at the beginning of Jesus' ministry when he was baptized[120] and then again at Jesus' transfiguration.[121]

In word and deed Jesus preached good news to the poor, freedom to the captives, recovery of sight to the blind, and announced the acceptable day of the Lord.[122] Jesus brought forgiveness for the oppressed sinners and opened the way to a new life with God.

Jesus' entire life and ministry was short on love words and long on love actions. In the love commands He did make love central to all he did and said. His life was certainly interpreted in this way and love words were increasingly used by other New Testament writers to interpret his mission and message as can be seen in the increased usage of love words to speechify the Jesus-event in the writings of Paul and John.

Love Aims and Love Energies

Jesus lived God's love aims and love energies that have creative transforming power. With persuasive gentleness God lures the world toward the fulfillment of these novel aims. Love's power lies in its absence of coercive force. True love in the human realm, like divine love, does not seek to control and force by threats. Tue love woos and invites. This love has risks of being rejected, but it is more adventurous and enjoyable.

Life guided by love aims and enlivened by love energies is a tremendous vision. The gentle Galilean glories that shone on the face of Jesus were fueled by these love aims and love energies. This is a vision that has the capacity to unite the universe and move it to a new level of evolution.

The gentle Galilean glories are a dream of a new and not yet realized world. God revealed in Jesus can enable us to see this vision. This is the

---

[119] Luke 10:35-37.
[120] Mark 1:11.
[121] Mark 9:7.
[122] Luke 4:16-20.

purpose of the Jesus-event. Jesus' bio-philic teachings are given not just to inform us about God's love aims and love energies, but to draw us into their glory. His gentle Galilean love actions pull us into a personal relationship with God, the ground of love, and transport us into a new world vision.

Since this new world vision is grounded in Jesus' love actions, it has a concreteness that will not go away. Paul said that this love constrains us or motivates us to action.[123] Over the centuries these love actions have altered the very structure of life as we have known it. These love actions have broken the shackles of slavery and liberated the masses. They are bringing equality to the sexes, to those of different sexual orientations, and different races, as well as giving dignity to those with disabilities.

To be sure, for many, this remains no more than a vision. Why is it so slow in coming to all? Many exercise their freedom and outright reject the vision. As self-actualizing individuals, we have the intrinsic capacity for good and evil and we have the instrumental possibility for influencing others for good or for evil. There is a correlation between the capacity to enjoy good and the capacity to suffer evil. As evolution advanced there was a gradual increase, a greater capacity, to enjoy love and goodness. Along with this came a greater freedom to enjoy life and a greater capacity to instrumentally contribute both good and evil to others. Evil in the form of fear and mistrust has the power to distort and breakup the vision for increased goodness. Evil disengages our imagination and saps our love energies. Evil prefers triviality and discord to the maximum enjoyment of the good and peace. Evil slows the transformation made possible by Jesus, the movement toward the union of all things in God's reconciling love.

Jesus' love actions in Galilee are not nullified by evil's love for triviality and disorientation or fragmentation. Triviality is not evil in itself; it is evil in the sense that it keeps us from enjoying maximum goodness. There is inevitable tension in the movement from what is to what can be. In the process of maturation there is always relapse and times of fragmentation which can be equated with evil.

This process of maturation and being drawn forward by the love energies of God exemplified by Jesus can also be seen in the life of Jesus' disciples. Jesus called them along the Sea of Galilee and began to instruct them as a peripatetic teacher (one who teaches while walking around). He taught them by words, but primarily by loving actions. At times the disciple's faith soared. At other times they groped in doubt; Peter denied knowing Jesus; and Judas betrayed Him. Yet, Peter became an evangelist, missionary, and saint.

Since discipleship is a life-long process of growth in love, it cannot escape the pull of evil with its momentary relapses into disorientation. This

---

[123] 2 Corinthians 5:14.

is the meaning of original sin; not that one man and woman, Adam and Eve, lived in an earthly paradise and fell from grace, thereby making us all sinners. In a scientific evolutionary world, one can no longer accept Adam and Eve as the parents of all mankind. The myth of Adam and Eve is theological, seeking in a metaphorical way to explain the pain and toil of life resulting in death. In this sense the Adam and Eve story is theologically true.

The theological truth of the Adam and Eve story is that we all sin and suffer. In its movement from infancy to maturation all life is marked by suffering, sin, pain, and death. A scientific evolutionary view of life and the world helps to answer the problem of evil. In this view, evil came into the world not because of some deficiency in the creative act but by the very structure of the process. Evil is introduced by the exercise of free choice inherent in the evolutionary process. Thus evil contradicts neither the goodness of God nor God's love. In an evolutionary process evil is an inevitable part of growth toward maturation.

The vision of reality seen in Jesus' gentle Galilean teachings and actions of love are integrating and unifying. The love energies generated by Jesus' life, death, and resurrection are like a power field that draws us into its creative transforming center. As we integrate God's love aims and love energies actualized by Jesus into our lives we are creatively transformed into sons and daughters of God.

In speaking of an integrating unifying center, I mean that the center of life for the Christian is a continual reorientation which heals brokenness and maintains wholeness, enabling us to love God fully and serve our neighbor freely. It is an internalizing of Jesus' vision of reality which opens us to creative transformation of ourselves and our world. This gentle Galilean vision of reality is too great for our small earthbound mind; only as we are gradually transformed into Jesus' likeness can we be enlivened by it and transformed with Jesus into its glory.

Chapter Seven

Gentle Teaching: Peace

Seek peace. Look deep into peace, and then you will understand everything else better. At the heart of a true vision of reality is the zest of adventurous peace-making.

Old Testament Vocabulary: The Hebrew word, shalom, as found in the Old Testament is difficult to translate into one English word. Its root meaning is "well-being," "completeness," or "wholeness," with an emphasis on the material side. It is used to signify bodily health. However, it refers more to national prosperity and health than it does to individuals. In the Old Testament, peace is a social concept.

Shalom and its New Testament counterpart, peace, is a gift of God. Peace is equated with the blessing of salvation in the land of promise. Since peace was never fully realized, it became an eschatological expectation. The Messiah will be the guarantor and guardian of peace. Peace is the antithesis of evil; it is synonymous with righteousness and salvation.

Peace in the Old Testament is closely related to covenant since the covenant relationship restores sinful persons to wholeness of relationship with God.

New Testament vocabulary: The Hebrew word, shalom, is translated as ειρηνη in the Septuagint, the Greek version of the Old Testament. *Eirene* has some of the depth and breadth of meaning of its Hebrew counterpart. The comprehensiveness of meaning of the Hebrew word, shalom, is seen in its use as a greeting, both on meeting and on parting.[124] Yet, in the New Testament, peace is much more than a greeting and a salutation. In these greetings God actually offers the bestowal of peace as a gift. In John 14:27, Jesus is quoted as saying, peace is what I leave with you; it is my own peace that I give you. So, peace is the gift of Jesus to his followers.

Beyond the inclusive significance of shalom, the New Testament has three more precise meanings of peace. First, the New Testament follows the classical Greek understanding of peace as absence of war and strife. This secular meaning of peace is seen in Luke 14:32, where a king finds himself

---

[124]Matthew 10:13; Luke 10:5,6 *Interperter's Dictionary of the Bible*, Vol. 3, p. 706. This greeting is found on the lips of Jesus as "Go in peace" Mark 5:34; Luke 7:50; 8:48.

outnumbered in battle and he "sends messengers to meet the other king to ask for terms of peace."

Secondly, the New Testament is strongly concerned for restoring right relationships between God and persons. Peace is used to describe this restored relationship. The Pauline letters make much of this usage of peace.[125]

In the third place, the New Testament word for peace may also mean "peace of mind" and "serenity". This is not characteristic of Hebrew or classical Greek where peace is more social and nationalistic. Again, this is a Pauline contribution. Its association with joy, patience, and self-control seems to speak of inner serenity.[126] In Philippians 4:7, Paul said, and God's peace. . . will keep your hearts and minds safe in union with Christ Jesus. Even though the emphasis here is on the relationship of the believer and Jesus as the source of peace, the sphere of heart and mind where peace rules would imply "peace of mind" and "serenity".

The Birth of Jesus and Peace

The announcement of Jesus' birth is couched in terms of peace. Luke's beautiful birth stories of Jesus in chapters one and two of his Gospel use the word, peace, three times in highly charged passages.

The first is found in Zachariah's prophecy. John and Jesus would be means by which God would guide the steps of God's people into the "paths of peace."[127]

This would be the fulfillment of the eschatological nature of peace as found in the Old Testament. The Messiah, the guardian and guarantor of peace, the bringer of salvation, and the restorer of the covenant, is now coming to God's people. His coming will be the light that illumines the path of peace.

The second significant passage that connects the birth of Jesus with peace is found in the angel's message upon Jesus' birth: Glory to God in the highest heaven, and peace on earth to those with whom He is pleased.[128] God's novel aim of peace that became immanent in Jesus of Galilee if actualized could save human civilization from destruction and bring the accompanying gift of zestful living.

While Jerusalem authorities and Temple hierarchy were blind to the "path of peace," there were simple folk like Simeon and Anna and lowly

---

[125] See especially Romans 5:1.
[126] See Galatians 5:22; Romans 14:17.
[127] Luke 1:79.
[128] Luke 2:14.

Galilean shepherds who had eyes to see and minds to understand God's visitation. The third highly changed passage in Luke's birth narratives about Jesus is found in the presentation of Jesus by Joseph and Mary to Simeon.[129] Simeon is described by Luke as a "God-fearing man" who was "waiting for Israel to be saved."[130] Simeon, filled with the Holy Spirit, took the baby Jesus in his arms and said, Now, Lord, you have kept your promise, and you may let your servant go in peace. With my own eyes I have seen your salvation, which you have prepared in the presence of all peoples.[131] The very same hour that Simeon spoke of his going in peace, Anna, a prophetess in the Temple, gave thanks to God and spoke about the child to all who were waiting for God to set Jerusalem free.[132]

The parables of Jesus revealed that shepherds were gentle and caring individuals who would search diligently for one lost sheep. Upon finding the lost sheep the shepherd would place it on his own shoulders and carry it back to the safety of the sheepfold. The shepherds spent time in quietness and meditation and therefore had eyes of faith to see and minds to understand the message of the angels that in the birth of Jesus there would be peace on earth. The shepherd's response was---Let's go to Bethlehem and see this thing that has happened, which the Lord has told us. So they hurried off and found Mary and Joseph and saw the baby lying in the manger.[133]

Jesus' Teachings on Peace

Some of Jesus' most serious teaching has been collected and presented in two key placed in the Gospels: "The Sermon on The Mount" in the Gospel of Matthew and "The Upper Room" in the Gospel of John.

The Sermon on the Mount

The Sermon on the Mount begins with the Beatitudes. At the heart of the Beatitudes stands Jesus' teaching---Happy are those who work for peace; God will call them God's children.[134] The Greek word, μακαριας, which introduces each of the Beatitudes is a designation of blessedness or happiness. It is not an inner felling or emotion, but a state of blessedness as seen by Jesus.

---

[129] Luke 2:22-33.
[130] Luke 2:25.
[131] Luke 2:29-31.
[132] Luke 2:38.
[133] Luke 2:15-16.
[134] Matthew 5:9.

Thus, peace is not a negative or passive trait that one has after the cessation of strife or conflict. It is not the feeling one has sitting in his chair after a good meal and watching a favorite sports team. Peace is positive and active. Jesus said, Happy are those who work for peace. Jesus came into a world where individuals "live in the dark shadow of death to guide their steps into the way of peace."[135] Jesus plunged into the midst of suffering humanity to bring harmony out of chaos, love out of hate, and light out of darkness. The "Prince of Peace"[136] calls his followers to be "peacemakers".[137] Although this implies the absence of conflict and the ending of war and strife, it is much more than this. It is becoming God's children and living in harmony in our earthly family, all our brothers and sisters on the face of the earth, and in harmony with God. Thus, peace is the "Harmony of Harmonies" to use a Whitehead phrase.

The Upper Room

During the last week of his life on earth Jesus met with his disciples in an upper room in Jerusalem to share his deepest and most important thoughts and concerns. Jesus could be described as making a living will with his loved ones. While he had no money or possessions to leave them, he had an eternal legacy to leave with his friends. In a final moment like this surely Jesus would speak only of the most important things. Thus when he said, Peace is what I leave with you; it is my own peace that I give you,[138] he was speaking of a concern close to his heart. Then to further highlight the significance of this gift of peace and indicate its source, he added, I have told you this so that you will have peace by being united with me. The world will make you suffer. But be brave! I have defeated the world![139]

Jesus' courageous strength in the final days of his life, even in the face of earthshaking events, stands out as one of the most remarkable features of the gospel story. While evil was doing its worst to try to destroy him, Jesus was giving his best to encourage and strengthen his followers.

Jesus lived out of a confident and secure relationship with his Father in heaven. His peace was found in living in harmony with what he felt to be God's call in his life.

Peace is self-control at its deepest level. Who can doubt that Jesus had tapped such peace at its source? He remained calm, serene, and self-controlled amid the turbulent crises of his last few days on earth. We see him

---

[135] Luke 1:79.
[136] Isaiah 9:6.
[137] Matthew 5:9.
[138] John 14:27.
[139] John 16:33.

in the Upper Room speaking words of love, joy, and peace to his disciples. We watch him in Gethsemane, calmly and serenely, rising from agonizing prayer to do the works of peace. He refused the way of the sword. We behold him on trial for crimes he did not commit but bearing himself with confident poise and calm dignity. We see him before Pilate, bruised, beaten, and mocked as a king with a crown of thorns and purple robe, yet fearless. Even on the cross when insanity fills the air and the pain of death racked his tortured body, we see concern for others---Forgive them, Father! They don't know what they are doing.[140] The suffering of Jesus attained its end in peace, the harmony of harmonies.

Peace and Permanence

Jesus' gift of peace to his disciples was given in the midst of tragedy and suffering. In an evolving universe evil as decay and loss is to be expected. The peaceable enjoyment of life becomes entwined with discord, decay, loss, suffering, and tragedy. What God intends does not often match what is. That is why Jesus said, "The world will make you suffer. But be brave! I have defeated the world."[141]

Jesus had the kind of peace that allowed him to stay sensitive to insensitivity and alive in the throes of death. His peace provided motivating power and calmness. His peace intuited stability and permanence in the maddening events that swirled around the cross. This eternal legacy of peace he gave as a gift to his disciples and all who would follow them. Thus, the travail, tragedy, and loss were not in vain. The Prince of Peace prevailed!

As the disciples looked back at these events of the trial, the scourging, the mockery, and the cross, they could have been filled with anger. And no doubt they were frustrated and angry prior to the resurrection. However, Jesus' gift of a gentle faith marked by grace, mercy, love, joy, and the crowning gift of peace purified their emotions.

The disciples in their youthful enthusiasm and zest caught the vision of the Prince of Peace and his gift of peace which energized and harmonized their activities with his own. This gift of peace lured them beyond personal ambitions and satisfactions and caught them up in the adventure of transformation, of bringing peace to the whole universe. Peace as used in this broad sense taps the source of all order and creativity broadening ones horizons and opening vistas of visions. In this sense peace is movement away from narrowness and toward the unification of multifaceted experiences that enrich and enliven life. With this gift of peace came a wider interest for the disciples---world evangelization.

---

[140] Luke 23:34.
[141] John 16:33.

The by-product of such worthwhile activity was their peace. Doing God's work of reconciliation is still the clearest path to peace. As each individual surrenders to the pursuit of peace, peace is extended in the universe.

At the heart of a true vision of reality is the zest of adventurous peace-making. The zest of self-forgetful transcendence belongs to the essence of a Christian vision of reality. Following this vision may involve suffering, but it attains its fulfillment in peace, the harmony of harmonies!

Chapter Eight

Gentle Parables

I will open my mouth to speak in parables; I will proclaim what has been hidden from the foundation of the world (Matthew 13:35).

Tug at Jesus' biophilic nature parables and you will find them attached to needy persons who find the loving care of God revealed in them.

Jesus was a master story teller who shared deep relational truths about God through simple parables like the lost coin, the lost sheep, and the lost son in Luke 15. These parable stories tell us that God is always searching for the lost, and when they are found God is as kind as a good shepherd and as forgiving as the waiting father of the prodigal.

These parables could be called "the gospel to the outcasts." Primarily, with the help of biophilic imagery that appeals to everyone as interconnected in the evolutionary process, they demonstrate God's care for the poor, lowly, and despised ones. Some of them are addressed to the scribes and Pharisees, and critics who are indignant that Jesus should associate with sinners and teach that God cares for them. Jesus' answer to these critics was: "People who are well do not need a doctor, but only those who are sick. I have not come to call respectable people, but outcasts."[142] This attitude would clearly place Jesus on the side of all disenfranchised individuals today, including people of different sexual orientations.

Focusing on the parables keeps us in touch with the human Jesus, and our over emphasis on the Christ of creedal faith often leaves out the life and teachings of the gentle Jesus. Creeds can lead to theological abstractions and need to be grounded in parables that uncover and teach life experiences. In this sense, Jesus is the parable who reverses human wisdom by incarnating the λογος and σοφια, the meaning and wisdom of God. To discover this meaning and wisdom of God is to become the children of God. We see these truths best in the parables of Jesus recorded in Luke's Gospel.

The three parables in Luke, chapter fifteen, show the sensitivity of God at its deepest level. Each parable pulls at our heart strings. All three, the watchful shepherd seeking a lost sheep, the weeping woman seeking a lost coin, and the waiting father seeking a lost son illustrate that it is God who seeks the lost and erring ones. God wills the joyful homecoming. God even seeks like the "Hound of Heaven" until the lost is found and saved.

---

[142] Mark 2:17.

In these parables Jesus is saying to the hard-hearted and blind religious leaders: "Behold the greatness of God's love for lost children, and contrast it with your own joyless, loveless, thankless, and self-righteous lives. Cease then from your loveless ways and be merciful. The spiritually dead are rising to new life, the lost are returning home, rejoice with them."[143] The parable of the workers in the vineyard, or better called the parable of the good employer, for the employer is the central figure, is also concerned with showing Jesus' action on behalf of the needy as a sign of divine action.[144] The message of the parable is this: look how good God is!

The parable of the Pharisee and publican deals with a favorite gospel theme, the great reversals in the divine scheme of things---God humbles the proud and exalts the humble.[145] This parable illustrates what we saw all through the Galilean ministry. Jesus lifts up the lowly ones and gives them new standing as God's children.

Finally, the simile of the Father and the child;[146] shows the parental goodness of God. Consider how you treat your children. If you, as bad as you are, give good gifts to your children. How much more will your Father/Mother in heaven give good things to those who ask![147] God is so merciful, especially to poor and needy children. The implied message in all of these parables for the religious leaders and others who heard them was this: it ought to be the same way with you.

A Father's Unconditional Love
Luke 15:1-3, 11b-32

As seen above Luke has some of our favorite parables like the Good Samaritan, the lost son, the lost sheep, and the lost coin. Luke also shows a special concern for the poor and outcast, and he lifts up women and gives them a special role in ministry. It is Luke's more gentle nature that can be seen for example in the parable of the great banquet (Luke 14:15-24) as compared to Matthew's version (Matthew 22:1-10) that led me to this insight. The parable comes from the Q Source and Luke left out Matthew's reference to how the invited guest who made excuses for not coming to the banquet grabbed and beat and killed the messengers. Luke also left out this violent sentence: "Then the host king sent his army to kill those murders and burn

---

[143] Jeremias, Jochaim. *The Parables of Jesus*. New York: Charles Scribner's Sons, 1963, p. 131.

[144] Matthew 20:1-15.
[145] Luke 18:9-14.
[146] Luke 11:11-13.
[147] Matthew 7:9-11

down their city." Luke also softens the wrath of the host king who according to Matthew was angry at some improperly dressed guests and had them thrown out into outer darkness. In Luke's account of the banquet, the king's anger is motivation for expanding the guest list to include the poor, the blind, and the lame who were all recipients of Jesus transforming gentle teachings.

There was a father who had two sons. Thus begins ones of Jesus' most popular parables. The story is about a father who loved his two sons with an unconditional love and wanted his sons to love each other. Jesus was a master storyteller. His parables were earthly stories with heavenly meaning. In this parable the earthly father models the unconditional love of God for all of God's children.

This is no doubt the most familiar of Jesus' many parables and it deserves a central place in our understanding of Jesus' gentle teachings. We find your story afresh in this Gospel parable.

I remember placing my children in front of a mirror and watching them study their reflection in the mirror. After a time of waving and smiling they begin to see some connection between the image in the mirror and themselves. Then it dawns on them, "That is I!" Perhaps, the same thing may happen to us as we hear this parable. We hear it, meditate upon it, and then exclaim more colloquially, "That's me!"

As I indicated in the beginning, the emphasis usually falls on the prodigal son. Could this be because we most readily see ourselves in the prodigal son? At one time or another we have all been like a prodigal son or prodigal daughter. Who was the prodigal?

In their book, Experiencing Spirituality, Ernest Kurtz and Katherine Ketcham, tell this story of a father and son in Spain who became estranged.

After months of futile searching for him, the father put an ad in a Madrid newspaper. The ad simply read, "Dear Paco, meet me in front of this newspaper office at noon on Saturday. All is forgiven. I love you. Your father." On Saturday eight hundred Pacos showed up, looking for forgiveness and love from their fathers. At one time or another we can all see ourselves in the prodigal.

In the first century Jewish culture the prodigal's request was unusual. Sons were taught to stay home and respect their parents and elders. Sons were expected to learn their father's trade and carry on the family business. The elder son in our parable dutifully carries out this role. The father's land or possessions were not usually divided among family members until after the death of the father. So, when the younger son, known as the prodigal, made his request, Father, give me the share of the property that will belong to me, he was saying in effect: "Dad, I wish you were dead so I could get my share now!"

Maybe we have not put it quite like that, but have we not all seen ourselves in the mirror of the prodigal? Have we not all wanted to be free from the bonds of home and family ties? After all, "Why shouldn't a person be his or her own boss. Why not break the chains that bind and restrict us?" The prodigal, like us, had heard all his life; "Thou shalt not!" Now he wanted to be free! And we understand, don't we? The pressures of family, jobs, and illness begin to feel like chains, and we want to break them and be free. However, running away seldom brings true freedom, as we will see.

You may see yourself mirrored in the elder brother. You may be the one who always stays home and takes care of others, maybe feeling a little smug and self-righteous as the result. The elder brother takes on the spirit of the Pharisees and commits the deadly sin of pride in saying to his father, Listen! For all these years I have been working like a slave for you, and I have never disobeyed your command. In other words, "Look at me. I am so good and so faithful! Yet, you have never rewarded me with a party."

Charlie Brown says that the only kind of pity you can count on to be sincere is self-pity. Before we get caught attending a "pity party" with the elder brother as the honored guest, let me call your attention to the father in our parable. The father mirrors the gospel for us in his unconditional love shown for both of his sons. When the younger son asked his father to give him the share of property that would belong to him as an inheritance, the father respected his request---his need for freedom. The father knew that his elder son and younger son were quite different, as they usually are; and he respected their individuality.

One thing I observed in my parents and from parents in Churches where I have served is that good parents give attention when and where it is needed. If one child is having difficulty, that child gets the most attention. I remember when one of my brothers got a divorce. Our father and mother invited him to come back home and live with them until he got his feet on the ground again. They did not judge him. They just offered unconditional love and acceptance. Did my parents love this son more than their other twelve children? No! He just needed more attention at that time. I saw in my parent's love the beauty of unconditional love.

Someone described home as the place where "when you return, they have to take you back." The ultimate Gospel truth of this parable is this: There is a homecoming for all of us because there is a home. The father who is mirrored in this parable drinks his coffee by the door each morning looking down the road, hoping to see the return of his son. One morning when he sees his son coming down the road weighed down with guilt, his father cannot contain his joy. Filled with compassion, he ran and put his arms around him and kissed him. His son began to give his speech he had rehearsed all the way home, Father, I have sinned against heaven and before you; I am no longer worthy to be called your son. His father would have none of this! His son's return was enough for him. He would not add to his guilt and shame by saying, "I told you so." No! His joy is breaking out all over in his message to his servants: Quickly, bring out a robe---the best one---and put it one him; put a ring on his finger and sandals on his feet. And get the fatted calf and kill it and let us eat and celebrate; for this son of mine was dead and is alive; he was lost and is found! And they began to celebrate.

A minister was telling this part of the story to some children and he asked, "Who was not happy about the return of the prodigal son?" A little boy quickly replied, "The fatted calf!" The elder brother was also not happy. In fact, he was angry and refused to go to the party, preferring his pity party to the family celebration.

The father's unconditional love is also shown for the eldest son. The father said to him, 'Son, you are always with me, and all that is mine is yours. But we had to celebrate and rejoice, because this brother of yours was dead and has come to life; he was lost and has been found.'

The father's unconditional love mirrors the love and acceptance of our heavenly Father. There is a homecoming for all of us because there is a home where our Parent God waits to receive us with a heavenly robe and ring. God is waiting to receive everyone into this family today.

This unconditional love of God surrounds us at all times. One of life's most basic needs is to be surrounded with the unconditional love of parents, extended family, and Church family. We should pray long and hard before ever leaving that circle of love.

When our children were growing up, Beth and I said to them often, "We hope your life will be filled with love and acceptance. Always remember this: No matter what may happen we will always love you. You are our son and our daughter, and we love you very much." Children need to hear those words and adults need to hear them. We never outgrow our need to be surrounded by this unconditional love. Thank God, we don't have to. We can always go home to God!

An Action Parable

In a dramatic acted parable Jesus modeled gentleness for all Christians when he came into Jerusalem on what has been called Palm Sunday, "gentle and riding on a donkey."[148] Luke said, that when Jesus saw Jerusalem he wept over her blindness and her failure to see the things that made peace.[149] If Jesus had come riding on a great white horse, using military imagery, the people would have gladly followed him as Messiah. They had to do some growing before they could see him as a weeping prophet, a Suffering Servant, riding gently on a lowly donkey toward the cross.

---

[148] Matthew 21:5, Williams translation.
[149] Luke 19:39-43.

We saw the shortest verse in the Bible in the Mary, Martha, and Lazarus story: "Jesus wept." Here Jesus weeps again. Behind this weeping over Jerusalem lies one of the longest verses in which Jesus put his feelings in these moving words: "Jerusalem, Jerusalem! How many times I wanted to put my arms around all your people, just as a hen gathers her chicks under wings, but you would not let me!"[150] If not the longest in words and sentences, it is the longest in sense and meaning. These words tell us that eternally there is a cross at the heart of God. God has gently been reaching out to gather people from the beginning of time.

---

[150] Matthew 23:37.

Chapter Nine

Gentle Actions of Jesus

Jesus' gentle words lead to tender actions that have transforming results for our lives.

It is somewhat artificial to divide Jesus' ministry into gentle teachings and gentle actions as we are doing. His teachings were like action sermons. His words act and his acts speak. Words were much more powerful in the Jewish culture of Jesus' time than they are today. We are bombarded with the media and almost drown in words. Our culture has sayings like "words are cheap" and "actions speak louder than words." In the Jewish religion words have almost a life of their own. To pronounce a blessing or curse is to set in motion actions.

Thus, one can speak of the ministry of Jesus as an action where God is present or as a Word-event where God is speaking. In learning to incorporate each moment of his life as an experience of God's life, Jesus fused human and divine love. Thus in Jesus' words and actions, we see and feel God acting in tender and caring ways. Whitehead was right when he said that God's nature is best conceived as a tender care that nothing be lost.[151]

In bringing the hurting of his day with infinite patience into his consciousness of God they experienced the immediacy of God's life and received wholeness. Thus, Jesus' gentle actions enabled transformation for the hurting who no longer perish but begin to live in the very being of God. Or as John expressed it, The Word was God. . .. And the Word became human and lived a little while among us, and we actually saw God's glory.[152] Gentle, Galilean glories are seen in both the teachings of Jesus and his actions. While they were united as one, we are dividing them for the sake of stressing both facets of his lowly service and glory.

Gentle Actions toward Women

Luke records a very moving story of Jesus raising from the dead a widow's only son. It occurred in a town named Nain, in southern Galilee. Jesus was with his disciples and a large crowd was following him. Just as he arrived at the gate into Nain, a funeral procession was coming out. The woman's grief was great. Not only was she a widow, but this dead man was her only son. When Jesus saw her, his heart was filled with pity, εσπλαγχνιζομαι, for her, and he said to her, Don't.[153] Then he walked over

---
[151] Whitehead, *Process and Reality*, p. 346.
[152] John 1:1, 14.
[153] Luke 7:13.

and touched the coffin, and the men carrying it stopped. Perhaps they stopped because the touching of a corpse was the most defiling thing according to the Jewish religion. They must have wondered, "What kind of man is this who goes around touching coffins?" Touching the coffin, Jesus said, 'Young man! Get up, I tell you!' The dead man sat up and began to talk, and Jesus gave him back to his mother. They were all filled with awe and began to glorify God saying: 'A great prophet has appeared among us! God has come to save!'[154] Jesus action sermon revealed the kindness of God coming to heal and to save people.

Jesus was in such a large crowd by the Sea of Galilee on one occasion that they were pushing him from every side. A woman came up to him who had suffered from severe bleeding for twelve years. She had spent all her money on doctors, and still got worse all the time. She had heard about Jesus and thought if she could just touch his cloak she would get well. The courage to touch was the difficult thing. In the eyes of the Jewish law, her bleeding defiled her and made her unclean. Also, it was not proper for a woman to touch a man in public, especially a rabbi. But she had seen something in Jesus that encouraged her to try. The Scripture simply says, She had heard about Jesus.[155] What she had heard moved her to touch him and at once her bleeding stopped. She was healed of her illness. Mark says that Jesus at once knew that someone had touched him. People were elbowing Jesus on every side, but he knew the difference in being elbowed and gently touched. 'Who touched my clothes!' he asked. The woman came trembling with fear, knelt down and told Jesus the whole truth. Instead of treating her harshly as a defiled person, Jesus treated her with dignity and tenderness: My daughter, your faith has made you well. Go in peace and be healed of your trouble.[156] To go in peace, shalom, is to go under God's care and loving kindness.

When Jesus addressed the woman as "My daughter," he was using a family name, a name this woman had not heard in a long time. Because of her illness she was shunned and called bad names. "My daughter" is a tender and loving name. Let me share this personal family experience with you to illustrate what I want each of you to experience in this Family of God when you hear the name, daughter or son.

When our son, Kevin, was born, Kimberly, our daughter, was staying with friends in our Church family while Beth and I were at the hospital. The evening after Kevin was born, I went home to be with Kimberly. She kept asking, "Where is Mama? I want Mama." I told her that Mama was in the hospital and that she had a new baby brother. She could not understand everything that was happening, and she kept saying "I want Mama."

---

[154] Luke 7:14-16.
[155] Mark 5:27.
[156] Mark 5:28-34.

The next morning, I took Kimberly to the hospital. That was when children could not go to the maternity ward, so I called from the front desk and asked Beth to come down to the lobby. When Beth got off the elevator and Kimberly saw her, she ran and leaped into her mother's arms, saying "Mama, Mama." Beth held her close to her heart and said, Kimberly, my wonderful daughter, Kimberly. How I love you." I joined in the family hug and we all wept tears of joy.

The Good News Jesus taught is that God loves us and comes to give each of us a new name, "Sons and Daughters" in the "Family of God." If you have had a bad name pinned to you in the past, or if you have lost a loved one, and your name is despair or depression, these are not your final names. Because of Jesus' gentle teachings and actions, we now have a new name: Wonderful Daughter, or Wonderful Son. And we are held close to God's heart in radiant faith.

According to Luke Jesus had been traveling through Galilee, from Capernaum to Nain, where he raised the widow's son. In this same vicinity he was invited into the home of Simon the Pharisee for dinner. A woman who lived a sinful life heard that Jesus was eating in Simon's house, so she went with an alabaster jar of perfume to anoint Jesus' feet. (Some scholars treat this as a doublet of a similar story placed in Bethany, outside of Jerusalem). She went in where the meal was taking place and anointed Jesus' feet with the perfume and with her tears, for she was weeping profusely. Then she dried his feet with her hair and kissed them.

To make such a daring move must mean that she had already experienced Jesus' forgiveness or she had known his attitude toward sinners. Jesus' host began to criticize him for his attitude toward the sinful woman. Jesus' answer to Simon was that the woman's great love proved that her many sins had been forgiven. Jesus sent this woman away forgiven, saying as he did to the woman with the issue of blood, Go in peace.[157] Both of these stories about Jesus' attitude toward women are the fulfillment of Luke's prophetic vision recorded in Luke 1:78, Our God is merciful and tender. He will cause the bright dawn of salvation to rise on us and to shine from heaven on all those who live in the dark shadow of death, to guide our steps into the path of peace. To both women Jesus said, Go in Peace.

While traveling in the same Galilean region, Jesus was accompanied by his disciples and some women who had been healed of evil spirits and diseases: Mary Magdalene, from whom seven demons had been driven out; Joanna, whose husband, Chuza, was an officer in Herod's court; and Susanna, and many other women who used their own resources to help Jesus and his disciples.[158] This is an amazing passage from Luke's Gospel. In the Greek

---

[157] Luke 7:36-50.
[158] Luke 8:1-3.

text, the three long verses form one sentence built around one verb--preaching the Good News of God. It is an evangelistic campaign through the towns and villages of Galilee, and the women are mentioned by name as participants. And they were not cooking and washing pots and pans. The only verb is "preaching the Gospel." Also, Luke's word for their service is "diakonos," which is usually translated in the New Testament as "servant," "minister," or "deacon."

Jesus' concern for elevating the role of women was evident wherever he went. We will now look at some of these gentle actions that occurred outside of Galilee, since they strengthen our overall case for Jesus' gentle ministry. One such story which circulated in the oral stage of gospel transmission and finally found its way into the Gospel of John (It is not even in the earliest manuscripts of John's Gospel) is about a woman caught in adultery. According to John the setting is in the Temple in Jerusalem. However, it comes after a lengthy discussion of Jesus coming from Galilee and whether the Messiah could come from such a place. The accusation of the chief priest and Pharisees seems to be this: Jesus do you expect to bring your simple Galilean teachings about sinners to the Temple and get a hearing? So while the story is in the Temple setting, it has the theological stamp of Galilee all over it. In bringing the woman to Jesus the religious leaders hope to trap him. "In our law of Moses," they said, 'such a woman must be stoned to death' Jesus bent over and wrote in the sand with his finger. Then Jesus stood up and said to them, "Whichever one of you has committed no sin may throw the first stone at her." Jesus bent over and wrote in the sand again and they all began to leave one by one, the older ones first. Whatever Jesus wrote had a very powerful effect. He stood up and said to the woman, "Is there no one left to accuse you?" "No one, sir," she replied, "Well, then," Jesus said, "I do not condemn you either. Go, but do not sin again."[159]

Jesus did not condone the sin of adultery. Rather, he rejected the double standard and turned the table upon the male accusers. Jesus rejected the sin and accepted the sinner. His acceptance of the woman challenged her to turn from her sin and toward a new life.

Jesus made a trip into Samaria, which bordered Galilee. Yet, if it was near in geography, it was a long way culturally. The Samaritans were a mixed race, and they were despised by the Jews. The story in John 4:1-42 centers on Jesus' conversation with a Samaritan woman at Jacob's well near Mt. Gerizim. The story is an example of how Jesus broke down sexual, racial, religious, and cultural barriers. Jesus restored the woman to wholeness, and she in turn became the first evangelist in John's Gospel by going and telling the Samaritans about Jesus. Because of her testimony many Samaritans were won to salvation. It is in this setting that Jesus stated his mission in the

---

[159] John 8:5-11.

strongest terms: My food is to obey the will of the one who sent me and to finish the work God gave me to do.[160] That work clearly involved liberating persons, especially women who had a low standing in Jesus' day.

Jesus had a close relationship with the sisters Mary and Martha. There are three major Gospel stories about their relationship. The first story is told in Luke 10:38-42. Jesus visited in the home of Mary and Martha and Martha wanted to make it a special visit. Soon she realized that she was doing all the work while Mary was sitting at Jesus' feet listening to his teaching. Martha became upset and said to Jesus: "Lord, don't' you care that my sister has left me to do all the work by myself? Tell her to come and help me!"[161] Jesus answered her: Martha, Martha! You are worried and troubled over so many things, but just one is needed. Mary has chosen the right thing, and it will not be taken away from her.[162]

Martha was doing what was expected in Jewish tradition, while Mary was breaking tradition. So Martha was justified in venting her feelings. Jesus does the unexpected and breaks with tradition himself. A rabbi was not supposed to teach a woman in this way. Not only did Jesus teach Mary, he commended her for choosing the one necessary thing. Women need spiritual food as well as physical food. Some have seen in this story the opening of the study for women.

The second story about Mary and Martha is found in John 11:1-44, and centers on the raising of Lazarus and Jesus' presentation of Himself as the resurrection and the life. The story records one of the most moving scenes from Jesus' life. When Jesus arrived at the home of Mary, Martha, and Lazarus, he found that Lazarus had been dead for four days. Jesus saw Mary and all those with her weeping and his heart was touched and he was deeply moved . . .. Then comes the shortest verse in the Bible, only two words: Jesus wept.[163] However, the shortest verse in the Bible has the longest meaning. Those tears take in the sorrows of the ages, from the Alpha of creation's beginning to the Omega point of its ending. Never again can we doubt that when we grieve and suffer, God is deeply moved and is in the presence of our grief and suffering.

The third story about Mary and Martha concerns the anointing of Jesus' head with expensive oil. As indicated earlier, some scholars see this as a doublet of the story of the anointing of Jesus' feet with oil by the sinful woman as recorded in Luke 7:36-50. The Gospels do report it as a separate anointing, and we will treat it as such. When Mary was criticized for wasting

---

[160] John 4:34.
[161] Luke 10:40.
[162] Luke 10:41-42.
[163] John 11:31-35.

the expensive oil, Jesus replied, "Leave her alone! Why are you bothering her? She has done a fine and beautiful thing for me . . . Now, I assure you that wherever the gospel is preached all over the world, what she has done will be told in memory of her."[164]

Not only was Mary permitted into the study; she was also made a part of the content of the gospel story. As we will see in the chapter on the resurrection, the women are also entrusted with telling the Good News about Jesus' resurrection. They were attracted to the gentle, Galilean glories, transformed by them, and proclaimed them in their own unique way.

Gentle Actions toward Children

The true character of a person is often revealed by the way children respond to him or her. Jesus attracted children. Matthew, Mark, and Luke tell of several occasions where children were blessed by Jesus. The disciples on one occasion wanted to send them away. They even scolded the people for bothering Jesus with children. Jesus said: Let the children come to me and do not stop them, because the agape glory of God belongs to such as these. I assure you that whoever does not receive the Good News of God like a child will never enter it. Then he took the children in his arms, placed his hands on each of them, and blessed them.

---

[164] Mark 10:13-16; Matt. 19:13-15; Luke 18:15-17; See also Mark 9:33-37; Matt. 18:1-5; Luke 9:46-48.

Chapter Ten

Gentle Invitations

Jesus' one consuming purpose was to invite others into the warm loving relationship he had with God.

We see the depth of this relationship in Jesus' prayers. In prayer Jesus talked to God as a child speaks to a loving parent, confidently and securely. The best image we have of this filial relationship is the way Jesus invited the children to come to him. Children were attracted to Jesus' spontaneous joy and laughter. Yet, when they came to Jesus the disciples wanted to send them away! Jesus' reaction was, Let the children come to me and do not stop them, because the agape glory of God belongs to such as these. Remember this! Whoever does not receive the Good News of God like a child will never possess it.[165] These are gentle invitations to trust in God.

Jesus was sometimes angry and had harsh words on a few occasions for those who kept anyone from this special relationship of love, but this just shows the humanness of Jesus and the depth of Jesus' compassion and desire to invite all persons into the agape glory of God. All of Jesus' gentle teachings and actions can be seen as just such an invitation. His parables are an invitation to discover the glory of God as treasure and the pearl of great price. Each act of kindness was like a magnet drawing the broken and hurting into the special relationship Jesus had with God.

Jesus could especially be harsh at times with the blindness of the religious leaders like the Scribes and Pharisees. Yet, it was after one of these harsh times that Matthew reports from Jesus one of the most inviting and compassionate invitations ever given to anyone. "Come to me, all of you who are tired from carrying heavy loads, and I will give you rest. Take my yoke and put it on you, and learn from me, because I am gentle (πραυς) and humble in spirit (ταπεινος): and you will find rest. For the yoke I will give you is easy (χρηστος, often translated as gentle or kind) and the load I will put on you is light.[166] In fact, Jesus himself at times carries the load. As the Good Shepherd, he carries the lost sheep on his shoulders to the safety of the fold.[167] To the Scribes and Pharisees who were staggering under the heavy demands of the law and to the outcasts Jesus taught gentle Galilean glories.

---

[165] Luke 18:15-17; Matthew 19:13-14; Mark 10:13-16.
[166] Matthew 11:28-30. Three key words for gentleness in Jesus' teachings, πραυς, ταπεινος, χρηστος, are found in these three verses.
[167] Luke 15:4-7.

What does it mean to come to Jesus and find freedom from the bondage of our sins? Perhaps an illustration will help us grasp this meaning. The Statue of Liberty stands on Liberty Island in New York Harbor. Its proper name is Liberty Enlightening the World. France gave the monument to the United States on July 4, 1884 as a symbol of friendship and the liberating power of a free form of government. The people of France gave about $250,000 for the construction of the statue that is made of more than 300 thin sheets of copper. The people of the United States gave about $280,000 for the construction of the pedestal of the statue. The statue stands 151 feet high and weighs 450,000 pounds. The torch rises 305 feet above the base of the pedestal and shines as a symbol of American freedom and as a beacon of refuge for immigrants.

A poem by Emma Lazarus was inscribed on a tablet in the pedestal in 1903. It reads:

> With conquering limbs astride from land to land;
> Here at our sea-washed sunset gates shall stand
> A mighty woman with a torch, whose flame
> Is the imprisoned lightning, and her name,
> Mother of Exiles. From her beacon-hand
> Glows world-wide welcome; her mild eyes command
> The air-bridged harbor that twin cities frame,
> 'Keep ancient lands, your storied pomp!'
> Cries she with silent lips,
> 'Give me your tired, your poor,
> your huddled masses yearning to breathe free,
> the wretched refuse of your teeming shore.
> Send these, the homeless, tempest-tost to me,
> I lift my lamp beside the golden door!'

In the foyer of John Hopkins University, facing the entrance, stands a marble statue of Jesus. It portrays Jesus leaning forward, arms outstretched as though he were reaching for some faltering individual. On the base of the statue are these words:

> Come unto me all ye that labor and are
> heavy laden, and I will give you rest.

Multitudes in all generations have responded to this gentle invitation of Jesus. Like the words by Emma Lazarus on the base of the Statue of Liberty, these words of Jesus are a precious invitation to feeble and fainting persons. As powerful and hope filled as the words on the statue are, the words of Jesus are even more powerful. Salvation, strength, and renewed courage are the gifts of those who come to Jesus.

    A statue has power to inspire and challenge, but it cannot forgive, cleanse, and save. Only Jesus can say with saving significance, "Come unto me, all you that labor and are heavy laden, and I will give you rest."

    I was sitting with a retired minister a few years ago, and we were discussing this passage. He told me about the death of his only son when he was seven years old. He said he and his wife had struggled with that loss for years. Then fighting back tears, he said, "Jesus knows all about burdens. He carried the cross up Calvary's Hill, a burden too big for anyone to bear. This invitation says that if he can bear the cross, he can help me bear my burden." And that is true for you---whatever your burden may be. Maybe you are burdened with your job, or family problems, or illness. This Gospel truth says that no one cares for you like Jesus.

    Since it is a highly significant invitation from the Gospels, let us look at the important phrases. To do this we must first examine the context. As the agent of creation and as God incarnate in human flesh, Jesus knew human nature. And this beautiful invitation comes after Jesus expressed frustration at how people could hear the Gospel and remain unbelieving. He was especially frustrated at how even believing people seem never to be satisfied. In Matthew 11:16 and following, Jesus said, Now to what can I compare the people of this day? They are like children sitting in the market place. One group shouts to the other, 'We played wedding music for you, but you wouldn't dance! We sang funeral songs, but you wouldn't cry!' Then Jesus explains what he means by this analogy of children playing. When John came, he fasted and drank no wine, and everyone said, 'He has a demon in him!' When the Son of Man came, he ate and drank, and everyone said, 'Look at this man! He is a glutton and wine-drinker, a friend of tax collectors and other outcasts!' At this point, I would have said, "You just can't please some people no matter what you do. If you are serious and reverent, people say, 'you are a sad sack.' If you smile and are happy, people say, 'no one could be that happy all the time. He must be on drugs or doing something he shouldn't.' You just can't please some people." But after getting their attention Jesus simply added, God's wisdom is shown to be true by its results.

    The people may have made fun of John the Baptist and called him a wild man who wore rough clothes of camel's hair and lived on honey and wild locusts in wilderness areas, but Jesus said he was greater than any man who has ever lived (Matthew 11:11). John came in the spirit of Elijah as the supreme witness to Jesus.

    The people may make fun of Jesus and say that he is drunk on wine, but the crowds heard him gladly. Yes, the wisdom of God is shown by its results (v. 19); and this precious invitation is one of the reasons Jesus had such great results with the poor and needy. I think you will see why as we look at each phrase.

Come unto me: One of the most characteristic words of the New Testament is the word, Come. "Come to me all you who walk in darkness," said Jesus, "I am the light of the world." "Come to me all who hunger and thirst, said the Master, "I am the bread of heaven and the water of life." "Come to me all who have lost their way," said Jesus, "I am the way, the truth, and the life." "Come to me all of you who are sick and needy, I am the Great Physician who has come to heal you, said our Lord. In a world where many voices call us, this is the one authentic voice that holds the answer to the mystery of life and death. Jesus still says, "Come to me if you are suffering from bad health, or family problems, or grief from the loss of a loved one." The words on the Statue of Liberty have greater meaning as they are under-girded by these words of Jesus.

All who labor: Jesus said, "Come to me, all of you who are tired from carrying heavy loads, and I will give you rest" (v. 28). No doubt Jesus was addressing this invitation to the Scribes and Pharisee who labored under the heavy burden of the law. Jesus' priority of individual needs over the demands of the law bothered them greatly. Right after the invitation is given, we are told in the next passage that the Pharisees criticized Jesus and his disciples for plucking grain on the Sabbath.[168] To Jesus, feeding hungry disciples took priority over the laws of the Sabbath.

The invitation is also to all who labor. Not all who have been loafing and refused to get involved. All who work hard, take risks, and carry heavy burdens, come to Jesus for rest.

I find great comfort and strength in laying my sermon on the altar each Sunday. In that act I am giving my labors of the week. I usually work twenty hours a week on that message. I begin by reading the lectionary passages from the Psalms, the prophets, the Gospel, and Epistle. I begin these readings a couple of months before the Sunday they are to be used. This way I have time to collect relevant materials that illuminate them. As I study, I pray that the light of God's Spirit will open my mind to understand the sacred scriptures, open my heart to feel the love of God flowing through them, and help me to apply them to the needs of my family of faith in the church.

I read them in Greek and study the key words and phrases in the Greek lexicons, commentaries, and other relevant books. I then begin to write the sermon on note pads and/or sitting at my laptop computer. It is revised throughout the week, sometimes receiving a final touch after reading the Sunday morning paper. Thus, when I lay it on the altar, I feel good that

---

[168] Matthew 12:1-8

it represents my best labor of the week, and I find the promised strength from God as I turn to prayerfully preach without the manuscript.

Take my yoke upon you: The yoke is an expression to denote subjection. Jesus is asking those who have been servants of sin, to obey him from the heart and be his servant. This is an invitation to exchange the yoke of Satan for the yoke of the Savior. To be a Christian is to accept a particular frame of reference; it is to bring one's life into the captivity of God actualized in the gentle teachings of Jesus! To take up the yoke of Jesus also involves the "bearing of one another's burdens."

Learn of Me: Jesus comes to us not only as Master, but also as Teacher and friend. Jesus' gentle truths of God need to be learned. All people need to be taught more tender ways of relating. The teachers I remember most fondly were the ones who were "gentle and humble in spirit." These are the qualities that Jesus used to describe his own teaching ministry. Those who come to Jesus are taught lessons of gentleness and humility. Living in a harsh and cruel world as we do, we all need to enroll in this school and sit at Jesus' feet as Mary did. Actually, his lessons are the required courses, not electives; they are lessons of life, love, joy, and peace.[169]

When refugees come to our shores, we ask them to learn about our constitution and American ways. We ask them to become American citizens. Even so, Jesus said, take my yoke upon you, and learn of me.

You will find rest: Imagine if you will, carrying a heavy burden on your back that is tied with cords you cannot sever. You carry it until you almost fall in your tracks. Then someone says to you, "Let me remove your burden." Would you not say, "Yes, please do. Please remove it." This is Jesus' invitation: "Learn from me, because I am gentle and humble in spirit; and you will find rest." After a time of exertion, there is nothing to compare to rest. "Rest" as used here is not escape from life and work, but "refreshment" for the exuberant living of life. Jesus knew such refreshment that enabled Him to live abundantly, joyfully, and triumphantly. The gift here is the security of knowing one is in the will of God, forgiven and accepted into the family of God. In addition to relaxation and refreshment, this "rest" is a synonym for salvation, associated with the Kingdom of God and eternal life. Sabbath rest had these overtones, and Matthew may be presenting Jesus as the true giver of Sabbath rest and all the gifts of worship that implies.

My yoke is easy: Tradition says that Jesus worked in Joseph's carpenter's shop where he made yokes that carried the sign, "My yokes are easy and light," meaning that they would not rub or chaff the neck of the

---

[169] This section should not be read or heard to say that Jesus is the only way to God. I am writing primarily for Christians, but our interpretation of Jesus as a human who self-actualized God's love aims and purposes opens the door for teachers in other religions to do the same.

oxen that wore them. Religiously speaking, Jesus' yoke is easy and light because he has born the heaviest burden on Calvary's Cross. Here we see the deep paradox that runs throughout Matthew's Gospel: salvation is gift and demand. It is the gift of gospel and the demand of service. Jesus the kind and gentle teacher places his yoke of service on us. The Christian is admonished to take up the cross and follow Jesus in a righteousness that exceeds that of the Scribes and Pharisees.[170] This is not a righteousness marked by superiority but characterized by gentle and lowly service. In the phase "My yoke is easy and light," the Greek word for "easy" is χρηστος, best translated as "kind and good." The Greek word, ελαφρον, translated as "light," means that His burden is not burdensome. The burden is light because Jesus bears our burdens with us and gives us strength to carry the burdens of others.

    A young boy was seen carrying an even smaller lad on his back who was crippled. "Son that is a heavy burden you are carrying." Shucks man, this ain't no burden. This is my wee brother!

    Now, one final question. What must one do to respond to this gentle invitation and come to Jesus? The answer is this---Come to Jesus just as you are! Don't wait until you feel ready. Don't think of getting prepared. Don't dream of being fit. The readiness, the preparation, and the fitness are all his gift to you. If you are burdened by sin or carrying a heavy load, Jesus invites you to come to God for salvation and rest. No one understands like Jesus. At the end his disciples failed him, but he forgave Peter who denied him three times. Jesus understands failure. I knew a family who saved all their life for their daughter to go to college, but she got married and didn't want to go to college. The parents were heartbroken. Another couple saved all their life so that they could buy a camper when they retired and tour the USA. The husband had a stroke the year he retired, and all their money was spent on nursing home care. Failed dreams are a part of our lives. No one knows about failure more than Jesus! And Jesus always stands with open arms, saying, Come unto me all you that labor and are heavy laden, and I will give you rest. If Jesus could take a burden from your life, what would it be? No burden is too great for God. Name a burden in your mind right now, and place your burden in the outstretched arms of Jesus with this prayer:

    Dear God, thank you for inviting me to come boldly to receive your grace. Yet, I confess that I come out of an often-dark world that has an evil grip on my life. So I come in confession acknowledging my sins and my need for your forgiving grace and love. Help me to throw off the yoke of evil and take on the yoke of Jesus. I come with confidence because you promise never to turn me away. Cleanse me now. Then teach me your lessons of gentleness and humility that I may be able to bear other's burdens. Give me now a

---

[170] See Matthew 5:20; 10:38; 16:24.

receptive mind to your sacred words, give me an open heart to your redemptive love, and give me a life inspired by your vision of reality seen in the life, death, and resurrection of Jesus. Amen.

Chapter Eleven

The Place of Miracles in Jesus' Gentle Teachings

Gentle words and actions have healing power.

Jesus' gentle and compassionate ministry of healing was an integral part of his good news. When the Pharisees criticized Jesus for associating with the outcasts, Jesus defined his ministry in these terms: People who are well do not need a doctor, but only those who are sick. I have come to show kindness to the outcast.[171] Kindness and healing are joined in this saying of Jesus.

The miracles of Jesus are action sermons that proclaim the gospel in terms of kindness and compassion. The Gospel writers included the miracles of Jesus as an integral part of his life and teachings---not to prove his divinity, but to share his love energies. Love's power lies in its desire to enrich the other. God's love is best seen as responsive love. Jesus as God's messenger could not walk through Galilee without responding to the broken persons he encountered. His gentle teachings and loving touch energized them and gave them new hope and new life.

Jesus' love was a suffering love. The Gospels were written after the suffering death and resurrection of Jesus. You and I know the end of the story. So when we see Jesus identifying with the brokenhearted, the lepers, and the blind, we see him as the wounded healer. Jesus so closely identified with the suffering that their wounds became his wounds; their pains were his pains. In speaking of the suffering death of Jesus for all persons, Matthew interprets this greatest of all miracles in these terms: "Jesus took upon Himself our sickness and carried away our diseases."[172]

The gentle teachings of Jesus show God coming to be partners with suffering persons to bring healing and wholeness. Miracles occur in cooperation with God, not in changing God or manipulating God. This follows from a relational understanding of God. In a relational world God is working for good in all circumstances, this is especially meaningful in times when we need miraculous love energies. As we join our love energies with God's miracles happen. In these moments we become co-laborers with God.

According to Mark, as soon as Jesus announced the coming of the Kingdom of God, He went out to meet the power of evil head on. This has

---

[171] Matthew 9:12-13.
[172] Matthew 8:17.

led some to imagine that Jesus performed these miracles to prove His divinity---to show that His power is greater than the demons. I would rather think that Jesus performed miracles to share His love energies to enrich the other. God's love in Jesus is responsive love. Jesus could not encounter those who were suffering without responding with compassion. His loving touch energized these helpless individuals and gave them new hope and new life. Stephen Speilburg's E. T. was not the first to touch with the finger and give energy and new life. Many of Jesus' miracles can be interpreted as miracles of compassion. Ten times in the Synoptic Gospels, Matthew, Mark, and Luke, Jesus is presented as the one in whom divine compassion is present. The Greek term translated as compassion, is the strongest word possible to stress the tender compassion with which God claims persons in saving acts. We get the expression "gut feeling" from this word. It speaks of a deep inner pity or compassion for a needy person.

As soon as Jesus announced the Kingdom of God was near, he began to perform miracles of compassion. He had compassion on the man with a dreaded skin disease and healed him. Jesus had compassion on the widow of Nain and raised her dead son back to life. Also, Jesus had compassion on the blind men and restored their sight. True compassion implies the willingness to suffer with the needy. In responsive love Jesus suffered with the leper, the broken-hearted mother, and the blind men. As the wounded healer, Jesus identified with the suffering. Their wounds were His wounds; their pains were His pains. Thus, the miracles of Jesus were acts of compassion that showed the Kingdom of God coming near.

We turn now from the why of Jesus' miracles to the how. How was Jesus able to perform such great miracles? The answer must surely be sought in the power of miraculous love energies.

The God who spoke and brought order out of disorder and cosmos out of chaos, spoke in Jesus to bring wholeness out of brokenness and life out of death. It was Jesus' total consciousness of God's presence in His life and ministry, exemplified by the confident way He spoke to God as a child speaks to a parent, that enabled Him to act with such authority and power.

So, how was Jesus able to cast this evil spirit out of this man in Capernaum? Jesus taught that perfect love casts out fear (I John 4:18). This includes fear of demons. His powerful Spirit filled love words and love actions evoked new levels of energy and power in the broken man. The fusion of these powerful love energies with the willing faith of the needy person brought catharsis and wholeness.

You and I can understand the power of Jesus' loving touch in this man's life, because we know the end of the Gospel story---We know the power of the cross and the resurrection. As Mark tells this story, he also knew the end. In fact, he wrote from the end back to the beginning. Mark and his community had experienced the creative and transforming power of the cross and the victory over evil on Easter morning. The cross and resurrection proved once and for all that the power of evil was broken!

With this knowledge and conviction, Mark can faithfully report Jesus saying to the evil spirit possessing this man's life: Be quiet and come out of the man! (1:25). It was a striking and astonishing act! Not because Jesus had the power to perform it; we know that from knowing the end of the story. No doubt the man was astounded because Jesus cared enough to come close to him. After all, he was shunned by the Jewish people. They felt that he had sinned and deserved his miserable demon possessed life. Jesus cut this Gordian knot and accepted him as a child of God who needed a loving word of acceptance. The word used to describe the man's life in classical Greek meant "to tear" or "rend," and here probably means "convulse." The poor man's life had been torn apart by the evil spirit and now the demon makes one last convulsing gasp before obeying Jesus and coming out of the man. He can do nothing else for he himself knows what we know---that Jesus is the Holy One of God!

The crowd is also astonished and amazed. They respond---What is this? Is it some kind of new teaching? The clue to understanding the crowd's amazement was not that Jesus could cast out the spirit. The magicians of the day could do the same. So why was the crowd amazed? Two words in the text give us the clue: καινη, meaning new, and ακαθαρτον, meaning defiled or unclean. Since the crowd saw the man as unclean, they would stay far away from him. To touch him, even accidentally, would mean they were defiled. They would have to go through cleansing rituals to purify their own bodies. So, their traditional laws allowed them to shout, "Stay away!" Even the unclean man was supposed to shout this as he walked along. Thus, the astonishing thing to them was that Jesus would come near to the man. It must be "a new teaching," for the old said loud and clear--- "Stay away!"

Now we are ready for the question, "What is the Word of God for us in this grizzly little story?" Central to our Good News story is the cry, the Holy One of God is with us! Our evil riddled society is wondering if there is any divine reality working for good in the world. Needy individuals are asking if there is any loving touch that can bring healing to their lives. Our world is filled with the "torn ones" --- the homeless fill our streets and the "demon possessed" fill our mental institutions. Just as the synagogue crowd shunned this torn and convulsing man, churches today shun the poor, the needy, women, children, those with AIDS, and the gay community. Jesus drew the man into the pure and un-coercive love of God, and that love had the power to heal and bring wholeness out of brokenness.

The crowd was amazed, and our world will be amazed once again when the church breaks down the barriers of race, gender, and poverty. When we love all people with the pure love of God, our world will once again be amazed and astounded! People today live with many demonic fears. And fear is the antithesis of trusting love and the parent of hate and retaliation. The demonic man in our gospel story was caught in the grip of this fear and cried out to Jesus, Are you here to destroy us! Notice the demon possessed man refers to himself as "us." He is a man of multiple personalities---his demons are many. In a very real sense Jesus was there to destroy the demons.

The daily fear of demons was a part of life in the time of Jesus. They feared that daily reality was controlled by demons. You could eat contaminated food and drink impure water and take in a demon. They believed demons lurked along the path of life in rocks and trees. Their daily lives were controlled by such fears. The fact that you and I can go a day without thinking of demons shows that Jesus did destroy the demons. He lived the creative, transforming power of the Kingdom of God. In His life, heavenly realities were shining in a dark demon infested world. In Mark 7:14-23, Jesus located evil in the human heart. This is a part of His new, fresh, and authoritative insight. And it is a discovery that makes evil manageable.

As long as evil is located outside of us, we can escape responsibility, saying, The devil made me do it! It is the inner life of persons that is divided and torn. Jesus knew the evil of the human heart and with love He sought to take possession of this heart for the Kingdom of God. Love unites and heals.[173] Our story closes with this happy refrain: And so the news about Jesus spread quickly everywhere in the province of Galilee (1:28). And why not. Galilean glories were shining with the light of Kingdom of Heaven realities, overcoming the dark evil forces that plague people's lives. Will you let Kingdom realities shine in your life? I wish for each of you a world free of demons and full of God's love and light.

Conclusion to Jesus As Creative Responsive Love

The New Testament Gospels are primarily about the call and response of Jesus to the love aims and purposes of God. Jesus chose to fully respond to God's call to love all persons and respect all persons. Thus, Jesus incarnated God's love in freeing, healing, and transforming ways.

The New Testament presents Jesus as being fully human and fully divine. In my theology of the New Testament, based on the gentle teachings of Jesus, there is no problem in making what is often seen as a contradictory statement---i.e., how can one person be both fully human and fully divine at one and the same time. Jesus was fully divine in the sense that he self-actualized fully the divine logos, the creative principle of God in loving and healing ways. The New Testament describes this actualization in two basic

---

[173] I am indebted to my mentor Frank Stagg and his book, *Polarities of Man's Existence in Biblical Perspective*, pp. 132-34, for many of the ideas and phrasing of this paragraph.

ways. Luke typifies one way when he reported the angel's message to Mary, The Holy Spirit will come on you, and God's power will rest upon you. For this reason, the holy child will be called the Son of God.[174]

Mary was obedient to God when she responded, I am the Lord's servant, may it happen to me as you have said.[175] The Apostles' Creed follows the Lukan perspective when it states that Jesus was "conceived by the Holy Spirit, born of the Virgin Mary." When God is seen in loving and relational terms, one has no problem accepting this Lukan perspective. This is an appropriate paradigm for understanding God as relating to God's people in new and redeeming ways.

John the disciple and Paul the apostle give different perspectives on the way God is present within the creative process. Both of them speak of the pre-existent wisdom or logos (Christ) coming from heaven above to dwell on earth below. Luke's perspective and John and Paul's perspective are relational ways of saying that God is near in Jesus in saving ways.

Jesus, when seen as fully human like us, opens up the possibility for all persons to self-actualize God's love in liberating and transforming ways. Faithfull self-actualization of God's love, enabling Jesus to become more God-conscious, was an ongoing experience for Jesus; and it was a transforming process in the followers of Jesus. Paul is an example of how open one can be to God's loving presence. The secret of Paul's life and ministry is the way he chose to embody Jesus-like virtues in his own life. We can acknowledge these fruits of the spirit in Paul's life and still wish he had grown more quickly in other areas, like overcoming his low view of women.

Jesus' uniqueness for the Christian is that he fully realized and lived God's loving presence, unlike any other person. Jesus' gentle teachings embody persuasive, luring love. When we learn to love God with our heart, soul, strength, and mind and to love our neighbor as ourselves, we are slowly but surely transformed by this love. Since we find these gentle teachings in the Gospels today, it is important that we prayerfully and devotionally study these teachings.

Paul surely recognized this truth when he continually admonished his helpers like Timothy to study the scriptures. Since the Gospels had not yet been written, Paul was referring to the Old Testament Scriptures, perhaps also to the oral Jesus tradition, for their spiritual growth. Paul wrote to the Philippians: "Finally, beloved, whatever is true, whatever is honorable, whatever is just, whatever is pure, whatever is pleasing, whatever is commendable, if there is any excellence and if there is anything worthy of

---

[174] Luke 1:35. See chapter on Father and Son for an understanding of this relationship.
[175] Luke 1:38.

praise, think about these things."[176] As we fill our minds with these Jesus-like virtues our lives are slowly but surely transformed. We can see this growth and development in Paul's life and teachings that is sometimes overlooked in our wish that he had grown more quickly. While his early letters show a low view of women, toward the end of his life he came to see that there was no distinction between male and female.

Jesus offers forgiving transforming love. In the New Testament Gospels, we see the power of Jesus' gentleness and compassion to heal crippling guilt. Guilt may be defined as "a painful feeling of self-reproach" that comes from feeling that "one has done something wrong or immoral." The paralytic in Mark 2:1-12 is an example of such forgiveness.

Guilt is overcome by accepting God's forgiveness. Forgiveness is a powerful therapeutic force. In accepting the paralytic as a friend when others rejected him as an untouchable sinner, the four friends initiated forgiveness. Jesus' acceptance of the paralytic as a child of God in need of forgiveness and healing made the miracle possible.

The Good News is that Jesus opens the way through the bondage of guilt and into forgiveness. Jesus' statement to the paralytic, "Son, your sins are forgiven," are powerful family words of acceptance. In these affirming words Jesus is identifying with the rejected "sinner" as his brother in suffering. Jesus' words, actions, and his death on the cross between two sinners demonstrate to us that God stands by us in spite of our sin.

Jesus' acceptance is the door to healing grace. To truly accept another person is to enter into their struggle to throw off the shackles of the old life burdened with guilt and creatively work toward the new self-envisioned by God. Acceptance by someone who cares is a powerful healing force. In Jesus' gentle Galilean teachings, we see God relating to us in forgiving and transforming love.

How do the gentle teachings of Jesus transform our lives?

Jesus expressed the creative love of God in his words and actions. Jesus' words acted God's love and his actions spoke God's love. When we receive Jesus' gentle teachings, believe them in our hearts, speak them in our words, and live them in our actions, we are open to God's creative responsive love. When we believe that Jesus was totally God-conscious, one with God, we are more open to God's aims and purposes for our lives and are more likely to respond to God's creative love more fully and positively.

Wherever authentic gentle teachings of Jesus are lived and spoken they interpret our life and our world, Jesus is embodied, and the church is present and the realization of the creative love of God occurs anew. Thus, the church exists to extend the gentle teachings of Jesus revealing the love of God in a broken world. As we are transformed by God's love actualized in

---

[176] Philippians 4:8.

Jesus, we make that love available for all other persons and things, we become as one in cosmic community. Where the gentle teachings of Jesus are faithfully taught and lived, there the gifts of love, joy, and peace are given. Is there anything our broken world needs more than this transformation?

God is in all acts of transformation, in our transformation and world transformation, feeling our joys and sorrows, our fears and hopes, taking them all into the divine life, and God is transformed in the process!

Chapter Twelve
Cross and Resurrection

Jesus' resurrection was the victory of love over death,
even the cruel death on a cross. Love triumphs over death.

The shadow of the cross fell early in the ministry of Jesus, at least by the middle of his three-year ministry, and it grew more serious as he journeyed toward Jerusalem. In the last week of his life, the gentle Jesus comes face to face with the cruel cross. And let us be clear, it is the gentle Galilean glories of Jesus that transform the cross from a symbol of betrayal, rejection, humiliation, and suffering into a great plus sign in the sky. Our faith story of Jesus includes the cross and resurrection. As we share our faith story of the cross (Jesus' death) we are drawn into its power and our future is revitalized (resurrection).

The story of the cross of Jesus is central to the New Testament. Indeed, there would be no Bible as we know it and no Christian Church without the story of Jesus' gentle suffering love. Our most crucial task is to learn Jesus' story, make it our own, and share it in a warm and personal way with others.

Jesus invites, lures, and welcomes us into his story. Jesus said, "If I be lifted up, I will draw all persons to me" (John 12:32). This is the greatest story ever told. It is based on the power of grace, mercy, and love seen in the cross. Telling this Gospel story of Jesus in a personal and warm way has a power and attraction for us today. Thus, we should spend far more of our time than we do telling this story. This is a miracle story. In the faithful telling and hearing of this story, Jesus steps off the pages of the New Testament and into our lives. When that happens, our life is never the same. The hymn, "Since Jesus Came into My Heart" says it best: "What a wonderful change in my life has been wrought, since Jesus came into my heart! I have light for which long I have sought, since Jesus came into my heart. Floods of joy o'er my soul like the sea billows roll, since Jesus came into my heart."

Come with me on this sacred journey and let the Jesus of history who suffered on the cross for you and me become the Jesus of faith for us. The story of the cross is about the transforming power of the gentle Jesus.

Mary Langford, a missionary to Hong Kong, tells of hearing outside her home peddlers shouting messages that describe what product or service they have to sell, like, "Flowers for sale" and "Come get your fruits and vegetables here." As she heard them, she wondered, "If Jesus were a peddler in Hong Kong today, what would He be saying?" The next message from the peddler gave her the answer: "I buy broken things, I mend broken things!" With His call of comfort, promise, and hope, Jesus says, "I buy broken things, I mend broken lives!" What better image could we find to describe the gentle Galilean ministry of Jesus? Jesus receives and mends broken things! We need to let his gentle touch heal our brokenness. Jesus loved each one of us enough to give his life on the cross for us.

How the cleansing of our sins and our salvation is accomplished at the cross remains one of the mysteries of our faith. Someone asked an older minister this question, and he replied like this: Just as blood is absorbed in a sponge, when we bring our sins to the foot of the cross, they are absorbed in a loving heart. In this process our sins are removed from our lives never to be remembered again.

In human terms, I like to think that the cleansing of our sins is like a parent taking a child in a warm embrace, cleaning away the dirt from a skinned knee and soothing away the ache and tears. I saw an example of this recently. An eight-year old boy fell on his skateboard and severally skinned his knee. He came running to his mother. She took him in her arms and went and got a warm bath cloth. She sat down and began to carefully clean the dirt from the wound. She put a large Band-Aid on the wound and then held her son until he felt much better. Then he ran out to play again. At the cross, a loving God embraces the confessing sinner, wipes away the tears, and cleanses and purifies the soul. Yes, just as blood is absorbed in a sponge, our sins are absorbed in the loving heart of God and we are forgiven.

To bring our lives to the cross is to experience transforming power within our inner self. The crucified Jesus in us is the change agent. Dr. Carl Jung, the great psychoanalyst, understood the power of the inner self as having the wisdom and drive to become the integrating center of optimal human health and wholeness. But he also saw that making the spiritual self the integrating center of life opens ones whole being to the influence of the energizing love of God.   In confessing faith in Jesus, the believer is exalted to a new level of existence. How do we account for such a high level of transforming love energies at the cross? With each successive actualization of the creative responsive love of God by Jesus, his love energies grew stronger. This is the inherent nature of radiant love energies in contrast to the mechanical energy of the solar system. Scientist generally acknowledge an entropy principle, the Second Law of Thermodynamics,[177] i.e., the slow depletion of energy in the solar system. This law, while apparently holding true for the solar system,[178] does not hold true with love energies. With each actualization of God's love, love grew in Jesus. Love is reciprocal in this sense. Jesus' voluntary sacrificial death on the cross transforms his love and

---

[177] Rudolf Clausius.
[178] Some scientist are taking a new look at this principle, questioning whether it is true.

the love of God. God is changed by the cross. This is the nature of love, and love cannot be silenced! Love triumphs! When the love energy of Jesus at the cross is united with the love energy of God, both are lifted to a new level of meaning consciousness.

Thus, the resurrection of Jesus cannot be understood apart from the love energies of the cross. When Jesus is lifted up on the cross, he is raised into this new existence, a new level of evolutionary energy expressing the love aims and purposes of God for the universe.

The Gentle Galilean Glories of Jesus, the Jesus love-event, was so powerfully transforming that it could not be stopped by a cruel cross. Gentleness trumps cruelty and a new evolution of love energies emerged as Jesus' followers gathered here and there and discovered this reality. As they joined their love energies with Jesus', a power field of energy was created.

A new body, the church, emerged with the resurrected Jesus as the mind directing the new body.[179] The Glory of God felt in the teachings of Jesus was more fully realized and unleashed for the future in this new body. In this evolutionary system such new emergences cannot be stopped. In this new resurrection emergence, Jesus escaped the time/space continuum and becomes present whenever and wherever his gentle agape teachings are taught and lived.

Thus, the first function of Christians is to form communities that harness and channel this new evolutionary consciousness, this power field of love, in creative and transforming ways. Instead of entropy after Jesus' death, in community love energies grow stronger and the power field is increased.

Let me tell you a story about transforming resurrection powers. My wife, Beth, gave me some tulip bulbs in my Christmas stocking once. She even bought the bone meal and had everything necessary for planting. I examined the bulbs a couple of times while we were waiting for the proper day for planting. I looked at those brown dead looking bulbs and shook my head half in doubt and half in wonder and awe. They could have been onions for all I knew. But no, the packet said tulip bulbs, and they looked like other tulip bulbs I had planted in the past, so we planted those in faith.

Right on schedule they put up a couple of inches of green blades that we admired like proud parents! Not long after that, Beth and I went out on the front porch and our tulips were blooming. We sat with our coffee and rocked in our Hinkle rocking chairs and enjoyed them.

As miraculous as this process was, it was completely natural. In spring the whole earth comes to life. You can feel the energy? The sap rises in the dormant trees, spring peepers start peeping, and trumpet lilies burst forth in bloom and spill their fragrance in the air.

---

[179] Paul describes the church as "the Body of Christ" throughout his Epistles. I use the risen Jesus instead of Christ for the sake of dialogue in a pluralistic age.

Jesus told parables like this. And it is in light of those bio-philic gentle teachings that we must understand the resurrection of Jesus. Jesus lived life out among the people. He spoke of the birds of the air and the flowers of the field. He spent his life trying to help people have a better life here and in the hereafter. He loved and cared for people, and he touched their lives in healing ways. The transforming healing power of Jesus' gentle teachings open the possibility for us to see the transforming nature of God at work in the resurrection of Jesus!

Jesus did not seek escape from this life and the Gospels will not let us think that his life was taken from him. He voluntarily gave his life as the completion of his sacrificial ministry. When the cross became inevitable, he willingly gave his life for others. When the evil of the world was doing its very worst, Jesus was doing his very best work. His resurrection was the vindication of the kindness that has always been at the heart of God. Jesus' resurrection continued his theme of strengthening and encouraging others for the living of life, here and now.

We discover this truth in the gentle teachings: Jesus called and taught his disciples so they could continue his gentle teachings based on the love commandment and extend them into the world. Jesus' resurrection makes love energies more real and possible on a continuing basis.

This is the testimony of the first followers of Jesus and Christians through the ages, and it is this personal experience and conviction that is hard to explain if Jesus is not a living reality and continuing presence. How we explain Jesus' presence may be secondary to this reality. The resurrection of Jesus as historical fact may be beyond proof, but the Easter faith of the first followers of Jesus is available for historical scholarship. While the Gospel stories vary and cannot prove the resurrection, they are historical evidence of Easter faith that Jesus was risen indeed!

The discovery of this amazing truth does not mean that we become passive observers but active participants of the good news. Our understanding of the resurrection also must take a back seat to the awe-inspiring mystery of the resurrection. What effect did the resurrection of Jesus have upon these early disciples? Clearly from the diversity of the resurrection stories found in the Gospels, they did not fully understand the implication of the resurrection, and we should not be surprised at this. The New Testament accounts fluctuate between understanding the risen Jesus as a spirit or ghost who can pass through doors,[180] a resuscitation of the human body that can be touched and even eat food with his disciples,[181] and as a

---

[180] John 20:19-20.
[181] Luke 24:36-49.

physical body in transition, as when Jesus said to Mary in the Garden, "Do not hold on to me for I have not yet ascended to my Father."[182]

In one sense the resurrection of Jesus is beyond human knowledge. It is in the realm of mystery, of faith, and we have no words to describe it. The energy we experience in nature in the spring help us to understand. However, its reality is not predicated on our understanding. Did humans understand when and why they began to walk on two legs instead of four? The resurrection of Jesus may be described as an advance or evolution of a new level of existence of which there have been many.

However, for the disciples, the crucifixion was too fresh in their minds to seek explanations. The crucifixion had sent them scurrying in many directions. They were disappointed and disillusioned. When Jesus came back to them, the message was "I am going to stay with you in a "higher" spiritual sense. John's Gospel quotes Jesus as saying to his disciples prior to his crucifixion, "My Father will send you a helper, the Spirit, who will remind you of all that I taught you."[183] In other words, Jesus says that my gentle teachings will continue to inspire you and guide you. The Spirit Jesus promised is best seen as his continuing presence. The risen Jesus and the Spirit are one.

So after the resurrection, like a mother hen gathers her brood, the risen Jesus began to gather his own. He met some on the Emmaus Road, others by the seaside, and still others in an upper room and asked, "Why are you troubled?" He dispelled their doubts and dissolved their fears. The risen Jesus molded them into his Body on earth, to continue his ministry of love and care. He gave to them his love, joy, and peace. Soon they were out in the byways of life sharing his "Galilean Glories." Belief in the resurrection molded the scattered disciples, women and men, into a fellowship of faith under the direction of the love energies generated by the gentle teachings of Jesus. We argue about whether men or women should lead the church today, making sexual preferences, racial distinctions, and social discriminations, missing how the gentle teachings overcome all of these barriers, and, we miss the main Gospel truth: Jesus is risen! He goes before you. The real leaders of the early Christian movement were not Mary, Martha, Salome, Peter, James, or John. Paul would not claim this role. All were subject to the authority of the gentle teachings. The Spirit of the risen Jesus was the real leader of the early Church. He is the Head of the new Body, the Church. Through this new transformation he continues his ministry of love and care. The crucified Jesus is alive in the church. The resurrection was like a bridge spanning his gentle earthly ministry and His ongoing ministry in and through the church to the larger world. The resurrection was like heavenly light shining in a new

---

[182] John 20:17.
[183] John 14:26.

and energizing way. The miracle for us is that Jesus' actualization of the creative love of God brought the heavenly light into our dark earthly existence. Our earthly life will never be the same again after the Jesus-event and the transforming resurrection.

While his earthly ministry was primarily with his own Jewish people, his ministry as the resurrected Jesus is worldwide. Jesus is now in the world and for the world with a new intensity! This transition did not come easily. It is a bold claim. But the resurrection empowered them for boldness! And this may be the greatest proof of Jesus' resurrection.

Some today would explain the resurrection stories as hallucinations. Many process philosophers and theologians, following the lead of Charles Hartshorne, who studied with Alfred North Whitehead and has advanced Whitehead's thought, interpret resurrection as the synthesis of our life in God, a living on in the memory of God. Liberal scholars have tended to see the resurrection as a powerful symbol, but not an actual event. Still others interpret the appearances of Jesus as psychic, like some loved ones think their departed family member appears to them. But can these ways of interpretation explain such boldness on the part of the disciples, a boldness that moved them from hiding behind barred doors to preaching courageously to the crowds?[184] As he promised, Jesus did go ahead of his followers to a hill in Galilee where he met them, commissioned, and empowered them:

> All authority in heaven and on earth has been given to me. . ..
> And remember! I will be with you always.[185]

What a tremendous promise! All the love energies of God that raised Jesus from the dead are available for his disciples and all disciples who come after them. Jesus goes before us in transforming loving kindness! Claiming this promise enabled the first disciples to become bold proclaimers of the Gospel in the face of martyrdom and death.[186]

Claiming this same promise and energizing love will enable us to boldly live the abundant life Jesus gives. With the resurrection the hope of tomorrow is here to dispel the despair of today. A little boy was on a train ride with his dad. The train entered a tunnel and they were plunged into total darkness. Soon the trained passed from the tunnel into bright sunshine again. The little boy was startled and exclaimed to his dad, "It is tomorrow, today." With God revealed in Jesus it is always tomorrow, today.

---

[184] See John 20:19-23; Acts chapters 2 and 4.
[185] Matthew 28:18-20.
[186] See my book on *The Book of Revelation: Jesus' Kindness Transforms Suffering*

One of the thieves on the cross next to Jesus said, "Remember me, Jesus, when you come as King!" The prayer implies a future rule, but Jesus' response offers a present reality: Jesus said to him, "I promise you that today you will be in Paradise with me."[187]

God relates to the world at every moment of its existence, remembering the past, feeling the present, and knowing the future as open to new possibilities; and the risen Jesus transcended these human calculations of time. The resurrection of Jesus brings God's love aims and purposes, God's dynamic future into our present, energizing and transforming it. And that is the mystery of transforming love. With Jesus God's tomorrow is our today!

In pursuing increased love energies, we may also find that Jesus is not the only way to transformation. Since Jesus as a human being responded to God's call and self-actualized God's love, it is possible to believe that all persons can respond to God's call to some degree; and it is possible to affirm that people in all religions like Moses, Mohammed, Confucius, Buddha, Gandhi, Martin Luther King, Jr., and others (including you and me) may also actualize these transforming powers in special ways in their unique culture as only they could do. Christians can affirm this and still give allegiance to the special role of Jesus for our faith.

Adherents in all religions need to learn more about miraculous love energies and how to live them in our broken world. The greatest threat to peace in our time may be that one religion becomes the enemy of another. These gentle love energies can break down religious and racial barriers, heal anger and hatred between those with different sexual orientations, and breach the growing divide between the rich and poor.

Theology at its best affirms that all things and all people are connected in a global society. Love energies generated by the cross and resurrection of Jesus enable us to see value in all persons and relate to them with a desire to learn from each other. The power of the cross lies in Jesus ability to love his enemies and even pray for them while he is dying. Jesus modeled inclusive love, and the path to living at peace in a global community lies in following his example. The more one sees Jesus, and indeed, all gentle peace makers, and is transformed by this vision, the more one sees ways to become a reconciler.

---

[187] Luke 23:42-43.

Chapter Thirteen

Is there Love on a Cosmic Level?

"There is only one supreme idea on earth---the idea of the immortality of the human soul." Dostoyevsky, Diary of a Writer

"There is another reality, the genuine one, which we lose sight of. This other reality is always sending us hints, which without art, we can't receive. Saul Bellow, Nobel Lecture, 1976

If one believes the universe has a face, a personality that directs the universe with novel love aims and purposes, then there is love on a cosmic level. We name this reality God who is best described as creative-relational love. We might also name this reality Spirit, within and beyond the created order. This Spirit guides, lures, creation forward to ever increasing joy, goodness, adventurous love, and a peace that passes understanding.

Jesus responded to the call of God and lived this creative-responsive love in word and deed. The union of Jesus' love and God's love created a new synthesis, a new consciousness for God and Jesus. The cross and resurrection of Jesus elevated this consciousness to a new level, a cosmic level of reality transcending time and space. My hope for the future is based on the nature of love to grow and be enriched with each new synthesis until the final transformation is heaven!

Is there life beyond death? This childhood experience expresses my view of heaven. When I was about ten years old, I was playing with two of my cousins at my grandparent's house. My mother had told me to be sure and come home before dark, since I would be walking through the woods alone. It was a well-known and well-trodden path about one mile long. As children will do, I forgot the time. Suddenly it was almost dark, so I hurriedly said good-bye and struck out through the woods.

In the beginning I was brave and felt good. Then it grew darker. At the half-way point I crossed the little brook I had spent many hours playing in---catching blue trout with red eyes, minnows with little horns on their head, and tadpoles. I caught so many tadpoles that my brothers and sisters gave me the nickname, "Tadpole."

Well, back to my journey through the dark woods. Crossing the brook, I was beginning to feel smaller than a tadpole. And I had a half- mile to go. I began to think of rattlesnakes, bobcats, and tales of a wild man who lived in those woods. Like many mythical tales there was a kernel of truth in this one. Jim could be seen on the dirt roads carrying a toad sack full of soup bones he had gathered behind the meat market in town. He brought the bones to his shack in the woods along the creek. There he boiled them in gallon cans on an open fire with vegetables given to him from people's gardens.

It was told, mainly by older brothers trying to scare younger brothers that Jim often frightened little children he found in his woods. Of course, I was thinking about Jim as I crossed the brook into utter darkness. I no longer felt brave. Every bush was alive and shaking and the leaves rattled from small animals scurrying about. Later in life I learned an African proverb that boldly states, "All things which make noise at the side of the path do not come down the path." This is a good proverb for seasoned sages, but meaningless to a frightened ten-year-old.

Besides, the noise I heard was coming down the path! There were definite footsteps ahead. Then I saw him coming down the path toward me! I froze in my tracks! My feet would not move, but my heart raced rapidly! Out of the darkness came a familiar voice, "Son is that you." Images of monsters melted away in the sunshine of those family words. I recognized the voice of my father who had come to meet me. My father hugged me home that night!

This childhood experience shaped my life and faith. According to an Irish proverb, "What the child sees, the child does, what the child does, the child is." Because of my kind father and gentle, nurturing mother, I grew up finding it easy to believe in God. God has always been to me like a kind Father and a nurturing Mother God---a loving parent if you will. This was a natural transference for me because of my parent's deep faith and loving example.

We need this kind of radiant faith. As Christians we bask in it at Easter and other peak moments of our lives. Other religious faiths do the same on their holy days. But this heavenly glow has a way of fading as we walk through dark woods and do battle with our fears. Thieves and robbers nibble away at our faith. So, we need re-assurance. No one knew this better than Jesus as he was preparing to leave his disciples. The Greek philosopher, Epicurus said, "The art of living and dying are one." Jesus had lived well, and now he wanted to die well by preparing his disciples for his death.

Beginning in the fourteenth chapter of John, Jesus bid his disciples farewell. The disciple's questions are like the questions of children when parents are leaving for the night. "Where are you going? When will you be back? Who will take care of us?" Recognizing their concern, Jesus said, "Let not your hearts be troubled. You believe in God, believe also in me" (v. 1). Jesus chose the most basic and central word in the disciple's religious vocabulary to ease their fears. Believe in God. In Jesus' Hebrew Scriptures, he'emin, usually translated in English as "believe," means "firm, constant, and reliable." The mental picture it carried and still holds for the Jews is of a child carried in the folds of the mother's garment close to her body where he/she is safe and sheltered. Jesus' words to his disciples could be restated as "My Father is hugging me home!"

On Ascension Sunday we celebrate Jesus' final victory. On a mountain top in Galilee Jesus bids his disciples farewell and the angels come and hug him home to heaven.

This faith image of the Jewish people, "belief/believing," became so precious to the disciples and early Christians that it occurs over 550 times in the Greek New Testament. The early Church was nurtured and held in this faith through many dark days and nights. To believe in God is to have hope.

I know how the disciples felt about Jesus preparing to leave them and return to His Father. There came a time when our father was preparing to leave our family. He was dying of emphysema. He was walking through the "valley of the shadow of death," and he was "troubled in heart." Afraid. I talked to him several times as Jesus talked to his disciples about his heaven going. I let him talk and I comforted him. Then, as he had done for me in the dark woods at the age of ten, I hugged him on his way home and handed him into the arms of Jesus who hugged him on home to heaven. Four years later my family and I did the same for our mother. These personal life and death experiences have been illuminated by the heavenly light of John 14.

This is my belief, my faith experience. I believe in heaven because Jesus said, You believe in God, believe also in me. There are many rooms in my Father's house, and I am going to prepare a place for you. I would not tell you this if it were not so. And after I go and prepare a place for you, I will come back and take you to myself, so that you will be where I am. You know the way that leads to the place where I am going.[188]

This news about Jesus going back to heaven to prepare a place for us and then coming back for us some day is almost too good to be true some say. Actually, it is too good not to be true!

We find comfort and security in this gospel truth from John 14. We have devoted our lives to learning this truth and living this life, as we walk the way of service. And one day we will walk through those dark woods known as the valley of the shadow of death. Our family on earth will hug us and hand us to the Good Shepherd of the Way who will guide us through that passage where the darkness gives way to heaven's bright light. And Look! There are my mother and father and your loved ones, our family of faith, to hug us home, and present us to our kind heavenly Father and nurturing Mother God.[189]

---

[188] John 14:1-4.

[189] Again, it is important to say that this belief that Jesus is the Way to heaven for me does not mean that Jesus is the only way. I believe that other religions also show

Chapter Fourteen

Spirit

Thesis: The Role of Spirit in the New Testament is to continue the work of Jesus by enabling his followers to remember and understand the gentle teachings of Jesus and extend them into the world with transforming power.

With this thesis in mind, go with me to an upper room in Jerusalem where the disciples are gathered with Jesus to discuss Jesus' last days of ministry with them. For months Jesus had been living under the shadow of the cross, trying to grasp its meaning for himself and his continuing ministry through his disciples. In this upper room, Jesus knows that it was time for farewells and final instructions. Tension is high. On the one hand, Jesus is talking of love, joy, and peace, the gifts that come from living well and dying well. Jesus is secure in his accomplishments and optimistic about his work going forward. The disciples, on the other hand, are shattered by the pain of possible separation and death. The hour is dark for them and despair is creeping into their hearts.

In that darkness Jesus' face shines with the light of heaven. And to his disciples he says, "I will not leave you Helpless! I will ask God to give you the Holy Spirit, a Helper, who will stay with you forever. The Spirit will remain with you and in you." The New Testament Greek word in this passage used to describe the Holy Spirit is παρακλητος. We get the English word, paraclete, as a direct transliteration of this Greek word. Translators of the Bible have often been in a quandary about how to translate this word. Some choose Paraclete, others seeking a warmer and more personal term, use Comforter, and still others use Helper. The word is too rich for any one word to carry its meaning. The Greek word is composed of two words: παρα, which means alongside of, and κλητος, which means called or summoned. Jesus who had responded to the call of God to walk along side of the disciples as their friend and helper is saying that he is leaving them, but he will come back to continue to be alongside of them as their Friend and Helper. And the best news of all is that as the risen Jesus he is not just alongside of them, but within them to empower, encourage, and instruct them in what they are to do. Indeed, Jesus promised as the Helper, the Spirit, I will teach you

---

the way to God. We can walk the way with each other and learn from each other along the way.

everything and make you remember all that I have told you.[190] Jesus' optimism in the upper room is tempered with realism. Jesus speaks to the disciples about his suffering, and adds, If people persecuted me, they will persecute you too.[191]

Do not fear! In all times and circumstances, no matter what happens, through thick and thin, in good times and bad times, The Helper will be with you! Each time the disciples begin to slip back into despair, Jesus says, "Help is on the Way." Four times in the span of three chapters, in each major movement, Jesus says, "Don't fear. Don't panic. Don't give up. Help is on the way."

On the Day of Pentecost, this promise of Jesus was fulfilled. The Spirit who was active in creation, who empowered the prophets of old, who energized Jesus' ministry, came in fresh ways upon the disciples like flames of fire from heaven and empowered them. As I read about the coming of the Spirit upon the disciples in the Upper Room, I am drawn into a deep feeling of mystery. This feeling is conveyed by the language like--- Suddenly there was a noise from the sky which sounded like a strong wind blowing, and it filled the whole house where they were sitting. They saw what looked like tongues of fire which spread out and touched each person there. They were all filled with the Spirit. Luke, in reporting this experience, wraps it up with words like "excitement," "amazement," and "wonder."[192]

I can't explain the Day of Pentecost, and thankfully I don't need to explain it. I can and do experience it. And we can experience the same excitement, amazement, and wonder as we worship. I experienced the power of the risen Jesus in unique ways in my pastoral ministry. For example, one Friday night Pat Underwood, an elder in the Church I was serving, called me and said that Betty Chapman one of our faithful members was worse. She has fought a brave fight with cancer for several years. Hospice has been called in and the doctors do not give her long to live. When the Hospice worker asked Betty if she needed a chaplain, she said, "No, I have a pastor." Thanks to Pat's call, Beth and I went to see Betty on Signal Mountain in Chattanooga, Tennessee. We had a good visit. Betty, who had spent over fifty years in our Church, wanted to know everything that was happening. She asked about the worship that Sunday. "What are you preaching about," she inquired? I told her that I was preaching a series of sermons on the Apostles' Creed, and that the one for Sunday was, "I Believe in the Holy Spirit." I gave her my interpretation of the Spirit as our Comforter, or Helper, and that Jesus will never leave us. She said, "Thank you pastor, I needed that." I quoted the

---

[190] John 14:25.
[191] John 15:20.
[192] Acts 2:1-13.

121st Psalm and prayed with Betty and her family. Surely God was with us, you could feel the Spirit.

There have been times in the past when I approached these great biblical truths like the Spirit as a student in the classroom playing the "Bible" game. Treating these great doctrines as texts to be analyzed and studied like history and culture. Now as I read about the Spirit in the New Testament, each word is like a sledge- hammer, pounding at my heart and soul. Each experience of the disciples and apostles becomes my experience as I shake hands with them, and experiencing the energy of that handshake, I come alive with excitement and wonder. How do you explain this difference? The Spirit opens my heart to the Scriptures and opens the Scriptures to my heart, and in these moments, I know that God is speaking! When God speaks, God acts! The Spirit is creative power. Where the Spirit is, creative energies flow and something miraculous happens. Our lives that are fractured and pulled in every direction by the voices of the world are quieted, and we experience God as peace. To the despairing and frightened disciples in the upper room Jesus said, Peace is what I leave with you; it is my own peace that I give you. I do not give it as the world does.[193]

I experienced this gift of peace as I was working on these thoughts on the Spirit. I felt that I was on the threshold of mystery. Through these Gospel passages the Spirit spoke to me saying, "Do not worry, do not fret, do not be afraid of what you will write, I will help you." What a wonderful gift of peace! And it is God's gift to God's people!

When the disciples were given this gift and empowered by God, they went out to continue Jesus' ministry of love and compassion, bringing the Help of God to people's broken lives. Given the New Testament message and the teachings of Jesus, how could it be otherwise?

The only question is, "Do we experience the Spirit as the gift of peace in our lives?" Or stated another way, do we need a Helper. In America we are given to rugged individualism, and are taught to say, "I can take care of myself." In the cartoons, Charlie Brown expresses our mood when he says, "The only pity you can rely on is self-pity." Charlie Brown is good for a chuckle, but he is wrong.

God is faithful and just. We can rely on God to help us in our time of need. If your heart is filled with sorrow and fear, Help is on the way. These human experiences of suffering, like Betty Chapman's, are times when we encounter the Spirit of the living God, in us and for us. Mystery, yes! The deeper the mystery, the greater is the possibility of divine revelation.

This connection of divine revelation with deep suffering is what attracts us to persons like Jesus and Mother Teresa. When an interviewer told Mother Teresa that she was doing a great work with the poor in Calcutta as

---

[193] John 14:27.

she went out in the mornings and picked up little babies and children who were left on the streets to die and brought them back to her clinic to be nourished back to health, she fiddled with her hands like a little child, and said, "It is Jesus." It was a short interview, but long on meaning. "It is Jesus." This crusty little nun does not pretend to solve the mystery of suffering. But by bringing the poor into her heart, she brings them to the heart of God. Thus, she helps to bring redemption to their lives. Mother Teresa knows that suffering and redemption have something to do with Jesus' suffering love. Indeed, her work is the work of the risen Jesus. This Saint knows and lives the truth that the Apostle Paul learned: God has shown us how much we are loved---it was while we were yet sinners that Jesus died for us. So we are happy to suffer with Jesus. We know that trouble produces endurance, endurance brings God's approval, and God's approval creates hope. This hope does not disappoint us, for God who is in us and for us has poured out love into our hearts by means of the Spirit, who is God's gift to us.[194]

The Spirit is about relationship, and I think Mother Teresa's comment above reveals something important to us. Summarizing her kind ministry as, "It is Jesus" is much warmer and connectional with those who suffer than speaking of the Holy Spirit or Holy Ghost, as many do when talking about Spiritual power. The name, Jesus, evokes kindness that transforms suffering.

Church leaders and theologians have always found it difficult to hold the truths about God, Jesus, and Spirit together and maintain the oneness of God. Here are some essentials for remaining true to the Bible, church traditions and creeds, and personal experience. **First**, Monotheism, the term for this oneness of God, is deeply imbedded in the Bible. This oneness of God is expressed in the Old and New Testaments in these words, "Our God is one, you shall love God with all your heart, soul, strength, and mind."[195] **Second**, Jesus actualized this love of God in his gentle and kind teachings. This actualization made it possible for God to be in Jesus healing ministry in transforming ways. Yet God is greater than God revealed in Jesus.

Third, Spirit in the Bible is about how God is in the world and for the world, in us and for us in saving ways. Spirit of God empowered Jesus' gentle and kind ministry as Jesus sought daily to actualize God's loving presence; and with Jesus' resurrection a new evolutionary stage is opened for all persons. The risen Jesus is raised in his new body, the church, to continue his kind ministry. The risen Jesus is the Spirit. Yet, again, God is greater than God revealed in the risen Jesus as the Spirit.

The key to seeing these relational Trinitarian aspects of God is accepting Jesus as truly human, and I have shown in previous chapters that

---

[194] Romans 5:1-11.
[195] See Deuteronomy 6:4 and Mark 12:29-30.

this is the main New Testament teaching. The temptation was to make Jesus totally divine from the beginning, perhaps because the Caesars claimed divinity. We have presented Jesus' divinity as a growth in God-consciousness. God was truly present in Jesus as God is present in all things, in us and for us. This insight is one of the contributions of process philosophy and process theology. This view maintains the oneness of God and maintains that Jesus was human and divine.

Glory be to the God of creative relational love who comes to us in saving ways in Jesus and empowering ways as the Spirit, our Friend and Helper. Peace be with you!

Chapter Fifteen

Trinity---The Way God Relates to Us

An elderly man took his ugly looking dog for his regular Sunday walk in the park. The little old man stopped at a park bench to rest, and his dog played at his feet. Soon another man appeared with his dog. The younger man's face had taken on the mean look of his bulldog, and they both were itching for a fight. The younger man began to taunt the little old man and his ugly dog. He commanded his dog, "Spike," and pointed at the ugly dog. The old man calmly said, "I wouldn't do that if I were you." This only irritated the young man, and he commanded Spike to attack the ugly dog. The old man reiterated, "I wouldn't have done that!" The battle raged in cartoon fashion with barking and hair flying. The result was unexpected. Spike lay defeated and before he could be seriously hurt, the old man reached down and pulled his dog off Spike. His humbled master said to the old man, "I am impressed. What kind of dog is that anyway?" The old man replied, "Well, before I cut off his tail and painted him yellow, he was an alligator!"

Things are not always as they appear. Situations are easily misread. This is especially true of the Bible that was written over a period of a thousand years and contains 66 different books. The Bible is used to support the handling of snakes and the drinking of poison as a test of one's faith in God. Some in Bible days saw Jesus as a drunkard and some even thought that Jesus was demon possessed, yet others saw him as the Son of God. Our views of God are often confused. The prophet Isaiah said, God's thoughts are not our thoughts and our ways are not God's ways!

Yet, there is an essential unity in the Bible. It is a unity in the midst of diversity. For example, there are two creation accounts in Genesis and four strikingly different Gospels, each with a different approach to telling the story of Jesus. However, the purpose is one: the Bible shows that God is for us in saving ways. There is no uniformity in details, but there is a unity of purpose: God relates to us in saving ways and that is the Gospel and the meaning of the Trinity.

The beloved disciple, John, quotes Jesus as saying, "If you love me you will keep my commandments. And I will ask God to give you another Advocate, to be with you forever. This is the Spirit of truth. . . and the Spirit will be in you."[196]

From beginning to end these verses from the Gospel of John, and others like them on the gift of the Spirit, are about God relating to the world

---

[196] Based on John 14:15-17.

and how people of the world experience God in saving ways. John testified to what he had seen and experienced in Jesus. He described his experience of God as creative responsive love. God is pictured as relating to all creation in loving ways---For God so loved the world that God gave us Jesus.[197] When taken together these verses speak of a love that is experienced in three distinct relational ways. First, God the Father/Mother/Parent[198] calls creation out of fullness, goodness, and love. The motive is to share that goodness and love with the world in relational ways. From the beginning God wanted the world to be like a beautiful garden where everyone related to each other in love and harmony. This is the theological truth of the mythic Garden of Eden story. Love does not force or coerce to get its way. Love grants freedom of choice and creates a climate of freedom. Instead of relating to God and each other in love, humans exercised their freedom of choice and rebelled against God and struck out at each other. In the first family, as told in the mythic story of Genesis, Cain even murdered his own brother, Abel, out of jealousy.

Yet, God did not give up. Like a good gardener, God nurtured a special relationship with Israel and formed a covenant of faith with Israel. God knew how the seed faith should grow and what it should produce. God the gardener knew how much sun, water, and nutrients were needed to produce fruit. In loving kindness God took care of Israel. God gave her the law through Moses and spoke tenderly to her in the prophets. In all of these ways God related to Israel like farmer Green Jeans or Mother Nature tenderly caring for the family garden.

The people of God still rebelled and refused to become a fruitful garden and give food to the hungry of the world. So, God, who spoke the beautiful garden into existence through a long evolutionary process, chose a second relational path. Jesus cleared this path by responding to God's call and self-actualizing God's love aims and purposes, enabling God "in the fullness of time" to relate in special ways. The logos, the creative principle that called creation out of chaos, is now realized in Jesus and lived in the garden world of Galilee. In the words and deeds of Jesus, the divine logos, the creative principle of God, God the Father/Mother now relates to the world in saving ways in Jesus. But God does not cease to be God. God is greater than God revealed in Jesus. This is not modalism, which was condemned as heresy by the early church councils. Modalistic views, stating that God is one and Jesus is God, not other than God, appeared in the East as early as 190 C.E. Those who stated this view were charged as Patripassians or Father suffering-ers. In the West, Sabellius (220-270 C.E.) was the strongest proponent of modalism. He said that God appeared successively as

---

[197] Based on John 3:16.
[198] You may choose whichever term you are more comfortable using, or choose another relational one.

Father, Son, and Holy Spirit, and not simultaneously. From creation to the birth of Jesus, God was manifested as Father---Creator and Legislator. From the birth of Jesus to the ascension of Jesus, God was manifested as Son. And from the ascension forward, God is manifested as Holy Spirit. Sabellius' concern was to safeguard monotheism. He did this by saying that there is one God in three modes. Thus, it was called modalism. Even to this day the West has tended toward modalism when it speaks of God as three persons. Karl Barth, often called the father of neo-orthodoxy, and the inspiration of many contemporary theologians, leaned toward modalism.

The New Testament Scriptures themselves do tend to open the door in this direction. The angels who announced Jesus' birth said, 'You shall call him Jesus, for he will save his people from their sins." An explanation of the name, Jesus, is added--- and they shall name him Emmanuel, which means, God is with us.[199] The message is: God is present in Jesus.

Jesus modeled tender loving care. In the rainy season, parts of Galilee, where Jesus performed most of his ministry, were like a garden. So, Jesus pointed to the flowers and said, "Consider the lilies of the field, how they grow; they neither toil nor spin, yet I tell you, even Solomon in all his glory was not clothed like one of these. If God so clothes the grass of the field. . . will God not much more care for you."[200]

In his creative responsive acts of love, Jesus gave a face to God. The disciples looked at Jesus and saw the glory of God in Jesus.[201] If you look at a picture of my daughter at age 12 and a picture of me at the same age, we look like identical twins. My daughter looks at me today and has nightmares about this genetic likeness; it doesn't bode well for her looks in the future.

In many ways the disciples saw God the Father/Mother in Jesus the Son. Phillip wanted to see more of God, and in the Upper Room he asked Jesus to show him God. Jesus replied, Philip, have I been with you all this time and you still do not know me? Whoever has seen me has seen the Father/Mother. How can you say, 'Show us the Father?' Do you not believe that the Father and I are one?[202] Jesus gave a physical face to God, and that face is love. In the face of the human Jesus, God's spiritual face shines bright; and it shines upon us as we turn our face toward Jesus and look full in his wonderful face. Everything in the countenance of Jesus reveals God. However, God is greater than God revealed in Jesus. This is the glory of Jesus and the glory of God. And this is the meaning of the Trinity!

Does our countenance reveal God? Henri Nouwen, the noted Catholic scholar, writer, and speaker, once told this story. A student came to

---

[199] Matthew 1:21-23.
[200] Matthew 6:27-29.
[201] John 1:14.
[202] John 14:8-10.

see him in his office. The student's request was different from most. "I have nothing to ask you or say to you. I just wanted to be silent with you." After they sat in silence for a while, the student said, "Whenever I'm in your presence, it is as if I am in the presence of Christ." Nouwen responded, "It is the Christ in you that sees the Christ in me."

As wonderful as this new relational activity of God in Jesus is for the early Christian community, there is a new transformation that occurs with the resurrection of Jesus. As the cross became immanent, Jesus made a wonderful promise: I am sending you the Spirit and the Spirit will be in you.[203]

The Spirit is the third way God relates to us. The Spirit is one with God and one with the risen Jesus. Jesus said that the Spirit will live in you. A wonderful transformation occurs here. Now we give a face to the Spirit or risen Jesus and to God. God has no other physical face than what is seen in the people of God. Where the people of God in all religions accurately reflect gentle teachings and actions, God has many friendly faces and encouraging faces; and they are all the face of God. The way Jesus became God-conscious lets us see how it is possible for God to be present in all persons. God transformed in the Risen Jesus or Holy Spirit and present in the people of God is without limits. God is now relating to people who open their lives to Spiritual Presence, spiritual transformation, in all times and places. Jesus made this promise in these comforting words: I am with you always, even to the end of the ages.[204] And this is the meaning of the Trinity!

The heart of all these teachings is saving love. The relational God who is like a Father and Mother, a Parent, loves the world enough to place good and loving aims in the creative process. Jesus who responded to the call of God and lived God's creative relational love in his gentle Galilean teachings and actions, becomes the Son of God. The Son radiates the love of the Parent and is willing to die for this love. God who was transformed by the suffering of Jesus is able to share creative responsive love more fully with others. So, the one constant is unconditional responsive love. The face of the triune God is revealed as creative responsive love in every instant of revelation and transformation, and Christian theology is most helpful to suffering humanity when it is formed around these agape truths.

What are the implications of this understanding of the Trinity as creative responsive love? Individuals may relate to God and experience God in different cultures and different religions. Wherever people come to God in love there is salvation. The Jewish person who comes to God through the Old Testament Scriptures experiences the love of God as the Christian experiences the love of God through Jesus. The one true God is revealed in Jesus, but not only in Jesus. God is greater than God revealed in Jesus.

---

[203] John 14:17.
[204] Matthew 28:20.

History would have been written differently if the church had only seen this polyphonic truth about God. All the hatred between Jews and Christians would be erased. All the rivalry between different religions would be useless. Racial hatred and gender battles would be eliminated. Love is the great equalizer. Christians could still witness in a spirit of love to the uniqueness of Jesus, without being judgmental of others who experience a deep love of God in their faith experience. By becoming totally God conscious and self-actualizing the creative responsive love of God in his gentle Galilean teachings, the human Jesus shows that God can also be present in others like Confucius, Mohammed, Buddha, Gandhi, Martin Luther King, Jr., and all who are open to the call of God.

The face of the Father/Mother, Saving love, and Spirit/Helper is One. The most central teaching of the Old and New Testaments is this: Hear, O Israel, the Lord, our God, is one Lord. The Spirit of God draws us to salvation. We relate to God as Creative Spirit who called all things into existence out of a long evolutionary process. We relate to God as Jesus who made the love of God tangible in human form.[205] And, we relate to God as the Spirit who is still active in reconciling the whole universe in saving ways. The Risen Jesus is also known as the Holy Spirit who is in all believers as Friend, Helper, and Comforter. These are all relational ways we experience God and God experiences us. And this is the meaning of the Trinity!

Does anyone see Jesus in you? Can you say of your work, "It is Jesus?" If people say, "You taught a good Sunday School Class," is your reply---"It is Jesus!" After I preach a sermon, can I say, "It is Jesus!" If we encounter needy individuals, do we see Jesus in them? When we reach that point, we can say that we understand the Trinity. Until we reach that level of maturity, we continue to worship in mystery and pray---

> Lord, my heart is not large enough,
> My memory is not good enough,
> My will is not strong enough:
> Take my heart and enlarge it.
> Take my memory and give it quicker recall.
> Take my will and make it strong
> And make me conscious of thee, ever present,
> ever accompanying.[206]

---

[205] See 1 John 1:1-3.
[206] The Oxford Book of Prayer.

Why Celebrate Trinity Anyway?

Now, I want to raise a practical and personal question: Why do we spend time with these old theological topics anyway, especially the trinity that is a controversial topic in religious dialogue? Why celebrate the Trinity? My answer is this: In the midst of a world of evil and suffering it is good to know that there is a God who is like a kind Father and nurturing Mother, a Parent God, if you will, who lures creation to ever enriching experiences, saves, and sustains us despite what evil may say. There is a mysterious, yet saving love (Jesus), an empowering Friend (Holy Spirit) who pervades the universe and our soul to console and reassure us that life is good, indeed, it is in the words of Genesis, chapters 1 and 2, "very good."

The Triune God is on the side of life and its joyous fulfillment. Because life is good, there is much to celebrate----much which can instill in us optimism, confidence, and a sense of well-being in spite of evil and suffering. We simply need to take time to be graced by those serene moments of beauty that are a part of our good creation.

The Psalmist leads the way for us. Psalm 8 is a hymn of praise to God's glory: "O Lord, our Lord, your greatness is seen in the world." What causes you to break out in praise like the Psalmist? What causes you to tingle with excitement? Sex! O.K. let's get that up front where it belongs. Sexuality is a marvelous gift. What else? I have harvested some special moments in God's good and beautiful creation and stored them in my memory bank. They are a part of the calm center out of which I live. One morning Beth and I sat on top of Clingmans Dome in the Great Smokey Mountains of East Tennessee, before pollution began to kill some of the trees, and looked at the mist from the valleys below. We took in the majestic view of the Smokies; and, as we did so, we felt a divine presence with us. Biophilic emotions welled up within us and we knew that we were one with God and a friendly universe. On another day we sat on the lip of the Grand Canyon and looked out across the chasm at the changing hues and colors of the rainbow. Again, we felt a Spiritual Friend with us, and we knew that life is good and beautiful. Our feeling of love for nature and all living things again nurtured our psyche and held us close to God.

My favorite place in this friendly, good, and beautiful creation is Hatteras Island and the Outer Banks of North Carolina when the sun first peeks up over the Atlantic Ocean. I enjoy standing in the surf and catching a speckled trout or flounder. That is a spine-tingling experience for me. In those moments I see "the greatness of God" and I feel close to God who is like a good Parent providing good and beautiful things for children to enjoy! In harvesting these moments, I was taking the pulse of the universe to see that all is well and let these psychetrophic (soul nurturing) moments perform their healing work.

Perhaps you are thrilled as you just look out over your land and recall the good times of your childhood, your wonderful parents, grandparents, and the raising of your own family on that good piece of earth.

You may be most worshipful when you step on "holy ground" at your place of worship where the "bush burns brightly" ----when you worship where your family for generations have worshipped. We ought to "take off our shoes" more often, for the whole earth is full of the presence of the Loving Triune God! God has been good to us. "O Lord, our Lord, your greatness is seen in the world!"

We hold these memories in our hearts and souls. Lest we forget, we have to relive and re-experience them ever so often. Even so, lest we forget, we have to celebrate the old stories of our faith. We have to celebrate Christmas and the birth of Jesus, The Gentle Galilean Teachings of Jesus, Holy Week and the suffering death of Jesus, Pentecost, and Trinity. Celebrating these truths helps us remember and relive them, and then reorganize and energize our lives around these core biophilic experiences of our Christian tradition. In remembering these core truths, evil is not any less real, but seen from this broad perspective of life's goodness and beauty, evil's power with all of its biophobic emotions that sap our energy, is diminished! And our dream of a transforming and liberating Gospel is revived.

So, "Glory be to God our Parent, who comes to us as Saving Love and empowering Friend: as it was in the beginning, is now, and ever shall be, world without end."[207]

---

[207]For more on the Trinity see my book, *A Relational Trinity of Kindness*.

CHAPTER SIXTEEN

The Role of The Church in Jesus' Gentle Teachings
What Makes A Church Effective?

The church is founded upon the gentle teachings of Jesus, culminating in his sacrificial death and resurrection. The goal and purpose of the church is to maintain, preserve, and extend these gentle teachings, with their power to transform lives, into the world. The sad history of the church is that it has often skipped over these gentle teachings of Jesus for the ways and power of Caesar.

Before the church can live and share these gentle teachings of Jesus it must become like Jesus. Paul recognized this when he encouraged the Philippians to have the "mind of Christ" in them.[208] Just as our minds direct our physical bodies, the spirit of Jesus is to be the guiding force for the church.

The birth of Jesus is described in the New Testament as the goodness and kindness of God coming to save us. Jesus' teachings dwelt on the tender things in life. Jesus' Galilean ministry was marked by compassionate love lifting up the needy. Jesus died with tender and forgiving words coming from his mouth. The power of Jesus' life is seen in the absence of force and the presence of persuasive responsive love.

If the church is to be effective today and have the same authority as Jesus had, it must recover Jesus' gentle Galilean glories. The church cannot adopt the ways of Caesar and the ways of big business, without losing the transforming power of the gentle ways of Jesus. An effective church is a Jesus centered church dedicated to maintaining, strengthening, and extending the gentle ministry of Jesus as lived out in Galilee as a model of God's novel love aims and goals for all people.

An effective church centered on the gentle teachings of Jesus will also be person centered. Jesus' life was an example of limitless love for all persons, especially the needy ones. This is seen best in the way Jesus accepted the very people society rejected. In Jesus tender ministry to these persons, God was near. Jesus' encounter with the woman of Samaria is a good example. In the Gospel of John, chapter four, we learn of Jesus stopping to rest at Jacob's well, while the disciples go into town to buy food. Jesus meets

---

[208] Philippians 2:5.

a Samaritan woman who has come to draw water and asked her for a drink. As the story unfolds, we become aware that we are in a world where there is deep conflict between the Samaritans and the Jews and a controversy is ongoing, focused on where one hears the word of God. The Samaritans feel that they hear the true word of God on Mount Gerizim and the Jews feel that they hear a true word of God in the Temple in Jerusalem. Each feels that the other is heretical and their teachings are the perversion of humans. Into the middle of this conflict comes Jesus, a Jewish stranger, to ask a drink from a Samaritan woman. Custom dictated that a Jewish man did not speak to a strange woman in public places and certainly not a Samaritan woman. Jacob's well was a popular and public place. The fact that the woman came there in the heat of the day instead of the cool of the evening when other women came indicates for some that she was considered as a sinful woman and shunned by others. However, Jesus does not call her sinful. She could have been getting water to give to the workers in the fields. The fact that she had lived with several husbands may indicate that she was the victim of levirate marriage, the compulsive marriage of a widow by the brother of her deceased husband.

Given the cultural conditions of Palestine in the time of Jesus, it is amazing that Jesus speaks to the woman without condemning or judging her! Instead Jesus speaks a true word of God that awakens new thirst and longing in the woman: Those who drink the water I give them will never be thirsty.[209] And what happens in this hearing of the word of God? The woman feels that her tangled life from many marriages and guilt is laid bare before Jesus. As Jesus offers the living water without judging her, the woman realizes that the source of eternal life is standing before her. She receives the promise and worships God in spirit and truth, then she runs to tell the whole town. In this story the mystery of God's true word and the words of Jesus are one. In the sharing of the story with the village, the mystery of the true word continues.

This compassionate and gentle story about Jesus tells us that God is Spirit. God is present with us in loving, healing, and saving ways. In his parable of the Good Samaritan that illuminates this story, Jesus is the Good Samaritan who brings this healing to all who are wounded.

If a church is centered on the gentle teachings of Jesus it will be person centered. Jesus' gentle teachings are filled with examples of limitless love. This is seen best in the way Jesus accepted all people, especially the people society rejected. The Gospel of Luke records for us the story of Jesus accepting, forgiving, and bestowing the gift of peace upon a woman shunned by others. There is a remarkable contrast between the attitude of the religious leaders and the attitude of Jesus toward the woman of the streets. Simon the Pharisee rejected the woman; Jesus accepted her. An effective church accepts

---

[209] John 4:14.

all people in love, especially persons of different sexual orientations, and all marginalized individuals today. The love of Jesus knows no bounds.

Jesus' life is the model for the church in caring for people. Jesus was the model for the parables like the Good Shepherd and as we saw above for the Good Samaritan. He was moved with compassion when he saw the crowds of people like sheep without a shepherd and as the wounded by the roadside. The church will recover its effectiveness when it learns to care for all people with the same compassion.

Jesus also gave himself to people. He gave his time, energy, and love to publicans needing to recover self-respect, beggars needing food, the blind needing sight, and lepers crying---"Unclean." An effective church as the embodiment of the gentle teachings of Jesus can do no less than give itself daily to needy persons. A church is at its best when it opens its doors on cold winter nights to house the homeless and feed the hungry with soup kitchens.

An effective church is also world centered. From the creation stories in Genesis we learn that God is in the world and for the world. Genesis 1:30 tells us that the world pleased God and God said that it was "very good." My faith in the Creator God who through evolutionary energies lures cosmos out of chaos over eons of time leads me to faith in the world that evolved and is evolving. The more conscious I become of the world and all its evolutionary energies, the more aware I become of God.

The creative, logos fully experienced in Jesus, forever joins God and the world together. In Colossians Paul wrote "Christ is the image of the invisible God, the first born of all creation, for in Christ all things in heaven and on earth were created, things visible and invisible. . . .. All things have been created through him and for him. He himself is before all things, and in him all things hold together.[210] In the prologue to the Gospel of John, we find that Jesus incarnated (perhaps self-actualized is a better term) this creative logos or wisdom principle in his life. By becoming fully God conscious, Jesus was able to reveal the glory of creation and the glory of the Creator God in his gentle Galilean Glories; and it is this union of heaven and earth that needs to be reflected in the life of the church. In and through the gentle teachings of Jesus the church is slowly but surely being redeemed and the world is being renewed. In Titus 3:4, Paul wrote that the kindness, love, gentleness, and mercy of God that was revealed in Jesus bring παλινγενεσις, palingenesis, regeneration to those coming under their influence.

The goodness and beauty at the center of life revealed in the gentle teachings of Jesus are also at the center of the physical world. To be at one with Jesus is to be at one with the world, and the world experiences cosmo-genesis.

---

[210] Colossians 1:15-17.

An effective church will be ecologically sensitive and responsible in caring for the world. Christians live not only for their own enjoyment but also for others. We are impoverished when any part of the world is harmed, depleted, or destroyed. God is in the world and for the world and enjoys the world. When the rich complexity of the biosphere is reduced, we are impoverished, and God is impoverished. We must learn to be good stewards of what has been entrusted to us so that we can pass it on to be enjoyed by future generations.

An effective church is joyfully involved with God in the adventurous work of being co-creators and co-redeemers of the whole universe. What a challenge!

Chapter Seventeen

Worship in The Gentle Teachings of Jesus

God is Worthy of Worship. (1John 4:7-21)

The words, "I love you," make all the difference in the world. These three words are life transforming, especially when we know ourselves as unworthy. Love is the energy or moving force in spiritual growth. In 1 John 4:7-21, the disciple Jesus loved, presents God's love for us as the positive image for understanding worship. God is love; and God's presence as love in the world through the life, teachings, death, and resurrection of Jesus, embraces relationship. We worship and serve God who is present in the world as creative-relational love. From the beginning God has been an active participant in the world, relating in personal caring ways. As Christians we affirm that God is best seen in the gentle Galilean, Jesus of Nazareth. This is the vision that inspires our worship and fills our lives with truth, beauty, adventure, and a wealth of inspiring relationships.

Jesus' relationship to God was so personal that he spoke of it as a child would talk to a parent, confidently and securely, yet at the same time reverently and obediently. This personal relationship with God was the energizing force and basis of Jesus' teachings and prayers. And it gives us an Image of God that is worthy of inspiring worship, shaping our prayers, and energizing all that we do as followers of Jesus. Jesus' gentle spirit-filled love words and love actions are life transforming. Jesus evoked new levels of energy and power in the shattered lives he touched. The fusion of these powerful biophilic energies brought catharsis and wholeness. Research today shows that staying close to nature has healing power.

Jesus grounded worship and all of life in the center of love when he gave the Great Commandment: You shall love the Lord your God with all your heart, and with all your soul, and with all your mind, and with all your strength. . ... You shall love your neighbor as yourself.[211] In worship our life and relationships are open to the transforming love of God.

In Jesus' tradition, heart was the center of the whole person, including will, intention, and intuition. Good and evil are seated in the

---
[211] Mark 12:30-31.

heart.[212] To turn the heart toward God is to be filled with beauty, truth, and goodness; to turn away from God is like walking in darkness and evil.

Understood in this way worship becomes the primary Christian practice or discipline. In asking us to love God with our whole heart Jesus invites us to live our lives in the context of God's goodness and love. People have worshipped God from many motives: fear, offering sacrifices, sometimes even of their own children, to appease an angry God. Fear of a wrathful God may force one into obedience, but this is not a worthy motive for worship. Sheer, coercive power may inspire awe. The gods of fear, greed, and war are not worthy of our worship. Only the goodness and love of God seen in Jesus Christ is worthy of our ultimate commitment and our "wholehearted" worship. It is easy and natural to worship when our lives are gripped by and centered in this ground of our being, God's love for us. Charles H. Gabriel expresses the feeling well in the hymn, "My Savior's Love," --- "I stand amazed in the presence of Jesus the Nazarene, and wonder how He could love me, a sinner condemned, unclean. How marvelous! How wonderful! And my song shall ever be: How marvelous! How wonderful is my Savior's love for me." Yes, we sing in "awe and wonder" in the presence of this love that is worthy of becoming the center of our lives.

I learned the importance of centering as I was growing up on a farm near a fruit orchard. For apple trees to produce well, they must be centered. During the first year of the tree's life, the gardener chooses a strong central trunk and cuts off all competing branches. In the second year the strong center trunk is maintained and a group of three or four lower branches are chosen to form a lower tier of fruit bearing limbs. All other competing branches above this tier are cut off as well. Each succeeding year another tier of branches is chosen and groomed until the tree reaches maturity. The secret to success and keeping the tree from splitting is maintaining the strong center trunk that supports and feeds all the fruit bearing branches.[213]

Worship centers our life on God's love for us and our love for others and keeps other things from becoming our ultimate concern. It is not hard to see how material things can become our major concern in life. Think of money and the whole economic enterprise. Money is necessary and inescapable, but it can easily become our ultimate concern. Jesus recognized this when he said, "Where your treasure is there your heart will be also."[214] Jesus warned against "storing up treasures on earth" and challenged us to "store up treasures in heaven." When all of our energy and time is used in gaining more money and material things, they become our God. The same

---

[212] Mark 7:21-23.
[213] Compare John 15:1-10, Jesus' teachings about the vine and the branches.
[214] Matthew 6:21.

could be said when pleasure and even social obligations become our primary concern.

In these and other related teachings about possessions, Jesus wanted to invite an open trust and reliance upon the goodness of God. God provides for the birds and creates beautiful flowers. God knows our needs, and we are important to God. Thus, Jesus said, "Seek first the Glory of God, and God will provide all other things."[215]

Corporate vs. Private Worship

In a relational world God is present in all things. This is not pantheism, the belief that all things are God. It is pan-en-theism, the recognition that God is in all of creation. Creation therefore reflects the beauty and goodness of God. Thus, we can worship God anywhere and everywhere. Yet, faith and love are relational concepts and involves one with other people. Liturgy binds us to God and to others.

We have defined God as creative, transforming love energies. In corporate worship we join our love energies with God, and they become a living flame of faith. The Quaker, Isaac Pennington, said that People gathered in worship "are like a heap of fresh and burning coals, warming one another as a great strength, freshness, and vigor of life flows into all."[216]

I once read of a minister illustrating this truth with a Church member. They were sitting around a fireplace with a roaring fire. The member had questioned the importance of corporate worship, saying that he could worship just as well by watching a preacher on television. As they talked the minister took the tongs and pulled a red coal from the fire and placed it by itself on the side of the hearth. They continued to talk, and as time passed the red coal grew dimmer, until it finally lost its glow and warmth. Pointing to the gray ember, the minister said, "That is what happens to one who tries to live a solitary Christian life. In corporate worship we join our love energies with God and other Christians, and they become a great flame of faith."

We gather to worship because we are a story formed community. In worship we use songs, sacred scriptures, sacraments, and the preached word to retell our story and reconstitute us as God's family.[217] These faith stories lead us through the seasons of Jesus' life. In the warm telling and hearing of these stories of Advent, Christmas, Epiphany, Lent, Easter, and Pentecost, we are drawn into Jesus' story and it becomes our life-transforming story. In this sense, worship holds a banner of love over us and draws us into God's saving grace and love.

---

[215] Matthew 6:24-33.
[216] Quoted without source in D. Elton Trueblood, *The People Called Quakers*, p. 91.
[217] Colossians 3:15-17.

While these faith stories are best experienced in corporate worship, they also have truths that can be experienced in private worship. One may walk in the footsteps of Jesus and discover the joy and enrichment his gentle teachings can bring to our daily living. Following in the footsteps of Jesus may also lead us deeper and deeper into God's beautiful world. There is a solace to be found in solitary places. Jesus faithfully engaged in corporate worship, but he often withdrew to solitary places to pray.[218] The more I experience and learn about the world, the closer I am drawn to God. On the other hand, following these solitary pathways is the surest route into corporate worship.

Learning to see the extraordinary in the ordinary Monday through Saturday strengthens our worship on Sunday. If the flames of faith are weak through the week, they will not burn very bright on Sunday. Brother Lawrence is a saint who learned the importance of *Practicing the Presence of God*[219] at all times. He learned to worship God in the clatter of the monastery kitchen as well as before the sacred altar. He said that the way to keep our mind from wander in prayer and worship is to stay focused on God at all times. As creative-relational love, God is with us at all times. In God's presence daily strength and discernment is available to us. Jesus' promise, "Come unto me all who are weary, and I will give you rest," is a promise for every day.

Worship and the Presence of God

In the gentle teachings of Jesus, God is present in the world and for the world. God is present in us and for us. It is the purpose of worship to usher us into the presence of God where we can grow spiritually and become who and what God wants us to be. William Temple's classic definition of worship supports this conviction: "To worship is to quicken the conscience by the holiness of God, to feed the mind with the truth of God, to purge the imagination by the beauty of God, to open the heart to the love of God, to devote the will to the purpose of God." In worship we experience the holy God as truth, beauty, and love.

A theological discussion of worship, grounded in God's loving presence, leads us into some of the richest veins of our theology. Look for example at the five basic forms of prayer and their implications for worship. Praise of God is the dynamic of prayer and worship. Praise of God springs

---

[218] Luke 5:16.
[219] Title of Brother Lawrence's book on his thoughts about prayer and the devotional life.

naturally from a life centered in the goodness, beauty, joy, love, and indeed, all the compassionate attributes of God.

As God's goodness and love become our ultimate concern it is natural to thank God. The Apostle Paul said to the Philippians that their expression of thanksgiving was like a sweet smelling offering to God, a sacrifice that is acceptable and pleasing to God.[220]

God is present in the world and for the world, in us and for us. This relational understanding of God invites us to participate with God in transforming the world. Worship draws us into this transforming love and spontaneously attracts others. Drawn into these love energies, it is natural to intercede for others. In prayerful worship we pull the suffering and pain of others into God's transforming love.

Worshipping God in the Temple, Isaiah petitioned God to forgive his sins and the sins of his people.[221] Confession is a vital part of prayer and worship. To experience the love of God revealed in Jesus is to realize how unworthy we are. Worship opens the door to confession and forgiveness. Being centered on God's love is the pathway to "perfecting love."

These five pathways of prayerful worship---praise, thanks, intercession, petition, and confession---lead us into God's transforming presence.

The Place of Prayer in Worship

I have known Church groups to weave beautiful quilts, sometimes working alone and then coming together to weave their individual pieces into a beautiful work of art. The quilt of faith is woven with the threads of prayer. In liturgical prayer the members of the Church come together to be woven as one with God revealed in Jesus' gentle teachings. Jesus' prayer in John 17 is a good model for the Church: Loving God, I am no longer in the world. I am coming to you, but my followers are still in the world. So keep them safe by the power of the name that you have given me. I am not praying just for these followers. I am also praying for everyone else who will have faith because of what my followers will say about me. I want all of them to be one with each other, just as I am one with you and you are one with me. I also want them to be one with us. Then the people of this world will believe that you sent me and that you love them as you love me.[222]

Actually, this is a very intimate prayer between Jesus and God. Jesus speaks to God confidently and intimately, as a child speaks to a parent, about love, care, and unity. As the disciples listen, they are drawn into this love and

---

[220] Philippians 4:18.
[221] Isaiah 6:1-8.
[222] John 17:11—21-23.

unity; and thereby, brought face to face with transforming grace that will hold them in perfect peace in the days ahead. Jesus knows that the community's security rests in and depends on God's care. As Christians pray together, they are drawn into this love and unity, grace and peace of God. When this happens, the Church has worshipped God in "spirit and truth."

    Beth, my wife, shared with me once that as she was growing up she heard her parents pray almost every night that she and her sister, Janice, would know and do God's will in their lives. Beth said that she was drawn into this prayer, and it became her pray as well. As Beth went away to college, she found that she was daily conscious of this prayer, and it gave her strength in her daily living to know what was right and wrong and make good decisions. After college she went to the seminary where she continued to pray for God's guidance and will. I met Beth in a Greek class at the seminary. We started dating and I was drawn into this powerful prayer. We introduced our wedding vows with the phrase, "Because God in infinite wisdom and providence has brought us to this moment, I, Dwayne, take you, Beth, to be my wife." "I, Beth, take you, Dwayne, to be my husband."

    In hearing her parents pray for her, Beth was drawn into their prayer. It became her prayer, and it changed her life for the good. That is the transforming power of prayer. In hearing Jesus pray for them, the faith community is drawn into the sacrificial love of God. This whole prayer is set in the context of the passion. The cross looms ahead. Thus, it is a High Priestly prayer grounded in the cross and resurrection. This, in fact, is the prayer's power. How would the church change if it took as its beginning point, "We are a community for whom the suffering Jesus prays?" In its liturgical prayers the church prays to become one with God and one with God's suffering and redeeming presence in the world.

Worship Leads to Service

    Jesus clearly prayed for the future of the church. That future is grounded in the unity of the Father and Son. And it is God revealed in Jesus who will assure the future of the church. So, this bold prayer entrusts the hope and future of the church, not in the disciple's hands, but in the care of the all wise, ever knowing, and always present God. It is good for the church to remember this Gospel truth: A church for which Jesus prays cannot fail! At times the church may look weak and faltering, but it is in God's care and grace. God cares for the church and God is working in the church for reconciliation. In liturgical prayers, the church prays to be one with God in this transforming action of grace, and this is the goal of all true worship. Worship should always lead to service.

    As the church becomes united in worship it embodies God's grace. Jesus recognized this when he said of his first followers, "God gave them to me. I gave them the words God gave me. God keeps them safe."[223] This does not mean that there is no responsibility on the part of the church. A gift of grace has to be kept in order to be effective. The disciples were to keep the unity of God and Jesus embodied in the gentle teachings. In worship the church is strengthened for its witness in the world; without unity, confusion and division disrupt and erode the witness of the church. When churches fail, it is usually a sign that they have not kept the gift in a spirit of prayer with Jesus.

The disciples, in recent days, had vied for chief places of honor. Jesus knew that a divided church could not win a broken world. Throughout the prayer found in John 17, Jesus prayed for unity. The unity spoken of is that which is informed and empowered by the unity of God and Jesus, as can be seen in vv. 20-23: I am not praying just for these followers. I am also praying for everyone else who will have faith because of what my followers will say about me. I want all of them to be one with each other, just as I am one with you and you are one with me. I also want them to be one with us. Then the people of this world will believe that you sent me and that you love them as you love me.

This is the purpose of the church: to be loved by God, to love one another, and to share that love in the world through both words and actions. To say it another way: the church exists to maintain, strengthen, and extend the gentle life transforming gentle teachings of Jesus into the world. In worship prayers the church is strengthened for this personal transforming ministry. People don't necessarily remember what they are told about God's love, but they never forget what they have experienced of God's relational love, especially when it was shared by a friend or loved one.

In this prayer Jesus lifts up the all-important oneness. As the ages come and as the ages go, there is one supreme requirement for the church: that we live close to God and close to one another.[224] Jesus is the bridge for this all-important unity and prayer supports the bridge. Denominational leaders, pastors, and elders are important in the unity of the church, but they are not the source of that unity. Actually church leaders may be the source of disunity. The church is strongest when God is allowed to lead through pastors and elders. Jesus' response to God in this pray is a model for us. Jesus shows an openness to receive God's word. He understands that God is the source of his strength. Jesus is committed to the mission of offering God's salvation to the world. In corporate worship the church prays to join with Jesus in this saving work.

---

[223] John 17.
[224] Philippians 2:1-5.

"I appeal to you therefore, brothers and sisters, by the mercies of God, to present your bodies as a living sacrifice, holy and acceptable to God, which is your spiritual worship. Do not be conformed to this world, but be transformed by the renewing of your minds, so that you may discern what is the will of God—what is good and acceptable and perfect."[225]

"The end of all things is near; therefore, be serious and discipline yourselves for the sake of your prayers. Above all, maintain constant love for one another, for love covers a multitude of sins. Be hospitable to one another without complaining. Like good stewards of the manifold grace of God, serve one another with whatever gift each of you has received. Whoever speaks must do so as one speaking the very words of God; whoever serves must do so with the strength that God supplies, so that God may be glorified in all things through Jesus. To him belong the glory and the power forever and ever."[226]

The mission of the church is to continue the work of Jesus. Jesus called his disciples to continue sharing the love of God. Jesus even said that his followers would do greater work than he had done.[227] How is this possible? God is always doing a new and transforming work. The Jesus of history became the future of faith. In the coming of the Holy Spirit, Jesus was still with his disciples. The followers of Jesus must not cling to the past but look to God's exciting future. In the risen Jesus God does something new and exciting.

I believe when Jesus was praying in the Upper Room with his disciples he was saying, "Father, you have sent me. I did your work. Now, God, do it again with my disciples. Do greater works than even I have done. God, do it again. God! Do it again!

Worship prepares the church to go out into the world praying, singing, and celebrating into God's future! God is not through with the world yet. God is always doing new things. Can't you feel it? Can't you sense that the Spirit is blowing through the church? Blow Spirit, blow. For this newness, Jesus is praying. And to be partners in this exciting adventure the church gathers to worship and departs to serve. As the church worships it is held close to the heart of God where there is security; and then it is hurled out into the world where it carries the world with God in infinite love.

---

[225] Romans 12:1-2.
[226] 1 Peter 4:7-11.
[227] John 14:12-14.

Chapter Eighteen

The Place of Prayer in Jesus' Gentle Teachings

When Jesus had finished praying, one of his disciples said to him, "Lord, teach us to pray."[228]

We worship and serve a God who is present in the world as creative-relational love. Our Bible begins in Genesis with the mythic story of God creating a good and beautiful world. God looked at all that had come into being and said, All of it is very good.[229] From the beginning God was an active participant in the world, relating in personal caring ways. We find biblical examples of this image of God in the Old Testament prophets like Jeremiah and Hosea and in the New Testament teachings of the gentle Galilean, Jesus of Nazareth.

The God to Whom We Pray: Images of God

Jesus' relationship to God was so personal that he spoke of it as a "Father/Son" relationship (See chapter on Father/Son for interpretation of this imagery). In this relationship Jesus talked to God as a child would talk to a parent, confidently and securely, yet at the same time reverently and obediently. This personal relationship with God was the energizing force and basis of Jesus' prayers, and it gives us an image of God that is worthy of shaping our prayer life.

The fact that Jesus used the term, "Father," and not "Father/Mother" or "Parent" is easy to understand. Jesus lived in the Jewish nation and culture. He spoke the Jewish language and adopted the Jewish patterns of thought. And while there were competing viewpoints on gender issues in Israel, Israel was primarily a patriarchal society. Jesus' intent in using the term, "Father," is to stress intimate relationship, not to describe God as male. Jesus spoke of God as a Spirit saying that those who worship must worship in spirit and truth.[230] As Creative-Spirit God understands male and female, but God is beyond physical characteristics of maleness and femaleness. Gentleness not gender is Jesus' concern.

---

[228] Luke 11:1.
[229] Genesis 1:31 CEV.
[230] John 4:24.

Jesus lived in this gentle relationship with God and others, and prayer was an important part of this relationship. Prayer was the habitual atmosphere of Jesus' life. Prayer was the breath of Jesus' soul. Jesus was found praying at all the major decision-making times and crises of his life. The Gospels tell us that Jesus often rose early to pray, and sometimes he prayed all through the night.[231] When the crowds pushed and shoved around him, he would lift his eyes to heaven as through to grasp the hand of God in prayer.[232] Prayer was not just a part of Jesus' life; prayer was his life.

Once when Jesus had finished praying, one of his disciples said, Lord, teach us to pray.[233] Apparently, the men and women who followed Jesus as disciples and learners were drawn into his prayerful relationship with God.[234] In response to this request, Jesus gave his followers the model prayer: Father, help us to honor your name. Come and show your glory. Give us each day the food we need. Forgive our sins, as we forgive everyone who has done wrong to us. And keep us from being tempted![235]

In this prayer we have an image of God as a personal parent who cares for us and provides for our daily needs. Jesus follows this model prayer with some teaching that continues to present prayer as a personal relationship of trust and faith.[236] It is this image that shapes our prayers.

Prayer as involvement in a personal relationship is not just talking with God; it is also walking with God. Prayer is cooperative living with a relational caring God. When Jesus linked faith and prayer, He made prayer cooperative living with God. In his teaching Jesus gave three imperatives to describe prayer. The first imperative word is "ask." Ask and it shall be given you. It is important to ask, because we are free persons in our relationship to God. But talk can be cheap. Jesus did not want us to think that we could just call God up and order our request like we would at a deli bar and stand by for delivery. This is an unworthy image for shaping prayer.

Jesus used two other imperative words, "seek and knock." Seek and you shall find. Knock and the door will be opened. These words are more active and intense. They involve active participation in the process. They involve putting forth effort and struggle.

When Jesus prayed, He always addressed God as a child speaks to a parent, confidently and securely. Jesus saw God like a kind Father and nurturing Mother who stands ready to empower us when we prayerfully cooperate. Only by cooperating are families able to help and strengthen one

---

[231] Mark 1:35; 6:46.
[232] Mark 7:34.
[233] Luke 11:1.
[234] This will be illustrated later in our discussion of Jesus' prayer in John 17.
[235] Luke 11:2-4.
[236] Luke 11:5-13.

another. In cooperative relational prayer we are able to actualize God's goodness for our lives.

Relational Prayer opens this door to the goodness of God. Earthly fathers desire to give good things to their children. Jesus said, "which one of you fathers would give your hungry child a snake if the child asked for a fish? Which one of you would give your child a scorpion if the child asked for an egg? As bad as you are, you still know how to give good gifts to your children"[237] This teaching brings us to the purpose and promise of prayer: "Your heavenly Father is even more ready to give the Holy Spirit to anyone who asks."[238] The greatest gift of prayer is God's energizing presence.

Prayer is cooperative living. It is asking, seeking, and knocking, persistently seeking to live in God's power field of good and helping others to do the same. The world has yet to see what a church can do when it prays like this: in a cooperative living way. For the prayers of good people have a powerful effect, says James (James 5:16). Jesus said, "those who ask receive, those who seek find, and those who knock have the door opened to them."[239]

Prayers for Forgiveness and Healing---Transforming Prayer

When the door is open to the transforming love of God, healing is possible. Prayer opens that door. And that is the place of prayer in healing. In the spirit of prayer, we present ourselves before God as a sinner in need of forgiveness and healing. John said, "If we confess our sins, God is faithful and just in forgiving our sins."[240] In the same spirit, we boldly bring our loved ones before the sacred throne of God and pray for healing. Physical healing does not always occur, but there is always spiritual healing of the soul and the gift of eternal life. Even when physical death occurs, the believer receives the greatest healing of all---resurrection to eternal life. So, we pray. In fact, all believers who prayed for physical healing one hundred years ago are now dead physically, yet they are alive spiritually with God.

Prayer is best seen as the personal appropriation of the faith that God is a personal God carrying out the divine purpose in the world and in the lives of people. In prayer, as in faith, we are given God's presence. Actually, there is a giving and receiving in prayer. God gives to us possibilities for enrichment and lures us with persuasive power toward the fulfillment of those possibilities. As we freely actualize these loving aims, we give back to God. When God clothes our dark and difficult experiences with a good and

---

[237] Luke 11:11-13.
[238] Luke 11:13.
[239] Luke 11:9.
[240] 1 John 1:9.

loving purpose, forgiveness and healing is possible. God is present in faithful prayer; therefore, as James said, "the prayers of good people have a powerful effect."[241]

Faith, love, prayer, and healing are tied together in the New Testament. One definition of miracles is an action or event in which you see or feel the presence of God. Webster's dictionary adds the qualifiers "extraordinary," "supernatural," and "unusual" in describing miraculous events. While these qualifiers could define some biblical miracles, this is not generally the case, as will be seen later. Wherever and whenever the creative-relational God works loving aims in the lives of people, there miracles happen!

Jesus is the greatest miracle of the New Testament. His life, ministry, death, and resurrection are all miraculous. Jesus was totally conscious of God's presence in his life. His mission and message was to bring God near to people. Miracles of healing are integral to both the mission and message of Jesus.

Jesus' miracles are action sermons that demonstrate the kindness and compassion of God. As action sermons, the miracles proclaim the coming of the glory of God. When Jesus gave the Lord's Prayer, he defined the glory (kingdom) of God. The phrase, "Your glory (kingdom) come" is followed by "Your will be done on earth as it is in heaven." This technique is called Hebrew parallelism. A statement is made: "Your glory (kingdom) come." The next or parallel phrase interprets the statement: "Your will be done on earth as it is in heaven." The glory (kingdom) of God is a time when God rules on earth as in heaven. In bringing God near, Jesus brings the glory of God near. Jesus' first recorded message was "The good news of God is at hand, repent and believe the Good News."[242]

The miracles of healing were not performed to prove Jesus' divinity, but to share his love energies. Love's power lies in its desire to enrich the other. God's love in Jesus is responsive love. Jesus could not walk through Galilee as God's servant without responding to the broken persons he encountered who were wasting away. His biophilic teachings and loving touch energized them and gave them new hope and new life. Many of Jesus' miracles can be interpreted as miracles of compassion. Ten times in the Synoptic Gospels Jesus is presented as the one in whom divine compassion is present. The Greek term, σπλαγχνιζομαι, is the strongest word possible to stress the tender compassion with which God claims persons in saving acts.

As soon as Jesus announced that the Good News of God was near, he began to perform miracles of compassion. In Mark 1:40-45, we are told that Jesus was moved with compassion toward a man with a dreaded skin

---

[241] James 5:16.
[242] Mark 1:15.

disease, possibly a leper. Jesus reached out and touched him and said, "Be clean." At once the disease left the man, and he was clean.

Jesus had compassion on the widow of Nain and raised her dead son back to life.[243] Also with compassion he restored sight to two blind men.[244] There are many other miracles of Jesus reported in the New Testament, and many that were not reported, but these have been cited because they are especially associated with compassion.

The English word, compassion, is a compound of two Latin words and means "suffering with." In responsive love Jesus suffered with the leper, the brokenhearted mother, and the blind men. As the wounded healer, Jesus identified with the suffering. Their wounds were his wounds; their pains were his pains. Matthew said that Jesus took our sickness and carried away our diseases.[245] In so doing, he was the true Suffering Servant, promised by God through the prophecy of Isaiah 53:4.

In Jesus' day disease was attributed to the power of the demonic, not just cases seen as "demon possession," but all manner of sickness. Wholeness and health implied the casting out of these malign influences. With the in-break of God's Good News in Jesus the whole kingdom of evil was being shaken to the foundation. Luke reports Jesus as saying, "if it is by the finger of God that I am expelling evil spirits, then the Good News of God has swept over you unawares!"[246] Thus, the miracles of Jesus were at the same time demonstrations of divine compassion and the breaking in of the glory of God. Both truths are a way of saying that the kindness of God is coming near.

Prayer as Miraculous Love Energies

We turn now from the why of Jesus' healing miracles to the how. How was Jesus able to perform such great miracles? The answer must surely be sought in the power of prayer energies.

The God who spoke and brought order out of disorder and cosmos out of chaos, spoke in Jesus to bring wholeness out of brokenness and life out of death. All the energy of God that called persons forth in creation radiated with new creative powers in Jesus. It was Jesus' total consciousness of God's presence in his life and ministry, exemplified by the confident way he spoke to God as a child speaks to a parent that enabled him to act with such authority and power.

---

[243] Luke 7:11-17
[244] Matthew 20:29-34.
[245] Matthew 8:17.
[246] Luke 11:20; Phillips translation.

The miracles of Jesus are distinguished from the Jewish and Hellenistic miracle workers of his day in at least four ways. (1) Jesus' miracles have no connection with magic, unlike the majority of miracles outside the New Testament. Webster's definition of miracles we gave earlier has more to do with these secular miracle workers than with Jesus' miracles. (2) The miracles of Jesus are evoked if not performed by his gentle words. His words carry transforming energy and are manifestations of the one Word made flesh in his life. The kindness and love of God came in saving ways in Jesus' proclamation and miraculous acts, overcoming and expelling malign spirits.[247] (3) The miracles of Jesus are energized by Jesus' pure love of God. (4) Jesus' miracles call forth faith and at times presuppose faith as a condition of the miracles. Thus, when faith is lacking, as in Nazareth, Jesus can only do a few miracles.[248]

How was Jesus able to perform miracles? His gentle spirit-filled love words and love actions evoked new levels of energy and power in the shattered lives he touched. The fusion of these powerful love energies brought catharsis and wholeness.

The Apostle Paul certainly understood healing miracles in this way. In speaking of the resurrection of Jesus, the greatest of all miracles, he combined the concepts of faith, power, prayer, and love. Following references to faith, prayer, and God's love, and the love of the Ephesian Christians, Paul wrote, "how very great is God's energy at work in us who believe (faithing). This power working in us is the same as the mighty strength which God used when Jesus was raised from the dead. . ." Ephesians 1:19-20, Paul used four different Greek words for power: δυναμις, ενεργιον, κρατους, ισκους. We get the English word dynamite from δυναμις and energy from ενεργιον. The other two Greek words are best translated as all-inclusive power. It is as though Paul was reaching for every word for power, he knew to describe God's love energies which raised Jesus from the dead. Paul was calling upon the Ephesian Christians to live in this tremendous power field of love created by the Jesus-event. For as Paul said, how very great is God's energy at work in us who believe, and not just intellectually but all who are held close to the heart of God.

Jesus brought God's gentle love energies near and made them available for all who seek God, believing. As many as believed in God were given power to become the children of God.[249]

---

[247] See Titus 3:4-7.
[248] Matthew 13:58.
[249] John 1:12.

When Thomas Kelly started to Haverford College, he said to Rufus Jones, one of his professors, "I am just going to make my life a miracle!"[250] And through the absolute commitment of his life to God, he did. He said to some of his students once, "I have been literally melted down by the love of God."[251] Trusting obedience was primary to Thomas Kelly. Kelly treasured Meister Eckhart's saying: "There are plenty to follow our Lord half-way, but not the other half"[252] Kelly practiced an "all the way obedience to God." Kelly's "holy obedience" unified his life around a "Divine Center" where he was gathered up in the love of God and transformed according to God's will. His will became God's will, and he became a blessing to a generation of students through his teaching and continues to bless many through his devotional writings he left behind. In a relational world each of us is a source of energy affecting others. Thomas Kelly's book, The Testament of Devotion, has certainly blessed my life. I first read it in the seminary years ago, and it continues as one of my favorite devotional classics. What would happen if we all prayed that God would make a miracle out of our life?

For those who have eyes to see, miracles may be happening now! In prayer God invites us into partnership of transformation, creating a more caring world.

Prayers of Intercession---Accepting Love is Transforming Love

In a relational world God's love energies effect how the universe unfolds. In prayer we are invited to be partners with God in this transformation. Our image of God as creative-relational love inspires us to join with God in this joyous adventure o bringing peace and harmony to the universe. It is awesome adventure. Others can respond to God's love and be transformed in the process.

When we live in a relationship of love and trust with God, we want to share what we have discovered with others. The early Christians felt compelled to share with their world what they had seen and heard in Jesus. The Book of Acts is filled with courageous stories of such sharing. Prayers of intercession are one way of drawing others into this loving relationship.

In intercessory prayer we draw our family, friends, and world into God's goodness and love. It is important to realize that God is already relating to these persons and events in love, even as we are in God's love. When I am making a visit in hospital, I silently breathe this prayer as I walk down the hall: "God, help me to slip into what You are already doing in this person's life. Let my words fit in with Yours to express acceptance,

---

[250] *A Testament Of Devotion*, p. 3.
[251] Ibid, p. 21.
[252] Ibid. p. 51.

forgiveness, and healing for this person." In this prayer we become conformed to God's loving will.

God's love involves God in the world. Responsive love is suffering love. God suffers with the world. We look upon the suffering of others differently if we see God in their suffering. We know from personal experience that love is a sympathetic response from one person to another. True love feels what the other person is feeling, rejoicing in their joys and hurting with their pains. We would doubt that a husband loves his wife if he were not aware of her feelings and if his feelings did not reflect her feelings.

This is the nature of relational love, whether we are speaking of God's love for us or our love for God and others. And it is this truth that forms the basis of intercessory prayer.

"I will be praying for you" is one of the most meaningful things Christians can say and do for another person. A young mother of two small children tells her pastor that she is going into hospital to be tested for cancer. Her pastor responds, "I will be praying for you." The young mother gains strength and encouragement in knowing that her pastor is remembering her in prayer. We all gain strength from the prayers and words of encouragement from others.

Liturgical Prayers and Christian Ministry

I have known Church groups to weave beautiful quilts, sometimes working alone and then coming together to weave their individual pieces into a beautiful work of art. The quilt of faith is woven with the threads of prayer. In liturgical prayer the members of the Church come together to be woven as one with God revealed in Jesus. Jesus' prayer in John 17 is a good model for the church: Loving God, I am no longer in the world. I am coming to you, but my followers are still in the world. So keep them safe by the power of the name that you have given me. I am not praying just for these followers. I am also praying for everyone else who will have faith because of what my followers will say about me. I want all of them to be one with each other, just as I am one with you and you are one with me. I also want them to be one with us. Then the people of this world will believe that you sent me and that you love them as you love me (vs. 11, 20-23).

Actually this is a very intimate prayer between Jesus and God. Jesus speaks to God confidently and intimately, as a child speaks to a parent, about love, care, and unity. As the disciples listen, they are drawn into this love and unity; and thereby, brought face to face with transforming grace that will hold them in perfect peace and then hurl them out into the world where they will carry it with God in infinite love. Jesus knows that the community's security rests in and depends on God's care. As Christians pray together, they are drawn into this love and unity, grace and peace of God. When this happens, the Church has found its ministry.

That is the transforming power of prayer. In hearing Jesus pray for them, the faith community is drawn into the sacrificial love of God. This whole prayer is set in the context of the passion. The cross looms ahead. Thus, it is a High Priestly prayer grounded in the cross and resurrection. This, in fact, is the prayer's power.

How would the church change if it took as its beginning point, "We are a community for whom the suffering Jesus prays?" In its liturgical prayers the church prays to become one with God and one with God's suffering and redeeming presence in the world.

Jesus is clearly praying for the future of the church. That future is grounded in the unity of the Father and Son. And it is God revealed in Jesus who will assure the future of the church. So, this bold prayer entrusts the hope and future of the church, not in the disciple's hands, but in the hands of the all wise, ever knowing, and always present God. It is good for the church to remember this Gospel truth: A church for which Jesus prays cannot fail! At times the church may look weak and faltering, but it is in God's care and grace. God cares for the church and God is working in the church for reconciliation. In liturgical prayers, the church prays to be one with God in this transforming action of grace.

There is no way to describe the Church fellowship except as an embodiment of God's grace. Jesus recognized this when he said of his first followers, God gave them to me. I gave them the words God gave me. God keeps them safe (John 17). This does not mean that there is no responsibility on the part of the church. A gift of grace has to be kept in order to be effective. The disciples were to keep the unity of Father and Son actualized in Jesus. In unity the church's witness to the world can be made effective; without unity, confusion and division disrupt and erode the witness of the church. When churches fail, it is usually a sign that they have not kept the gift in a spirit of prayer with Jesus.

The disciples, in recent days, had vied for chief places of honor. Jesus knew that a divided church could not win a broken world. Throughout the prayer found in John 17, Jesus prayed for unity. The unity spoken of is that which is informed and empowered by the unity of God and Jesus, as can be seen in vv. 20-23: I am not praying just for these followers. I am also praying for everyone else who will have faith because of what my followers will say about me. I want all of them to be one with each other, just as I am one with you and you are one with me. I also want them to be one with us. Then the people of this world will believe that you sent me and that you love them as you love me.

This is the purpose of the church: to be loved by God, to love one another, and to share that love in the world through both words and actions.

To say it another way: The Church exists to maintain, strengthen, and extend the gentle life transforming teachings of Jesus into the world. In its liturgical prayers the Church is strengthened for this personal transforming task. People don't necessarily remember what they are told about God's love, but they never forget what they have experienced of God's relational love, especially when it was shared by a friend or loved one.

In this prayer Jesus lifts up the all-important oneness. As the ages come and as the ages go, there is one supreme requirement for the church: that we live close to God and close to one another. Jesus is the bridge for this all-important unity and prayer supports the bridge. Denominational leaders, pastors, and elders are important in the unity of the church, but they are not the source of that unity. Actually, church leaders may be the source of disunity. The church is strongest when Jesus is allowed to lead through pastors and elders. Jesus' response to God in this pray is a model for us. Jesus shows an openness to receive God's word. He understands that God is the source of his strength. Jesus is committed to the mission of offering God's salvation to the world. In its liturgical prayers the Church prays to join with Jesus in this saving work.

Our mission is to continue the work of Jesus. Jesus called his disciples to continue sharing the love of God. Jesus even said that his followers would do greater work than he had done. How is this possible? God is always doing a new and transforming work. In the coming of the Holy Spirit, Jesus was still with his disciples. The followers of Jesus must not cling to the past but look to God's exciting future. In the Spirit God does something new and exciting.

Each Church has had its exciting missional moments when some daring members have done something generous and different. God is about to do something new now. Jesus' ministry was like new wine in old wineskins. It was like fresh water in a dry and arid land. It was like bread offered to starving souls. Would we not expect Jesus to be praying for his church to do the same today?

You might say the Church was born in a spirit of prayer in the Upper Room. The Cumberland Presbyterian Church is an example of how a Church is born in a spirit of prayer. In July 1995, soon after I became a Cumberland Presbyterian, I went to Bethel College to study the history and theology of Cumberland Presbyterians, taught by Dr. Hubert Morrow. While there I went into the archives and did research for a paper on the Great Revival of the 1800's that I was writing for the Committee on the Ministry of the Nashville Presbytery. I was captivated by the Great Revival that swept across Tennessee in the early 1800's and gave birth to the Cumberland Presbyterian Church. Our Church grew rapidly and rode the crest of that revival westward. There in the archives with McDonald's history reverberating down the corridors of my soul, I prayed, "God, do it again. God, do it again. God! Do it again!

Later that summer, I visited the Birth Place Shrine adjacent to Montgomery Bell State Park. I visited the log home of Samuel McAdow and envisioned Samuel McAdow, Finis Ewing, and Samuel King kneeling before a roaring fireplace and praying through the night about the birth of a new church. I stood there just "rocking the cradle of our Church." I walked around the grounds and visited the spring out back, just "rocking the cradle of our Church." Vernon Burrow told Maury Norman and me that if you drink from this spring you will live forever. I almost believe him. Maury Norman retired from the "full-time" ministry at the age of 65. He accepted the call of McAdoo Cumberland Presbyterian Church, saying that he would give them 10-12 years. McAdoo grew strong enough to call a "full-time" pastor. After serving this Church for 11 years, Maury accepted the call of the Hendersonville Mission, saying that he would give them about 10-12 years! Maury who was then 81 continued to preach and the Hendersonville Church grew.

Leaving the fount of living water, I entered the little chapel, knelt before the altar---just "rocking the cradle of our Church" ---and I prayed, "God, do it again. God, do it again. God! Do it again! And as I prayed, I felt new spiritual energies being birthed in my soul!

I believe when Jesus was praying in the Upper Room with his disciples he was saying, "Father, you called me. I did your work. Now, God, do it again with my disciples. Do greater works than even I have done. God, do it again. God! Do it again!

So, dear friends come from tired old ways! Come from fears that divide and weaken the church! Come from old quarrels unresolved! Come from old sins that have scarred and wounded the church! Come from old memories that have become graven images! God is about to do something new and exciting!

We may not know yet the shape of this newness, and we may live a while between the times. But I believe God will lead us into a freshly formed new life together. We will watch, wait, and pray believing that---

• The mission of the church is not finished. Our best days are ahead of us. Jesus is praying for the church.

• The church cannot circle in a holding pattern. With the Human Genome Project mapping and sequencing the twenty-three chromosomes of the human body, there is a biological revolution going on in medicine and science; and, our theology is lagging behind. We need a theology that engages the biological revolution and deals with medical ethics, evolution, ecology, and new technology. Jesus is praying for the Church.

• The future of the church cannot be business as usual. Gifted women are responding to the call of God and preparing for the ministry in our seminaries with increasing numbers, but our churches are not calling them as pastors. In reference to needing more ministers in our churches, one denominational executive said at a Minister's Conference, "God may not give us anymore ministers until we use the ones already given." Jesus is praying for the Church.

• It is not a time to be parochial, as some are, and cut back on missions. The fields are ready for harvest! Jesus is praying for the church.

• It is not a time to write memorials and pass resolutions that exclude some from ministry based on sexual preference. It is a time to be sensitive to all the marginalized ones in our society. Jesus is praying for the Church.

In its liturgical prayers the Church is preparing to go out into the world praying, singing, and celebrating into God's future! God is not through with the world yet. God is always doing new things. Can't you feel it? Can't you sense that the Spirit is blowing through the world? Blow Spirit, blow. For this newness, Jesus is praying. And to be partners in this exciting adventure the church prays.

Chapter Nineteen

The Place of Prayers in Healing

29 As soon as they left the synagogue, they entered the house of Simon and Andrew, with James and John. 30 Now Simon's mother-in-law was in bed with a fever, and they told him about her at once. 31 He came and took her by the hand and lifted her up. Then the fever left her, and she began to serve them.

32 That evening, at sundown, they brought to him all who were sick or possessed with demons. 33 And the whole city was gathered around the door. 34 And he cured many who were sick with various diseases and cast out many demons; and he would not permit the demons to speak, because they knew him.

35 In the morning, while it was still very dark, he got up and went out to a deserted place, and there he prayed. 36 And Simon and his companions hunted for him. 37 When they found him, they said to him, "Everyone is searching for you." 38 He answered, "Let us go on to the neighboring towns, so that I may proclaim the message there also; for that is what I came out to do." 39 And he went throughout Galilee, proclaiming the message in their synagogues and casting out demons. (Mark 1:29-39).

When I was a young minister, my brother, Michael, and his daughter, Kay, were in a car accident. Michael was not seriously hurt, but Kay was penned under the car for a while and was taken to the hospital in critical condition. My family---father, mother, six brothers, six sisters, in-laws, nieces, nephews, and I---gathered at the hospital for prayerful support.

Several times during the night the doctors told us there was very little hope, and if my niece lived, she would suffer brain damage. We refused to give up hope and prayed through the night, sometimes verbally out loud, but mostly silently, each in his/her own private way. Kay not only lived through the night, she fully recovered without any permanent damage.

For my family this was a miracle of prayer, and even the doctors admitted it was miraculous. I am aware that some would explain this experience differently. Perhaps, saying that the doctors were fallible and misdiagnosed. Maybe adding that youth are tenacious in holding on to life and that the human body is amazing in its ability to heal, all of which are true.

Yet, "miracle" was the most appropriate word for the feeling of God's presence we experienced.

Three characteristics of miracles are seen in this experience. First, there was an acute crisis or threat to the life of a loved one that was totally beyond our ability to help. Second, there was a turning to God in prayerful trust. Third, there was help available. The love energies that flowed from family and the medical profession were awesome. And I do not believe that this miracle would have occurred apart from using the best medical help that was available to us. We felt God's love energies permeating the whole experience and making the miracle complete. In and through our prayers and the loving actions of the medical professionals God came to us. This is the gift of prayer and essence of miracle.

Jesus' gentle healing ministry supports this faith experience. Approximately one third of Marks Gospel is about miracles, healing, and exorcisms. Mark reports thirteen specific healing miracles, five nature miracles, and makes many general references to healing. Mark 1:29-39 tells of the healing of Peter's mother-in-law and the casting out of demons. In the middle of these stories we find the verse: In the morning, while it was still very dark, Jesus got up and went out to a deserted place to pray (v. 35). The healing stories pivot on prayer!

Jesus' popularity is growing and the demands on him multiply. Mark says, The whole city was coming to Jesus (v. 33). In order to find quietness and prayerful meditation Jesus had to rise early in the morning, while it was still dark.

My mother once said that she began and closed each day of her life as a mother with prayer. One of my fond memories is seeing her sit each evening with her Bible in her lap and a prayer on her lips. Remember, she had thirteen children. So, you might ask, "How did she have time to pray?" I am sure she would answer, "I do not have time not to pray!" She found her serenity and strength in those times of Bible reading and prayer. They were a center for her when things were falling apart in her household.

She could have learned that lesson from Jesus. Prayer was the habitual atmosphere of Jesus' life; prayer was the breath of Jesus' soul. Jesus was found praying at all the major decision making times and crises of his life. Every part of the Gospels seems to demonstrate this prayer activity of Jesus. Our text reads, Jesus rose early to pray. Often, he prayed all through the night (Mark 6:46). When the crowd pushed and shoved around him during the day, Jesus would lift his eyes toward heaven as though to grasp his Father's hand in prayer (Mark 7:34). Prayer was not just a part of his life; it was his life.

The model prayer that Jesus taught his disciples was couched in family terms. Jesus spoke of God as Our Father who wants to give us our daily bread. When we come to believe that God is as personal as a parent and that God cares for us as a friend, prayer becomes as natural as breathing. The most natural thing in the world is for a parent and child to sit and talk together. Our faith offers us the privilege of a personal talking relationship to God, and our prayers appropriate that faith.

Prayer is not just talking with God; it is also walking with God. Prayer is cooperative living with God. When Jesus linked faith and prayer, he made prayer cooperative living with God. Jesus followed this faith statement with three imperatives to describe prayer. The first word is "ask." Ask and it shall be given you. It is important to ask, because we are free persons in our relationship to God. But talk can be cheap. Jesus did not want us to think that we could just call God up and order our request like we would at a deli bar and stand by for delivery.

Jesus used two other words, "seek and knock." Seek and you shall find. Knock and the door will be opened. These words are more active and intense. They involve active participation in the process. They involve putting forth effort and struggle.

When Jesus prayed, he always addressed God as a child speaks to a parent, confidently and securely. Jesus saw God like a kind Father and nurturing Mother who stands ready to empower us when we prayerfully cooperate. I learned in a home of fifteen people, only by cooperating are families able to help and strengthen one another.

Prayer opens the door to the goodness of God. Earthly fathers desire to give good things to their children. Jesus said, Which one of you fathers would give your hungry child a snake if the child asked for a fish? Which one of you would give your child a scorpion if the child asked for an egg? As bad as you are, you still know how to give good gifts to your children (Luke 11:11-13). This teaching brings us to the purpose and promise of prayer: Your heavenly Father is even more ready to give the Holy Spirit to anyone who asks (Luke 11:13).

Prayer is cooperative living. It is asking, seeking, and knocking, persistently seeking to live in God's power field of good and helping others to do the same. The world has yet to see what a church can do when it prays like this: in a cooperative living way. For the prayers of good people have a powerful effect, says James (James 5:16). Jesus said those who ask receive, those who seek find, and those who knock have the door opened to them (Luke 11:9).

When the door is open to the power of God, healing is possible. Prayer opens that door. And that is the place of prayer in healing. In the spirit of prayer we present ourselves before God as a sinner in need of forgiveness and healing. John said, If we confess our sins, God is faithful and just in forgiving our sins (I John 1:9). In the same spirit, we boldly bring our loved ones before the sacred throne of God and pray for healing. Physical healing does not always occur, but there is always spiritual healing of the soul and the gift of eternal life. So, let us pray in that spirit always.

Wishing to encourage her young son's progress on the piano, a mother took her boy to a Paderewski concert. After they were seated, the mother spotted a friend in the audience and walked down the aisle to greet her. Seizing the opportunity to explore the wonders of the concert hall, the little boy rose and eventually explored his way through a door marked "NO ADMITTANCE." When the house lights dimmed and the concert was about to begin, the mother returned to her seat and discovered that her son was missing. Suddenly, the curtains parted, and spotlights focused on the impressive Steinway on stage. In horror, the mother saw her little boy sitting at the keyboard, innocently pecking out "Twinkle, Twinkle, Little Star." At that moment the great piano master made his entrance, quickly moved to the piano, and whispered in the boy's ear, "Don't quit. Keep playing." Then leaning over, Paderewski reached down with his left hand and began to fill in a bass part. Soon his right hand reached around to the other side of the child and he added a running obbligato. Together, the old master and the young novice transformed a frightening situation into a wonderfully creative experience. And the audience was mesmerized.

Whatever your situation in life, God comes to sit beside you and whisper, "Don't quit. Keep praying. You are not alone." Then reaching loving arms around you, says, "Together we will transform the broken patterns into a masterwork of creative art."

Is there someone here near to fainting? Are you losing Heart? Is your faith growing weak? Place your hand in the hands of a personal God. In faithful prayer tell God all about it! Faith is kept alive by prayerful communion with God.

Chapter Twenty

The Place of Forgiveness in Healing

> *2 When Jesus returned to Capernaum after some days, it was reported that he was at home. 2 So many gathered around that there was no longer room for them, not even in front of the door; and he was speaking the word to them. 3 Then some people came, bringing to him a paralyzed man, carried by four of them. 4 And when they could not bring him to Jesus because of the crowd, they removed the roof above him; and after having dug through it, they let down the mat on which the paralytic lay. 5 When Jesus saw their faith, he said to the paralytic, "Son, your sins are forgiven." 6 Now some of the scribes were sitting there, questioning in their hearts, 7 "Why does this fellow speak in this way? It is blasphemy! Who can forgive sins but God alone?" 8 At once Jesus perceived in his spirit that they were discussing these questions among themselves; and he said to them, "Why do you raise such questions in your hearts? 9 Which is easier, to say to the paralytic, 'Your sins are forgiven,' or to say, 'Stand up and take your mat and walk'? 10 But so that you may know that the Son of Man has authority on earth to forgive sins"—he said to the paralytic—11 "I say to you, stand up, take your mat and go to your home." 12 And he stood up, and immediately took the mat and went out before all of them; so that they were all amazed and glorified God, saying, "We have never seen anything like this!" (Mark 2:1-12)*

The Gospel of Mark clearly paints Jesus as a healer. One third of this earliest Gospel is about miracles, exorcisms, and healing. The last chapter dealt with the place of prayer in healing, focusing on the healing of Simon Peter's mother-in-law. Following that healing, Jesus' popularity grew, and many were brought to Jesus for his healing touch.

In Mark chapter 2, Jesus is in the house of Simon and Andrew, which is like Jesus' second home after his rejection at Nazareth. To Simon Peter's credit, after Jesus healed his mother-in-law, he still became Jesus' disciple. After all, when his mother-in-law became ill, he was already dreaming of getting up in the morning and seeing a picture of her on the milk carton! You laugh, but I heard that one of our elders went to buy a new car, and the salesman asked if he wanted a car with an airbag. The elder replied, "No thanks, I already have a mother-in-law." Yet, mothers-in-law are not all bad. Few mistakes can be made by a mother-in-law who is willing to baby sit! How can you not like a mother-in-law who gets up out of the sick bed like Peter's mother-in-law did, and starts serving you food?

All joking aside, these healing miracles caused Jesus' popularity to grow, and the demands on him multiply. Just before this healing story, Mark says, "The whole city was coming to Jesus" (1: 33). When Jesus came to Simon Peter's home, a large crowd is present, so much so that it is impossible to get to the door of the house. Among the crowd is a paralytic who is being carried by four friends, and what friends they are! When they cannot get in by the door, they devised a second plan. Most of the houses had flat roofs and the more sturdy ones had steps and were used for additional living space. Some roofs were formed with flat boards often separated by three feet and the space was filled with branches, twigs, grass, and sod. They may have grass growing on them.

When blocked by the crowd at the door, the four friends take the paralytic to the roof, remove a portion of the roof, and proceed to lower their friend down into the house at the feet of Jesus. It was an astonishing descent, no doubt preceded by falling dirt, twigs, and sod. I can imagine that Jesus looked up with astonishment at the audacity of the friends as they carefully lowered the paralytic to the floor. Mark's account tells us that Jesus was impressed by their bold faith and said to the paralytic: "My son, I forgive your sins" (Mark 2:5).

The kindness of the four friends is only surpassed by those tender words of Jesus. These gentle words, "My son, I forgive your sins" are at the heart of Jesus' Galilean glories. Remember, Jesus' God consciousness allowed him to walk under an open heaven. The radiant light of heaven that fell upon Jesus at his baptism shines through that crude hole in the roof and falls upon Jesus the Son of God and this son of suffering. It is such a beautiful and tender moment that I want to climb on that roof and scale down the rope to sit at the feet of this miracle worker who has the power to forgive sins. And the story does pivot on these tender and gentle words about the forgiveness of sins.

Before we get too enthralled in the miracle, there is an abrupt interruption. Seeing and hearing something out of the ordinary, the religious leaders quickly call a session meeting and start whispering disapproval: "He can't talk like that can, he? This is supposed to be a healing service, not the confession of sin time! That is blasphemy! God and only God can forgive sins." The religious leaders were right in understanding that only God can forgive sins, but wrong in their failure to see that God was in Jesus' words and actions bringing forgiveness and healing.

Jesus, who knew what was in the hearts of all persons, knew right away what they were thinking; and, he said, "Why are you so skeptical? Which is simpler, to say to the paralyzed man, 'I forgive your sins,' or say, 'Get up, take up your mat, and start walking?'" Well, just so it is clear that the emphasis of this Gospel story is on the power of Jesus to declare God's forgiveness of sin, Jesus says to the man who is perhaps paralyzed by guilt, "Get up, pick up your mat, and go home." With all eyes upon him, the paralytic got up, picked up his mat and walked out. The crowd was completely amazed and praised God, saying, "We have never seen anything like this!

If we had been on the roof top that day and had slid down the rope to witness this miracle, I am sure we too would be filled with awe and wonder. God revealed in Jesus forgives sins and heals, and forgiveness has a central place in this healing story. Yet, this is not to say that all illness is the result of sin or that the forgiveness of sin always results in healing. Some religious teaching in Jesus' day did connect sin and suffering, but Jesus cut that Gordian knot. A disciple pointing to a blind man asked Jesus once, "Teacher, whose sin caused this man to be born blind? Was it his own or his parent's sin?" Jesus answered, "His blindness has nothing to do with his sins or his parent's sins." Jesus went on to show how in his blindness the glory and power of God could be revealed. Jesus used this teaching opportunity to reveal himself as the light of the world (John 9:1-5).

However, in some cases forgiveness is necessary for healing to take place. Psychoanalysis has demonstrated that deep-seated guilt and self-loathing can contribute to serious physical illnesses. At such times we need loving caregivers like the four friends of the paralyzed man. The faith of these care-giving friends initiated the healing encounter with Jesus. Sometimes the care and forgiveness of humans can contribute to healing. Yet this Gospel story moves us to a deeper lever: Only God can forgive our crippling sins! This is the truth that Jesus lived. As one who became totally God-conscious, Jesus was endowed with divine dynamis (explosive power) ---the power and authority to forgive sins.

What can we learn from this Gospel story today? First, we see the importance of care-giving, tenacious friends who can help us move from the crippling past to the new future made possible by God. In the middle of this road we call life, many become disabled and cannot rise by themselves. In fact, our high-tech, fast paced life seems to be casting off many such individuals. Without the necessary skills and the help of friends they simply cannot make it. All caregivers like Mother Theresa recognize this truth, and this recognition is one of the motivating factors in volunteer service and career training programs.

This insight leads to a second truth: In this Gospel story we see the power of gentleness and compassion to heal crippling guilt. Webster defines guilt as "a painful feeling of self-reproach" that comes from feeling that "one has done something wrong or immoral." The paralytic in our story would have been rejected by almost everyone in his life and labeled as a sinner, and this rejection would have created strong guilt feelings.

Some guilt is the normal part of living in a moral society and is necessary for our well-being. In fact, it is sad to see the erosion of moral accountability among political leaders and corporate executives today. A sense of moral accountability has been replaced by a "sleaze factor" when leaders betray public trust and show no guilt or remorse!

On the other hand, some guilt grows to exaggerated levels. This sometimes occurs after divorce or failure in some other significant relationship. A strong sense of failure triggers depression and a feeling of worthlessness. Sometimes guilt is so strong that it is repressed into the unconscious. This may happen after sexual abuse as a child.

This leads us back to the importance of friends and care-givers like the ones in our Gospel story. Exaggerated guilt or repressed guilt needs special care-givers who can help us do two things: face our guilt and confess our guilt. Sometimes we are not able to stop destructive behavior without special friends and care-givers. Sharing your struggle with a friend can help you take the first step toward healing. In our Gospel story the four friends initiated the healing encounter with Jesus.

Friends may have to be combative to move us toward healing. In Second Samuel, chapter 12, we find the prophet, Nathan, confronting King David with a gripping, heart-throbbing parable that moves David to see his own guilt and sin. After David faces his guilt and is moved to confess that he has sinned against the Lord, Nathan is able to say to David, "The Lord forgives you" (v. 13).

Here at the end we return to the very heart of our Gospel story. Guilt is overcome by accepting God's forgiveness. Forgiveness is a powerful therapeutic force. In accepting the paralytic as a friend when others rejected him as an untouchable sinner, the four friends initiated forgiveness. Jesus' acceptance of the paralytic as a child of God in need of forgiveness and healing made the miracle possible.

The Good News is that Jesus opens the way through the bondage of guilt and into forgiveness. Jesus' statement to the paralytic, "Son, your sins are forgiven," are powerful family words of acceptance. In these affirming words Jesus is identifying with the rejected "sinner" as his brother in suffering. Jesus' words, actions, and his death on the cross between two sinners demonstrate to us that God stands by us in spite of our sin. Paul recognized this truth when he wrote, "God shows love for us in that while we were yet sinners Jesus died for us" (Romans 5:8).

Jesus' acceptance is the door to healing grace. To truly accept another person is to enter into their struggle to throw off the shackles of the old life burdened with guilt and creatively work toward the new self envisioned by God. Acceptance by someone who cares is a powerful healing force.

Many worship services have a special time of confession to convey this acceptance of God and the assurance of forgiveness. In fact, I see the confession of sin and the pronouncement of forgiveness as the heart of any worship experience. In the assurance of forgiveness, we are invited through the power of the Holy Spirit to move from crippling guilt to a wonderful new life.

Chapter Twenty-One

The Role of Ethics in Theology

"A thing is right when it tends to preserve the integrity, stability, and beauty of the biotic community; it is wrong when it tends otherwise"
Aldo Leopold, conservationist

"Words lead to deeds.... They prepare the soul, make it ready, and move it to tenderness" (Saint Teresa).

Ethics may be defined from a utilitarian perspective as the discipline that seeks to further the interest of those affected. The goal is gaining the "best consequences" for those affected by the decision. From a selfish perspective this view is often narrowed to finding what is best for me, my family, friends, and associates. For too many ethical decisions have been make from this perspective, and often so-called Christian ethics.

The danger here is that we are living in a world where there is radical evil. Evil has become so horrendous that the word "radical" is the best word to describe it. An evolutionary principle is that we are good to insiders, those like us, our kind; and nasty to outsiders. It is human nature to seek self-love with a predisposition to one's own preservation and survival. One is never free from the luring power of evil. We are never beyond temptation. Personal desires for happiness and success get in the way of making ethical decisions that truly result in "best consequences" that further the interest of those affected by the decisions we make.

The social character of evil, displayed in games of superiority and one up-man-ship, demonstrates how crucial it is that we have some compass or moral principle that guides "best consequences." However, to introduce the word "moral" waves a red flag for many. It is not used here in its narrow sense that is often focused on judging and condemning certain actions, with the words "Thou shalt not." Also it is not "social will" or doing what is culturally acceptable, as important as these are to success and happiness. Societal views may themselves be narrow and negative.

There does seem to be the need in ethics for a universal point of view or a moral principle that is universally approved. In fact, one might ask, of a decision one is making, "Would I want this to become a universal principle that guides all societal decisions?" The Hippocratic Oath serves as an example of such a moral principle: "I will give no deadly medicine to anyone if asked, nor suggest any such counsel." This universal moral principle has served as guide for doctors of medicine for generations.

Acknowledging the corrupting power of radical evil, one may define ethics as the capacity to control the inclination to self-love and be guided by universal moral principles. Other moral principles are the value of all persons and one's right to health and happiness. Moral principles trump self-love. By moral principle I do not just mean a character trait, but a principle of character---that is the moral values that guide the growth of maturation of one's character.

Christians need guidance and training in ethics for there is no absolute "social will" or "innate will" to ascribe responsibility for ethical decisions. Apart from the Christian's faith perspective, the only will involved is one's own, and as seen above one's will can be shaped by evil intent.

The following are some reasons why one should be guided by moral principles:

(1) Each of us is a contributing member of a society that commits radical evil.

(2) There are universal moral principles that produce untrumpable value.

(3) As a person capable of making decisions based on moral principles, I am responsible for making these principles authoritative for me and my profession.

(4) I am a dependent person who seeks happiness and success and measure my worth in light of these moral principles. These principles also lead me to value all other persons regardless of social status.

(5) My evolutionary human nature gives me the tendency to place my pursuit of happiness and self-love over my commitment to moral principles.

(6) I am inter-connected with all world entities, including animals; but especially other humans who share the same capacity for corrupting tendencies I find in myself.

(7) Despite these tendencies I affirm that universally accepted moral principles found in psychology, philosophy, theology, and above all found in the gentle teachings of Jesus grounded in the unmerited love of God take precedence over my self-love and search for happiness, and I am committed to letting them guide me in making my ethical decisions.

Societal expectations and laws serve as motives for making ethical decisions but are not in themselves a guarantee of right action. Since we are self-actualizing individuals, and this is an accepted principle in maturation; we need to internalize moral principles for them to be maximized. Human beings seem to have an innate need for self-actualization that involves growth toward goodness, kindness, love, unselfishness, honesty, and courage. When we fulfill this need we feel, joy, zest for living in meaningful relationships, and a greater sense of happiness.

Christians certainly need to internalize and actualize the moral and ethical principles that are grounded in the gentle teachings of Jesus. When we act contrary to this need of self-actualizing benevolence, we feel anxiety, despair, shame, and a feeling of unhappiness. This feeling might lead to a false sense of humility grounded in self-degradation and self-contempt.

However, a proper appreciation for the role of moral principles can clear away undue self-love and pave the way for forming an equal worth of all persons. Pride can easily become the mega-value shaping moral and ethical decisions based on self-love.

What is needed is a humility gained through quieting the concern for self-love and freeing the ability to see value in others. Humility, grounded in the gentle teachings of Jesus is the one mega-value that frees us to see merit and worth in all persons and gives us a greater respect for moral and ethical principles. The humble person will grow in his or her appreciation of moral principles for guiding ethical decisions.

Humility leads the follower of Jesus to ask, "Have I felt the full sweep of God's creative relational love actualized by Jesus. The first commandment for gaining humility is to know oneself as transformed by God's love. That is, to know your innermost thoughts. Are your motives pure or impure, good or evil; and to know yourself as inter-connected with all persons and bound as one under moral and ethical imperatives.

Nothing is greater for the follower of Jesus than the quiet humble confidence that one is living with the peace of mind that comes from knowing that one is doing one's best according to the moral values one finds in the gentle teachings of Jesus.

Is it possible for Christians to achieve this epistemic humility in the pursuit of everyday living? Or is it possible only for those like Jesus? I do not intend to under value Jesus' example. I only intend to emphasize that it is possible for all who are transformed by Jesus' gentle teachings to live as Jesus did and demonstrate equal dignity for all persons, including the poor like the Haitians of our day who have been devastated by radical evil, poverty, and natural disasters. In Dr. Paul Farmer's medical work in Haiti we see one who has found in his moral imperatives the strength to make ethical decisions that give health care and dignity to all persons, especially the poor.

Humility provides a sort of integration of these competing drives for self-love and making moral ethical decisions that brings the best results for all concerned.

Chapter Twenty-Two

Saving the Environment

"When we try to pick out anything by itself, we find it hitched to everything else in the universe."[253] John Muir

Thesis #1: That Jesus' gentle Galilean teachings showed special concern for the poor and outcast; and by wrapping these concerns in nature imagery, like birds of the air and flowers of the field, Jesus brought all of nature, plant and animal life, into his concern for the poor. Using these gentle teachings to show God's intimate loving care for the birds and flowers, as well as for humans, Jesus showed that God's concern includes nature.

For Christians, saving the environment starts with the conviction that God is intimately related to the world. Psalm 65 beautifully shows God's delightful involvement in the world:

> Our God, you deserve praise. You take care of the earth
> and send rain to help the soil grow all kinds of crops.
> Your rivers never run dry.
> You water all of its fields and level the lumpy ground.
> You send showers of rain to soften the soil
> and help the plants sprout.
> Wherever your footsteps touch the earth, a rich harvest is gathered.
> Desert pastures blossom, and mountains celebrate.
> Meadows are filled with sheep and goats;
> Valleys overflow with grain and echo with joyful songs.

As a minister I have lived with the Bible, the sacred scriptures of Christians, for fifty years. From Genesis, through the Psalms, the Gospels, and all the way to Revelation, I have experienced God within the world working like a gardener cultivating nature and people from these mythic, poetic, and prophetic writings. In Genesis, the beginning of the Bible, the Spirit woos creation into being, bringing order out of chaos, creating a Garden of Eden with all kinds of vegetation, plants, and fruit trees. Beautiful birds flew in the skies, playful creatures swam in the oceans, animals filled the land, and humans walked in the Garden with God. God was pleased and blessed all living things in the Garden, saying it was good.

---

[253] Quoted in *John Muir. And The Ice That Started A Fire.* by Kim Heacock. p. xv.

In Revelation, the end of the Bible, the same Spirit calls forth a new heaven and a new earth that is also a fruitful place for God's people. A river flows through the new garden with trees of life bearing healing leaves. God will walk in this new garden, wiping tears from crying eyes, removing pain, and restoring peace. What is lost in the first garden is restored in the new earth.

At the heart of these scriptures, the Gospels show Jesus self-actualizing God's redemptive all-inclusive love, becoming totally God-conscious, and opening the door for all of us to follow in his footsteps. These scriptures, especially Jesus' gentle Galilean teachings, reveal a God who is compassionately involved in world transformation, giving to the world and receiving from the world; and calling all of us to a deeper relationship with God and each other, giving and receiving wooing love. In the spring, parts of Galilee were like a beautiful garden; and, as a peripatetic teacher, Jesus used the garden imagery of birds and flowers in his gentle teachings, inspiring his followers to trust in God's care for them, as God cares for the birds and flowers.

John 3:16 is often seen as the heart of the Gospel: For God so loved the world (cosmos) that God gave us Jesus. That everyone believing in Jesus will have eternal life (Author's paraphrase). This key verse clearly frames the Jesus event as a cosmic event and defines God's love as all inclusive, including the whole universe.

Christian theologians have erred in seeing God's involvement with the world as creatio ex nihilo, creation from nothing. This view stresses God's controlling power and clashes with evolutionary scientific theories. Also, Genesis and much of the Old Testament seem to support the view of God creating out of chaos. This supports an evolutionary view of creation. Instead of compressing time and space as the mythic story of creation in Genesis does, evolutionary science sees the universe evolving over billions of years with God luring creation toward more complex actualities enjoying more value and satisfaction. Another problem with interpreting the myth of Genesis in a literal way with humans and the earth as the center of the universe is that it devalues everything else.

Using scientific imagery, we might say that in each stage of the evolutionary process, God's love aims and purposes serve to guide enduring electrons, protons, neutrons, etc., providing the necessary conditions for the emergence of atoms, and the atoms in turn providing the appearance of molecules and the emergence of living cells. Each stage of the evolutionary process actualizes the divinely set possibilities until human life appears.

Continuing to use nature imagery from the garden, we might say that God the Gardener loves natural beauty and has a desire to create and share goodness. The Gardener hovers over every blade of grass and whispers, "Awake. Grow. Grow beautiful and green." Meadows grow, giving way to gurgling streams, water plants, butterflies, hummingbirds, flitting from red, orange, and yellow flowers. Beautiful gardens answer the call and over eons of time, all nature is lured toward ever enriching possibilities until conditions are right for life forms to emerge. Over billions of years God called forth a world able to support human beings. Humans are a new song that nature hums, the music swells with each new stanza, giving purpose and meaning. Humans moved from being gatherers in the garden to being gardeners, ever singing nature's song.

Throughout this process God's power is persuasive and luring not coercive and controlling, and God is best described as creative responsive love. Since creation is processive and not fixed, we are called to participate with God, as were the first human participants in the garden, in an unfinished universe, bringing beauty and adventure out of chaos, ever reflecting God's redemptive love.

God's relationship to the world is best described as creative responsive love and is best seen in the gentle Galilean teachings of Jesus. Yet, the Jesus event is but one attempt from one point in time and history to speak about the mystery of the universe. As Christians we can say this allowing for God's saving action in other religions and other religious leaders like Mohammed and Buddha; and we can at the same time affirm that for us as Christians Jesus is a special and distinct perspective of reality.

In Jesus' unique God-consciousness, he self-actualized God's unconditional and unmerited love and opened the door for all persons to do the same, while showing special concern for the poor and outcast. Jesus' biophilic teachings (biophilia is a theory developed by E. O. Wilson, scientist and naturalist at Harvard University that says there is an innate tendency in each of us to be attracted by other life forms and to affiliate with natural living systems.) broadened this concern for the poor to include all of nature, plant and animal life. Affirming Jesus' unique consciousness of God says that God's concern includes nature.

After carefully reading the Gospels of the New Testament, no one would doubt Jesus' concern for the poor and vulnerable and his faith that God cares for the birds of the air and the flowers of the field. What we fail to see is that nature is the vulnerable new poor. It is not a case of whether humans or nature should be seen as the poor in Jesus' gentle teachings, rather we should say that nature is also included with the poor. Persons, animals, and plants all have intrinsic and instrumental value to God and should have value for us as well. All give and receive from one another and are interconnected in a diverse web-like universe.

Society's failure to see this interconnection and interdependence has led to our making nature poor. Can we doubt this with massive soil erosion, water pollution and depletion, global warming, air pollution, coastal erosion, deforestation, and species extinction? This tragic failure led E.O. Wilson to call us humans, "Planetary Killers."

Thesis #2: As poor persons need liberation and healing, so does nature, for we have made nature our servant, and nature has grown poor, weary, and sick.

Native Americans taught us, but we forgot, that when we humans use for our sustenance, plants, fish, and animals, we should do so with humility, thanksgiving, and prayerful respect. The gentle teachings of Jesus teach us to look at nature with loving eyes rather than arrogant eyes. Jesus' gift of abundant life includes the health, wholeness, and harmony of the universe.

The Role of the Church in Saving the Environment

A church that affirms God's involvement in the world as creative relational love will be conscious of our role in saving the environment. Using the garden imagery gleaned from the scriptures, we have seen that God is in the world and for the world. Genesis 1:30 tells us that the world pleased God and God said that it was "very good." My faith in God who through evolutionary energies lures cosmos out of chaos over eons of time leads me to faith in the world that evolved and is evolving. The more conscious I become of the world and all its evolutionary energies, the more aware I become of God.

The creative energy of God experienced in Jesus' gentle teachings forever joins God and the world together. In the prologue to the Gospel of John, we find that Jesus incarnated (perhaps self-actualized is a better term) this creative energy or wisdom (σοφια) principle in his life. By becoming fully God conscious, Jesus was able to reveal the glory of creation and the glory of the Creator God in his gentle Galilean Glories; and it is this union of heaven and earth that needs to be reflected in the life of the church. In and through the gentle teachings of Jesus the church is slowly but surely being redeemed and the world is being daily recreated. In Titus 3:4, Paul wrote that the kindness, love, gentleness, and mercy of God that was revealed in Jesus brings, παλιγγενεσιας (palingenesis, regeneration, birth again) to those coming under their influence.

The goodness and beauty at the center of life revealed in the gentle teachings of Jesus are also at the center of the physical world. To be at one with Jesus is to be at one with God and the world, and in this unity, we experience cosmo-genesis.

An effective church will be ecologically sensitive and responsible in caring for the world. Christians live not only for their own enjoyment but also for others. We are impoverished when any part of the world is harmed, depleted, or destroyed. God is in the world and for the world and enjoys the world. When the rich complexity of the biosphere is reduced, we are impoverished, and God is impoverished. We must learn to be good stewards of what has been entrusted to us so that we can pass it on to be enjoyed by future generations.

An effective church is joyfully involved with God in the adventurous work of being co-creators and co-redeemers of the whole universe. What a challenge!

Strategies for Protecting the Environment

During the last few decades Scientists and conservation professionals have put together a strategy aimed at protecting the remaining ecosystems and species. Here are some of the key elements:

*Salvage immediately the world's hotspots, those habitats that are at the greatest risk and shelter the largest concentrations of species found nowhere else, like the remnants of rainforests in Hawaii, the West Indies, West Africa, and Southern California.

*Keep intact the remaining five frontier forests like the Amazon Basin and the conifer forests of Canada and Alaska.

*Cease logging of all old-growth forests everywhere---shift to tree farming on already converted lands.

*Concentrate on the river and lake systems everywhere for they are the most threatened ecosystems of all.

*Define the coral reefs, the rainforests of the sea that are at the greatest risk---like parts of the Caribbean and the Philippines.

*Complete the mapping of the world's biological diversity. Scientists estimate that 10 percent of the world's plants, a majority of animals, and a huge majority of microorganisms remain undiscovered and unnamed.

*Initiate restoration projects to recover more land for saving nature.

*Increase botanical gardens and facilities to breed endangered species.

*Support population planning and guide humanity everywhere to a lighter footstep with biodiversity flourishing everywhere.

Accomplishing these strategies will require the cooperation of the private sector with churches joining hands and hearts, science and technology, and government. Success or failure will come down to an ethical decision: it is right that we save our planet and the marvelous life it nourishes (These strategies were taken from E.O. Wilson, *The Future of Life*).

Summary: The world does not exist apart from God. God the Gardener loves natural beauty and has a desire to create order out of chaos. The gardener imagery used earlier is worth repeating. The Gardener hovers over every blade of grass and whispers, "Awake. Grow. Grow beautiful and green." Meadows grow, giving way to gurgling streams, water plants, butterflies, hummingbirds, flitting from red, orange, and yellow flowers. Beautiful gardens answer the call and over eons of time, all nature is lured toward ever enriching possibilities until conditions are right for life forms to emerge. Over billions of years God called forth a world able to support human beings. Humans are a new song that nature hums, the music swells with each new stanza, giving purpose and meaning. Humans moved from being gatherers in the garden to being gardeners, ever singing nature's song.

God did not create the world and then abandon creation as the Deists once thought. God is in the creative process, placing novel love aims and goals within all parts of creation. God is supremely socially related with the purpose of sharing goodness and love with all of creation. God, all nature, and humans are interconnected. As God is immanent in the world, I am in nature and nature is in me. As I write these words, I am looking at the snow-capped Chugak Mountains of Alaska. I am in the mountains and the mountains are in me, singing their song, filling every part of my body and spirit with a wealth of beauty. If any part of this beautiful creation is diminished, I am diminished; and since God is in the world and the world is in God, God feels the loss.

During the week I was working on editing this chapter, Beth and I were driving our grandchildren, Cole and Clara, to swimming lessons. As we drove along, we were talking about politics in Alaska that gets tied up with oil and pollution. Our news and newspapers were filled with the tight governor and senate races that were still undecided two weeks after election day. The topic of pollution came up as we noticed a hazy atmosphere ahead that was somewhat screening the beauty of the snow-capped Chugach Mountain range that spans 250 miles of Alaska. The caravan of cars all around us brought up pollution and the environment. Ten-year-old Cole said, "If I made cars, they would put out butterflies instead of pollution." He laughed and we all joyously laughed at the image of beautiful butterflies wafting about in a spring garden.

The next morning, I was sitting in my recliner with a view of the snow-capped Chugach range, only now they were taking on a rosy color from the morning sun; and I was filled with awe and wonder. I was also still feeling the warm glow of Cole's butterfly pun. I began to think of the butterfly as a metaphor for interpreting the environment. Much of nature is enclosed in a womb of suffering much like the butterfly in the caterpillar awaiting new birth. Maybe the metamorphosis, the whole change process from the butterfly, to the egg, to the larva, to the pupa, and finally to the beautiful multicolored butterfly, is an apt metaphor for saving the environment.

I went from laughing about cars putting our butterflies instead of pollutants to sadness when I discovered that monarch butterflies are on the brink of extinction. Over the last 20 years, 90% of monarch butterflies in North America have died due to pollutants, primarily Monsanto pesticides that are killing off milkweed---the only plant on which the monarchs lay their eggs, and the primary food source for monarch caterpillars (National Geographic, August 26, 2014). Unless we act now to save the environment, the future looks grim.

Surely, the Psalmist was right when singing, "God delights in creation" and God "cares for the earth" (Psalm 65). Do we care? If so, we need to join the chorus and sing in harmony with God who seeks to heal our lives and our environment. God and future generations await our choice!

Conclusion

An Unrealized Dream

The gentle teachings of Jesus are filled with optimism, transforming love energies, and dreams of abundant life, here and forever. Yet, in one sense the dream is unrealized. But it will not die. The gentle teachings of Jesus have enduring appeal and staying power.

Humans seem to have a Platonic yearning for immortality, born even for life everlasting. If we feel at home here it is because it reminds us of another place from whence we were born. Our yearning encompasses body and soul. Body (soma) and soul (psyche) are united in the gentle teachings of Jesus and are envisioned as forever linked in love, joy, and peace.

Jesus' consciousness of God is not a violation of human nature, but its wondrous fulfillment and completion. In Jesus' growth and development, the fullness of God dwelt (Colossians 2:9, "God lives fully in Jesus"). God was in Jesus and for Jesus, as God is in us and for us. In this sense Jesus was human and divine---true God and true human.

My world view that shaped this book affirms the achievements of science, especially evolutionary science. While there is tension and some disagreement between science and faith, I see no reason they cannot work together, and many do. Religion needs evidence-based science to keep it grounded and honest. Religion has a tendency to adapt to culture and be shaped by its world view, as one would expect. Thus, the church has sanctioned at times slavery and sexist views. If not actually sanctioning, the church has too often been silent when it needed to speak a challenging word. And eventually the church, armed with philosophical insights affirming the dignity of all humans, did challenge these dehumanizing tendencies in society.

I also read and acknowledge the insights of atheists. They take God more seriously than many religious people, and I believe God loves them. I find that many atheists are rejecting conservative beliefs, perhaps that they grew up with, that do not fit their science; and they have not explored inclusive integrating views like process theology.

This book is the result of my own personal struggle with conservative Christians who were closed to science and how God is involved in the world as an evolving universe. In process thought I found a unity of God and the world, existing in a dynamic becoming, inter-related and inter-dependent in an open future of process.

Conservative Christians often place more emphasis on ideas and beliefs, than on a dynamic relationship with God. The gentle teachings of Jesus expounded in this book are not so much about belief as they are about action. The goal has been to evoke actions and behaviors in us and in our relationships with others. This is especially needed in global dialogue with other religions, especially Buddhism and Islam. We hear from them frequently that they want Christians to be more like Jesus and stay centered on his love for all people. Dialogue requires an openness to learn from each other. Kindness is an archetypal image that is found in all religions. It is a powerful healing concept when wrapped in the love of Jesus for all people. Other religions are looking for love actions from us, not faith judgments and creedal rigidity.

Gentle teachings slowly heal our lives on a personal level and are intended to help us build our patterns of existence, especially when our life falls apart and we have to pick up the shattered pieces and put them back together as a renewed and redeemed psyche in new relationships with a renewed sensitivity to an evolving universe.

More liberal Christians, especially in university and seminary settings that have dealt with the continuing search for the historical Jesus, tend to discard most of the Gospel material as being the product of the writers of the Gospels and the community. They would leave us with very little that is actually from Jesus. By focusing on the gentle teachings of Jesus, this book has taken a more balanced approach between the conservative and liberal views. We can all agree on the need for kindness.[254]

My major thesis has been that it is precisely in Jesus' gentle words and actions that we find Jesus' history as occurrence, as a word-event that brings God's presence into our lives. Jesus' uniqueness is not proven by the use of titles like Christ or Messiah which may be attributed to the evangelists or early church. Jesus' uniqueness is found in his gentle words and deeds.

Finding common ground and new relationships, not just between conservatives and liberals, but with all those who profess faith in God offers hope for our global age; and the greatest danger to our survival is one religion set against another. The gentle teachings of Jesus are the seed bed for this route to peace and our hope of survival.

Thus, having shown us what it truly means to be human, we can, in the spirit of the Gentle Galilean Glories, conclude this book with hope of transformation of this world, this life, for eternity. The urgent call that comes from the tender teachings is to lose oneself, surrender coercive power, in order to live transforming love that others may find the treasure of the Good News and a new heaven and new earth.

As we live the gentle Galilean glories of Jesus, his gentle teachings are still at work in the world. In this sense the gentle words of Jesus are eternal, uniting past, present, and future; and they are appropriate to any life and any world.

---

[254] See my book, *A Relational Hermeneutic of Kindness*.

Energy is transmitted in this word-event, enlivening our lives and our world. Wherever Jesus' gentle words are spoken and lived, Jesus comes to us as he came to his disciples by the Sea of Galilee long ago. He calls us to follow him and learn from his gentle and kind ways (Matthew 28:19-20; 2 Cor. 10:1; Eph. 4:2; Col. 3:12; Titus 3:2).

So, come Jesus! Be kind to us (Rev. 22:21, CEV) as we live Galilean Glories.

Glossary of Terms

biophilia- is the transliteration of two Greek words I find in the New Testament, βιος-life, φιλια-love. Biophilia is the theory popularized by E.O. Wilson, Professor of Science at Harvard University, that we as humans have an innate love of life, of all of nature, as a result of our evolutionary history. Humans prefer to live in natural environs, near mountains, streams, or lakes. This theory has had great impact in many fields, most notably among environmentalists and architecture. Frank Lloyd Wright's house, Falling Waters, is a prime example of biophilic design. I have found the theory helpful in explaining Jesus' teachings and why they have had appeal through the centuries

Concrescence- is the act of becoming by unifying possibilities from the past into the self-actualizing entity or person. Humans are partially created by their heredity and environment, what is given to them from the past, and the lure of the future (God); but humans exercise personal choice in the final act of becoming psychologically speaking, this is self-actualization.

God Consciousness: As used in this book "God-consciousness" refers to Jesus learning to incorporate each moment of his life in an experience of God's life. This creative rhythmic responsiveness brought a fusion of human and divine love. Thus in Jesus' gentle words and actions we see and feel God acting in tender and caring ways that nothing be lost. Jesus' consciousness of God was also God's consciousness of Jesus and this process of rhythmic responsiveness changes Jesus and God, for this is the nature of love. This is also the essence of Jesus' "Good News" announced in his first sermon according to Mark (Mark 1:14-15). In bringing the hurting of his day with infinite patience into his God-consciousness, they experienced the immediacy of God's presence and were saved. Thus, Jesus' gentle words and actions enabled transformation for the hurting who no longer perish but begin to live in the very immediacy of God's glory (kingdom). The glory of heaven is now on earth, and Jesus's compassion for the hurting ones is seen as God wiping away their tears and making all things new. God's home is now with God's people!

psychetrophic- In the gentle teachings of Jesus the Greek word, τρεφει (troph), is joined with psyche, the Greek word for life or soul. Thus when joined psychetrophic means feeding or nourishing the soul. Translators and commentators have missed the importance of finding these two Greek words in Jesus' gentle Galilean teachings given by a peripatetic teacher, one teaching while walking in nature, along the Sea of Galilee with the beauty of flowers and birds. I have coined psychetrophic to gather-up this important aspect of Jesus' teaching. I have also used philiatrophic and agapetropic for nurturing love and somatrophic for the nurturing of the body.

Appendix A
Jesus And God Consciousness

The heart of this relational theology is Jesus and his gentle Galilean teachings. Throughout there are references to Jesus' unique God consciousness, a concept first popularized by the philosopher, Fredrick Schleiermacher. The concept has been used by many theologians since Schleiermacher, often with increasing richness. As used in this book "God-consciousness" refers to Jesus learning to incorporate each moment of his life in an experience of God's life. This creative rhythmic responsiveness brought a fusion of human and divine love. Thus in Jesus' words and actions we see and feel God acting in tender and caring ways that nothing be lost.

The psychiatrist C.G. Jung is known for his work on archetypes, the personal consciousness, and the collective unconscious. For Jung the collective unconscious is the deeper layer of consciousness that lies under the personal consciousness and does not derive from personal experience; it is not a personal acquisition but is inborn. It is collective in the sense that it is not individual but universal. Recently, human consciousness has been at the center of much psychiatric study focusing on new understandings of the human brain.

Today scientific theories are moving consciousness outside of the human brain. Giulio Tononi and his colleagues at the University of Wisconsin-Madison have the goal of understanding how the brain generates consciousness. They are using state of the art brain scanners and the latest computer programs to produce torrents of information on brain function. Tononi's quiet reflection after amassing this information is that each split second of awareness is a unified experience that is completely new and different from any experience before or after it.

Tononi's theory defines consciousness as the capacity of a person or any system to connect and use information. Each moment of existence has the potential of playing out in a limitless number of ways. Yet, the instant an experience is integrated and gels, the options vanish. The next moment brings new possibilities, new options, and new experience forming consciousness. The many options produce the one new experience. So Tononi's theory is information +integration=experience (consciousness).

Integration is what makes every conscious experience a unified whole. These two concepts: information and integration describe consciousness. If this equation is correct, then Tononi untethers the theory of consciousness from the physical brain. Silicon chips integrating information zooming around the World Wide Web produces consciousness.

It is interesting to see that ancient religions and current panpsychism says the same thing. Other scientists today say that the only systems that we know that fulfill Tononi's theory are biological.

My own belief is that the possibility of consciousness is inherent in the fabric of reality as God's initial love aims and purposes for an evolving universe. Consciousness is woven into the very fabric of cosmos as possibilities, as information to be experienced by emergent creatures.

Consciousness is grounded in God best known as creative relational kindness. As God calls creation out of chaos over eons of time, the evolving creation is conducive to the formation of human consciousness. As God's novel love aims and purposes were experienced and unified, consciousness emerged. The ethical quality of consciousness and the presence of moral law in many cultures support this view. Thus, the origin of consciousness is primarily in the Divine and secondarily in humans. Since God's Spirit is in all things, then consciousness can be experienced in varying degrees at many levels of evolution.

Jesus' gentle Galilean glories, his gentle teachings, are unique in that Jesus became totally obedient to God's call. In each succeeding act of obedience, Jesus became more conscious of God's love aims and purposes until he became fully God conscious. Jesus' consciousness was God's consciousness, and both Jesus and God were changed in the process; thus he could say as he faced the cross, God and I are one (See John 17). Divine consciousness is greater than that experienced by Jesus.

Jesus' consciousness was the totality of all his sensory experiences. He was aware of his religious past, how God was revealed in the consciousness of the prophets like Isaiah. Seeing God revealed in the prophets opened the way for Jesus to become God conscious. Jesus received the information of God's actions in the world from the past, preserved in his sacred scriptures and buried in his consciousness, integrated this information into his experience of God, and became more fully God conscious with each self-actualization. This is in harmony with Luke's understanding of Jesus when he wrote, "Jesus increased in wisdom and stature, in favor with God and persons" (Luke 2:52). Also, the writer of Hebrew says that Jesus learned obedience (Hebrews 5:8).

Gentleness as actualized by Jesus is like an archetype of consciousness, rooted in the nature of God and layered in many religions from ancient times. The Hebrew/Greek words for gentleness could be called archetypal words for gentleness set forth in the secrets of Jesus' consciousness in glorious images that can inspire and transform, making gentleness accessible to every believing heart.

These images of gentleness be they Jewish, Christian, or Buddhist are mysteriously, richly intuitive. In their archetypal nature these images of kindness often covey mythic qualities as they are associated with the birth of

Jesus. As in Luke 1:78-79, where the Gospel writer says about the birth narratives, God's love and kindness will shine on us from on high.

Jesus incarnated these images of kindness and the early Christians were gripped by these images, as can be seen in the New Testament literature of the early church. I am afraid that for the church today these archetypal images of gentleness have been worn smooth by usage and have become superficial and banal, replaced by correct belief set in the concrete of creeds. Thus, dogma takes the place of gentle consciousness and the gentle Jesus is replaced by the ways of Caesar. Gentleness, if not cast out of the psyche into cosmic space, lies buried in the layers of personal consciousness, waiting for a reawakening.

Having ceased to think theologically, the contemporary church doesn't have the remotest conception of the treasure buried in these human vessels. When the church ceases to think seriously about these images of gentleness and how the Trinity reveals the love and kindness of God coming to save us (See Titus 3:4), the church is stripped of mystery, its walls collapse, exposing the evil winds of the world.

The modern church members enlightened consciousness leads him/her to look elsewhere for what has been lost in the archetypal image of collective kindness. The success of the mega-church is due to its effective use of theatrical imagery and pabulum feed theology that satisfies the restlessness of heart and mind.

Meanwhile, the archetypal image of gentleness that Jesus incarnated in his God-consciousness remains an unrealized dream. Reawakening this gentle conscious is the route to zestful love, joy, and peace, the harmony of harmonies.

Jesus' God-consciousness is a model of how the world might be. It came to fruition in Jesus' consciousness after being shaped over time with the sacrifice of many including the sacrifice of the prophets of Israel as told in the Old Testament; it was born more fully in the life and gentle teachings of Jesus, his sacrificial death on the cross, and his glorious resurrection.

Without the inner glow of this God-consciousness there would be no real sight or the light that unifies human consciousness. Go and seek that light!

Appendix B

New Testament Churches Living the Gentle Teachings

In the New Testament God's word has become one with Jesus' word. Indeed, according to the Gospel of John, God's word became flesh in Jesus. Jesus was the Word and the Word was with God and the Word was God (John 1:1). The Word became a human being and, full of grace and truth, lived among us. We saw his glory, the glory which he received as the Father's only Son (John 1:14).

We have seen the significance of the Father/Son imagery for interpreting the life and teachings of Jesus, and we have seen the heart of those teachings as gentle Galilean glories. It now remains for us to explore the impact of the gentle teachings on the decision-making process in our lives and in the life of the Church. We have stated several times that the gentle teachings slowly but surely operate by love to change and transform our lives and our world. This is their authority. A common theme in the gentle teachings is that "Jesus taught as One who had authority and not as the scribes." "Authority" means His direct divine authority. It is this divine authority that is present and effective in the gentle teachings.

This divine authority can be felt and experienced in the words that promise the kingdom of God to the poor, forgiveness, love, joy, and peace to the lost who are like sheep without a shepherd. There is no parable, no interpretation of the parables to the disciples, no healing miracle of Jesus that does not shine with the sovereign power and authority of God. Even the controversies that often seem harsh and condemning are in the contest of these gentle teachings. Jesus is most concerned when these gentle teachings are kept from the lowly ones, especially women and children. So, even in the most human words and emotions of Jesus, God's sovereign words shine through. He who has ears to hear and eyes to see can hear, see, and experience the presence of God in saving ways.

No wonder the crowds were amazed and saw authority in Jesus' humble life and gentle teachings. The Jewish religion in the time of Jesus had devised a sacrificial system based on hierarchical ordinances and sacred traditions that had to be followed to come into the presence of God. The poor, the *amhaares,* were virtually excluded from this religious system. Jesus' gentle teachings brought this whole ironclad social and religious structure tumbling down. This accounts for the controversies with the religious leaders and the plots to get rid of Jesus. These humble and gentle teachings of Jesus enrage some and bring unbounded joy to others. Jesus brings the kingdom of God near. In Jesus God is present to help and to heal. "Blessed are" the sorrowing, the hungry, the sick, the poor, for God is present!

The gentle teachings of Jesus convey at the same time the radically earth-shaking nature of God's word and the amazing wonder, mystery, and authority of God's presence. This is Jesus' unique authority: God's words have become one with Jesus' gentle teachings.

The gentle teachings of Jesus had great authority for New Testament Churches. Jesus' miraculous birth, gentle teachings, death on the cross, and resurrection retained their power and effect in the life of the early church. The Apostle Paul interpreted the whole Christ event in terms of gentleness and kindness with these words to Titus:

When the goodness and loving kindness of God our Savior appeared, he saved us, not because of any works of righteousness that we had done, but according to his mercy, through the water of rebirth and renewal by the Holy Spirit. This Spirit he poured out on us richly through Jesus Christ our Savior, so that, having been justified by his grace, we might become heirs according to the hope of eternal life. The saying is sure, I desire that you insist on these things, so that those who have come to believe in God may be careful to devote themselves to good works; these things are excellent and profitable to everyone (Titus 3:4-8).

Paul's earliest correspondence to New Testament Churches is found in the letters to the Thessalonians. In this correspondence Paul recognized the authority of God's word in the life of the Church. Paul's one desire was to live in Christ, a prayer found throughout his letters, and challenged the Churches with these words:

We also constantly give thanks to God for this, that when you received the word of God that you heard from us, you accepted it not as a human word but as what it really is, God's word, which is also at work in you believers. For you, brothers and sisters, became imitators of the churches of God in Christ Jesus that are in Judea (1 Thessalonians 2:13-14).

In this passage Paul has grounded his own authority and the authority of the Church in the word of God revealed in Jesus Christ. Jesus' authority was seen in the way God's words were one with His gentle words, and now Paul is saying that his authority and the authority of the Church is the way God's word is at work in the followers of Christ---God's word is at work in you believers (1 Thessalonians 2:13).

Paul defends his right to speak the word of God to the Corinthians in these words: For we are not peddlers of God's word like so many; but in Christ we speak as persons of sincerity, as persons sent from God and standing in his presence (2 Corinthians 2:17). For Paul and the Corinthian Church the locus of authority is in the crucified and risen Christ. The Church is the Body of Christ in the world living out the gentle teachings with their power to transform.

To be in Christ is to be in a power field of the Spirit and energized by Jesus' gentle teachings, sacrificial death, and resurrection. The power of Jesus' gentle teachings opens the Church to creative transformation. To be in Christ is to conform in some measure to the gentle teachings. They shake the Church up when it becomes complacent and comfort the Church when it is shaken. And God is present and near in the shaking of the foundations.

Paul summarizes the mystery of the word of God being near to us in Jesus and in the Church gathered to hear and celebrate the word: Do not say in your heart, 'Who will ascend into heaven?' (that is, to bring Christ down) or 'Who will descend into the abyss?' (that is, to bring Christ up from the dead) . . .. The word is near you, on your lips and in your heart (Romans 10:6-8). The word of God is near to you. So near that you if you "confess with your lips that Jesus is Lord and believe in your heart that God raised him from the dead, you will be saved (10:9).

In a world where astrology, stoicism, Gnosticism, and the mystery religions were vying for followers, Paul says that the aimless running is not necessary. God's mercy and grace has come near to us---When the kindness of God came, God saved us! (Titus 3:4). God is near to us!

Paul binds God's speaking and our hearing and believing and confessing in the Church and when the Church hears that word of God it has authority for its life and ministry. Paul asked the Roman Christians, How are we to hear without a preacher? (Romans 10:14). Wherever the word of God is faithfully preached and heard, there is the Church. And Jesus' gentle teachings are the past, present, and future of the Church. While Paul interpreted the Christ event as the goodness and kindness of God coming to save us, John expressed it these words: For God so loved the world that he gave his only Son, so that everyone who believes in him may have eternal life (John 3:16). Jesus' gentle ministry is the past of the Church---God did not spare the Son but gave Him up for us all! This is the present of the Church---If God in Christ is for us, who can be against us! The gentle teachings grounded in the love of Jesus are the future of the Church---Nothing will be able to separate us from the love of God in Christ Jesus our Lord (See Romans 8:31-39)

All authority for the Church is located in the goodness and mercy of God revealed in the gentle teachings of Jesus. When we ask the questions, "Where in the Bible is God's word?" and "Where in the Bible are we encountering human words?" is a false dichotomy. In the New Testament we find the mystery of God's saving words in the humanity of those divine words made flesh in the gentle ministry of Jesus and embodied in the continuing gentle ministry of the Church.

Appendix C

The Influence of Psychology and Consciousness in Interpreting the Gentle Teachings of Jesus

Look deep into Jesus' gentle love teachings, and then you will understand everything in your life better.

These thoughts on the gentle teachings of Jesus have also been filtered by the author through a life time interest in reading psychology as a way of understanding human consciousness, human development, and social action; and the greatest influence comes from C.G. Jung and his writings on the archetypes, collective unconsciousness, and personal consciousness. For Jung the collective unconscious is the deeper layer of consciousness that lies under the personal consciousness and does not derive from personal experience; it is not a personal acquisition but is inborn. It is collective in the sense that it is not individual but universal.

Serving as a parish minister and encountering the best and the worst in Christians, I often wished that we could become more like Jesus. A Muslim once said, "I wish I had met Jesus before I met Christians." The heartbeat of my theology is Jesus, and more specifically, the gentle Galilean glories of Jesus that reveal God as creative relational love. I would say that I experienced the church at its best when hearing children sing, "Jesus loves me this I know, for the Bible tells me so." As mentioned above, if I found my spirit sagging, all I had to do was recall the words of this childhood song, and my spirit was immediately lifted. Kindness works. Love matters. Jesus' unconditional gentle love is transforming and heart- warming. In fact, the purpose of this book may be summarized in this one sentence: Simple acts of kindness to ourselves, our family, and all living things are the most powerful transformers in the world.

The heart of this book is Jesus and his gentle Galilean teachings. Throughout this book there are references to Jesus' unique God consciousness, a concept first popularized by the philosopher, Fredrick Schleiermacher. The concept has been used by many theologians since Schleiermacher, often with increasing richness. For me consciousness is the heart beat of Jesus' gentle teachings, the grammar and poetry of the word that became flesh in Jesus, a creative word that speaks ultimate meaning.

Recently, human consciousness has been at the center of much psychiatric study focusing on new understandings of the human brain. Today scientific theories are moving consciousness outside of the human brain. Giulio Tononi and his colleagues at the University of Wisconsin-Madison have the goal of understanding how the brain generates consciousness. They are using state of the art brain scanners and the latest computer programs to produce torrents of information on brain function. Tononi's quiet reflection after amassing this information is that each split second of awareness is a unified experience that is completely new and different from any experience before or after it (As in process philosophy).

Tononi's theory defines consciousness as the capacity of a person or any system to connect and use information. Each moment of existence has the potential of playing out in a limitless number of ways. Yet, the instant an experience is integrated and gels, the options vanish. The next moment brings new possibilities, new options, and new experience forming consciousness. The many options produce the one new experience. So Tononi's theory is information +integration=experience (consciousness).

Integration is what makes every conscious experience a unified whole. These two concepts: information and integration describe consciousness. If this equation is correct, then Tononi untethers the theory of consciousness from the physical brain. Silicon chips integrating information zooming around the World Wide Web produces consciousness. Other scientists today say that the only systems that we know that fulfill Tononi's theory are biological.

My own belief is that consciousness is inherent in the fabric of reality as God's initial love aims and purposes for an evolving universe. Consciousness is woven into the very fabric of cosmos as possibilities, as information to be experienced by emergent creatures.

Consciousness is grounded in God best known as creative relational love. As God calls creation out of chaos over eons of time, the evolving creation is conducive to the formation of human consciousness. As God's novel love aims and purposes were experienced and unified, God-consciousness emerged. The ethical quality of consciousness and the presence of moral law as experienced by humans in many cultures support this view. Thus, the origin of consciousness is primarily in the Divine and secondarily in humans. Since God's Spirit is in all things, then consciousness can be experienced in varying degrees at many levels of evolution.

Jesus' gentle Galilean glories, his gentle teachings, are unique in that Jesus became obedient to God's call seen in prophets like Isaiah and Hosea. Isaiah 55:12 serves as background and inspiration for the gentle teachings of Jesus: "For you shall go out in joy and be led back in peace; the mountains and hills before you shall burst out into song, and all the trees of the fields shall clap their hands." Hosea 11 is like a springboard to Jesus' gentle teachings: "When Israel was a child, I loved him, and I called my son out of Egypt... I took Israel by the arm and taught them to walk. I led them with kindness and love." In the spirit of these prophets Jesus responded to God's love aims and purposes until he became fully God conscious. Jesus' consciousness was God's consciousness; thus he could say as he faced the cross, God and I are one (See John 17). Yet, it is important to see that Divine consciousness is greater than that experienced by the human Jesus.

Jesus' consciousness of God's presence was the totality of all his sensory experiences and linked Jesus with his religious past, linking past, present, and future into a unity. Jesus was aware of his religious past reflected in his scriptures, especially how God was revealed in the consciousness of the prophets of Israel like Isaiah and Hosea as seen above. In Jesus' consciousness, there is a shaking of hands with the prophets and psalmists, synapses occurs (In Greek, synapses is "clasping together"). Seeing God revealed in the prophets as the Father of Israel and Israel as God's first-born son (See Exodus 4:22 and Hosea 11:1 above) opened the way for Jesus to become God conscious and self-actualize this relational filial concept in his Gentle Galilean Glories. Jesus received the information of God's actions in the world from the past, preserved in his sacred scriptures and buried deep in his collective unconsciousness, to use Jungian terms, integrated this information into his personal consciousness of God, and became more fully God conscious with each self-actualization. The gentle Galilean glories are birthed, shining forth with new radiance from the weaver of biophilic and psychetrophic words (See intro for definition of biophilic and psychetrophic).

This emphasis on Jesus as a human is in harmony with Luke's understanding of Jesus when he wrote, "Jesus increased in wisdom and stature, in favor with God and persons" (Luke 2:52). Also, the writer of Hebrews says that Jesus learned obedience (Hebrews 5:8). Living intimately with the four Gospels for the past fifty years has convinced me that the purpose of the New Testament writers was to show the humanity of Jesus more than his divinity.

Gentleness as actualized by Jesus is like an archetype of consciousness, rooted in the nature of God and layered in repetitive patterns in many religions from ancient times. The Hebrew/Greek words for love and gentleness could be called archetypal words for love and gentleness set forth in the secrets of Jesus' consciousness in glorious images that can inspire and transform, making gentle love accessible to every believing heart. That Jesus wrapped these secrets in beautiful biophilic images from nature make them all the more appealing and psychetrophic, for we all have an innate need to affiliate cognitively and emotionally with these nature images which have restorative powers.

These images of love and gentleness have found their way into Judaism, Christianity, Islam, Confucianism, Buddhism, Hinduism, and other world religions and are mysteriously, richly intuitive. In their archetypal nature these images of kindness often convey mythic qualities as they are associated with the celebrations in all religions, and especially in Christianity with the birth of Jesus and theological concepts like the Trinity. As in Luke 1:78-79, where the Gospel writer says about the birth narratives, "God's love and kindness will shine on us from on high." It is this sense of mystery, awe, and wonder that needs to be recovered in our daily lives and especially in worship.

Jesus ministry was inspired by these images of kindness and the early Christians were gripped by these images, as can be seen in the New Testament literature of the early church. Kindness worked for Jesus, and I know gentleness works for me in times of brokenness. I also saw it transform many in the churches where I served as minister. Simple acts of kindness to ourselves, our family, and to all living things are the most powerful transformers in the world. I am afraid that often in the church today these archetypal images of gentle love have been worn smooth by usage and have become superficial and banal, replaced by "correct beliefs" set in the concrete of creeds. Thus, dogma takes the place of gentle consciousness and the gentle Jesus is replaced by the ways of power, politics, and big business, the military-industrial complex.

Gentleness, if not cast out of the psyche into cosmic space, lies buried in the layers of personal consciousness of this Christian generation, waiting for a reawakening and nurturing anew. The biophilic and psychetrophic teachings of Jesus have the power to awake and transform.

Having ceased to think theologically, the contemporary church has lost the sparkle of the treasure buried in these human vessels. When the church ceases to think seriously about these images of gentleness and how the Trinity, for example, reveals the love and kindness of God coming to save us (See Titus 3:4), the church is stripped of mystery, its walls collapse, exposing the evil winds of the world.

The modern church member's "enlightened" consciousness leads him/her to look elsewhere for what has been lost in the archetypal images of collective loving kindness. The success of the mega-church is due to its effective use of theatrical imagery and pabulum fed theology that superficially satisfies the restlessness of heart and mind.

This restlessness leads many to stock pile guns and ammunition and issues in statements like this: "the only way to stop a bad guy with a gun is a good guy with a gun" (from an address of the Executive Vice-President of the National Rifle Association, Wayne Lapiere). A better statement would be: gentleness not guns transforms society and is the long-term solution for overcoming evil actions.

Meanwhile, the archetypal images of gentle love that Jesus self-actualized remain an unrealized dream, flickering here and there. Reawakening this gentle conscious and fanning the flame is the route to zestful love, joy, and peace, the harmony of harmonies, to use a Whitehead phrase.

Jesus is central to all Christian theology for he revealed God as the totally related One, in all things, for all things, and before all things sharing the experience of the whole universe in transforming love. Jesus' gentle teachings reveal God as relating through agape persuasion, not coercion, and this is their greatest contribution and strength. God knows the future to be open and free with many different loving aims and possibilities, and then God of the future lures us and all creation toward the fulfillment of those agape aims that give purpose and meaning to life (See Lewis S. Ford, *Transforming Process Theism* for an intriguing view of God as the creative activity of the future).

The biblical writers and Christian theologians have used many images for God's presence in the world. Jesus used the image of Spirit in his dialogue with the woman of Samaria recorded in John chapter four, saying, "God is Spirit and the one who worships God must worship in Spirit." Jesus knew the concept of "Spirit" from his scriptures, especially in the creative process (Genesis 1:1) and in the activity of the prophets (Isaiah 42:1). As used by Jesus, Spirit is an experiential and relational concept grounded in love. Spirit came upon Jesus at his baptism. Also Spirit as a way of understanding God is used in many religions, especially Native Americans; therefore "Spirit" is used in this book as a way in which God relates to us and all of creation. As Spirit God moves throughout the universe as wind blows gently through the trees.

Jesus' gentle teachings invite us to join our spirits with God's Spirit in prayer, worship, and service. The central purpose of Christian theology is to hold up the gentle Galilean glories of Jesus as the guiding light for our lives, our churches, and our world. Prayer is central to how God relates to the world and to us. Prayer, as a form of healing energy (See James 5:15), was essential in the way Jesus related to God and was as habitual in his life as breathing. Jesus spoke to God as a child would speak to his parent, confidently and securely, and is a key to understanding his God-consciousness and his transformation into one who was a Son of God. God is present with all who pray. Jesus was familiar with this truth from Isaiah: "They that wait upon the Lord shall renew their strength; they shall mount up with wings as eagles; they shall run, and not be weary; they shall walk and not faint" (Isaiah 40:31). So let us pray that we may be transformed as children of God and that we may work with God in transforming the world as one family of God. That is the hope of this book.

Appendix D

The Search for The Historical Jesus

I am more confident than many current biblical scholars and theologians that one can find the historical Jesus in the Gospels of the New Testament. The critical question is to what extent is the proclaimed Jesus of the Gospels identical to the Jesus of Nazareth? Answering this question raises the issue of the inspiration of scriptures. Who is speaking in scripture? Is scripture the word of God and inspired by the Spirit of God? Does the historical Jesus speak the words of Matthew, Mark, Luke, and John? Should these writings even be considered as history or seen as novels about Jesus and the early Church? If they contain history, are the Synoptic Gospels, Matthew, Mark, and Luke, more historical than John? These are hermeneutical questions. Each Gospel writer found himself in a special hermeneutical situation with new needs.

After the crucifixion of Jesus, his teachings circulated in oral form for about 40 years before some of them were written down by Mark about 70 C.E. These stories in their oral stage were fluid and changed some with each new telling. However, with little printed media, the people of the time depended much more on memory than we do today when we are awash with printed words. They sought to be faithful in the retelling of stories of faith. The Jesus tradition was an important influence in shaping the life and thought of the early church.

Matthew and Luke, writing about 80-85 C.E. are even further separated from Jesus of Nazareth. John writing as late as 90-100 C.E. is even further removed. It is commonly believed that Matthew and Luke used Mark in the writing of their Gospels. About 95 percent of Mark is reproduced in Matthew and Luke. Matthew and Luke also have material in common that is not in Mark and is called the Q source, from the German word, quelle. Since the material is so similar in both Matthew and Luke, it was probably a written source, but we have no copy that has been found. Matthew also has material that is unique to his Gospel that scholars label as M, and Luke has unique material that is labeled, L. Matthew, Mark, and Luke are so similar that they have been laid out in parallel columns and called the Synoptic Gospels.

John's Gospel coming at the end of the first Christian century is distinctly different from the synoptic Gospels in language, style, and theological concerns. The Fourth Gospel, as John is called, presents Jesus in long narrative discourses with persons like Nicodemus and the woman of Samaria. John presents Jesus as a new interpretation of the traditions of the early Church.

The time interval is significant. The demands of John's community create different needs and lead John to give a new interpretation of the Jesus tradition. Does this make it less historical?

The miracle of the Gospels is that in and through the inspired words of the four Gospel writers, Jesus' words continue to live and speak. Gospel writing may be called an anamnesis form of writing. Anamnesis comes from the transliteration of a Greek word best translated as "remembering". As acts of remembering, the gospels are not strictly speaking historical biographies about Jesus. However, this could be said for all biographical writing, for all are interpreted remembrance and seldom if ever "pure" facts. There is no un-interpreted and un-biased remembering and putting remembering into written words. To be a faithful witness does not simply mean passing on tradition. The New Testament evangelists in announcing good news were responsible for letting the good news meet the changing needs of their present communities. The vital needs of the early Christian movement changed quickly and drastically following the crucifixion and resurrection of Jesus. All the Gospels look back at the life of Jesus through the lens of the crucifixion and resurrection of Jesus.

In the anamnesis form of writing, the faithful telling of the past stories of Jesus are united with the faithful proclamation in the present worshipping community of the evangelist. The time interval is bridged, and a living word of Jesus is experienced. What links the past and present creating a new future is the experienced presence of God in each new situation.

The same symbiosis action can be seen in the life and teachings of Jesus. The consciousness of God's presence linked the human Jesus with Israel's prophets and psalmists, his religious past. The linking of past and present creates a new unity in Jesus' teachings, and those who hear Jesus hear the word of God. The sacred past is remembered and re-enacted in Jesus' teachings. As Jesus' mode of vision renders the past as present, when the followers of Jesus remember his words and actions they are linked with the historical Jesus. In remembering all are drawn into the "we circle." The core of the "we circle" are the eye-witnesses who saw and heard Jesus speak. In remembering we are linked with the "we circle" and thereby linked with the historical Jesus who becomes present to us today. Remembering overcomes the time interval. As Jesus is remembered he becomes a once for all time event. In the Church's liturgy the generations are united as one as we become one with "the great cloud of witnesses."

The act of remembering and the "we circle" formula are supported by the role of the paraclete or Spirit in the New Testament. The Spirit of God infuses and inspires the Church's proclamation and the words of Jesus continue to speak, become more deeply understood, and grasped in faith. In the faithful linking of past and present, the historical Jesus steps out of the

New Testament stories as they are proclaimed and into our lives as the living word of God!

As we live the gentle Galilean glories of Jesus, his gentle teachings are still at work in the world. In this sense the gentle words of Jesus are eternal, uniting past, present, and future; and they are appropriated to any life and any world.

Energy is transmitted in this word-event, enlivening our lives and our world. Wherever Jesus' gentle words are spoken and lived, Jesus comes to us as he came to his disciples by the Sea of Galilee long ago. He calls us to follow him and learn from his gentle and kind ways (Matthew 28f:19-20; 2Cor. 10:1; Eph. 4:2; Col. 3:12; Titus 3:2).

So, come Jesus! Be kind to us (Rev. 22:21) as we live Galilean Glories.

Appendix E

My Process Hermeneutic: The Gentle Teachings of Jesus

Thesis: the gentle teachings of Jesus slowly but surely transform our lives and our world. Jesus' loving kindness has transforming energy. This is my hermeneutic from Alpha to Omega, from beginning to end. Here is the heartbeat of my hermeneutic: The kindness we show to ourselves, our family, and to all living things is the greatest healing force in the world.[255]

Using the gentle teachings of Jesus focused on loving kindness as my hermeneutic is the result of a selective process where Jesus' relevant past, the faith stories of the prophets and poets of Israel, are creatively brought together by Jesus through a process of selective prehension, feeling, to become Jesus' new gentle teachings. The reality of the transforming power of living kindness is conceived as a process of creative advance in which many past faith events are integrated in the events of Jesus' present healing ministry, and in turn are taken up by future events. The universe creatively advances as a sequence of integrations at every level and moment of existence. This creative advance is especially seen in the cross and resurrection of Jesus.

In self-actualizing the creative love of God, Jesus found a security to transcend his own suffering on the cross. As the worthy model for all persons, God lifted Jesus to heaven where his suffering is absorbed in creative responsive love. In this transforming act the victim becomes the victor---satisfaction is completed and transformed into heavenly reality as the risen Jesus passes back into the world as a new creation. Jesus is given a new body, the church where he lives and continues his new ministry empowered by the Spirit of God. This transformative action in the life of Jesus also transforms God. What was done in the world is lifted to heaven where all things become new and passes back into the world making all things new. God is now in the world in new ways and for the world in new tidal waves of saving love.[256]

Alfred North Whitehead, the father of process philosophy, affirmed that the temporal process is a momentary transition from one actual entity to another. These entities are themselves momentary events which perish

---

[255] For a fuller treatment of this thesis of kindness see my book, *A Relational Hermeneutic of Kindness*.

[256] See *Process and Reality, Corrected Edition*, edited by David Ray Griffin and Donald W. Sherburne, pp. 350-51).

immediately upon coming into being. The perishing marks the transition to the succeeding events. We see this in Jesus' transforming loving kindness. Time is not a single smooth flow but comes into being as a series of events: the old covenant with Moses and the new covenant with Jesus, the old earth and heaven and the new earth and heaven. In this sense, time moves from the past, through the present, and into the future. Every moment is new and cannot be reproduced. Each unit of the old process provides the datum for new processes to happen.

Process theology is a form of process philosophy that seeks to explain God and how God relates to the world from this metaphysical perspective of experiential events rather than enduring substances. This is in contrast to traditional theology that is based on a mechanistic model that sees the world as made up of unchanging building blocks that bounce like billiard balls when hit by the cue stick. Protons and atoms bounce off each other unaffected in this static view, giving a view of cosmic and biological evolution as re-arrangement of the building blocks.

This vision of God being in the gentle teachings of Jesus in saving ways has implications for how God is in the world and for the world in creative transformation. Thus, the gentle teachings of Jesus as a hermeneutic for interpreting the whole Bible also has implications for saving the environment. Process theology says that in the course of evolution change occurs in subjects, not objects.

Process theology sees all things inter-connected and inter-related, seeing God in the world and for the world, in us and for us acting in saving ways. Process theology stresses individual freedom in the evolutionary process and sees individual self-determination and self-actualization as key to understanding human existence. In Jesus' gentle teachings, filled with nature imagery like birds of the air and flowers of the field, we learn that God understands and cares for the all of creation. God is in our lives and in the world setting novel aims and purposes, luring all creation toward redemption. Jesus' gentle teachings are the fulfillment of these aims and purposes that are always good and loving and never violent.

God is not coercive in this relationship but persuasive and luring. God relates to the world from within as persuasive activity. In Jesus we see this divine activity in his miraculous ministry and his new ministry as risen the risen Jesus directing his new body, the church, in transforming ways.

Whereas traditional theology saw God as passionless, as a perfect unchanging being, process theology says that God feels the feelings of all creation as responsive beneficiary, not benefactor only. Thus process strongly emphasizes the immanence of God, seeing God as synthesis of all our feelings and all feelings of the universe, and God is changed by this concrescence. God both gives and receives love and reciprocal love changes all coming into its warmth and glow.

In summary, the following are key concepts in process theology and my process hermeneutic used in interpreting all of life.

(1) Internal-relatedness. All things are internally related, one entity among the many in a cosmic community of becoming.

(2) Panentheism. God is in all things. Not pantheism which says that all things are God. Panentheism says that God is in all things as immanence, but God transcends all things as well, having creative power of persuasion, distinct from the universe. In stressing the relatedness of all things, process comes down heavily on the side of immanence.

(3) A reciprocal relationship between God and the world. According to Whitehead there is full symmetry, "it is as true to say that the world is immanent in God, as that God is immanent in the world" (Process and Reality, p. 348).

(4) Integrity of the natural order. For autonomous self-actualizing entities (humans) to emerge in the evolutionary history, it is necessary that the natural order be organized and regular, and therefore comprehensible to the evolving entities, including persons.

My hermeneutic based on the gentle teachings of Jesus adds to this "integrity of the natural order," the insight that humans have evolved with an innate need to relate to all of nature and to all other life forms. I use two Greek words found in the New Testament to convey this need, βιος and φιλια, joined together, "biophilia" means love for all life forms.

(5) God is the supremely related entity. Panentheism makes it possible to see God as the "Spirit" relating to the universe as creative responsive love.

(6) God's relational love is the ground of all ethical actions. In process thought each entity has intrinsic value.

(7) Jesus as relational love. Jesus' life and death, to have transforming power for us, must not violate the integrity of the natural order as defined in number four above. (For more detailed analysis of process philosophy see *Process and Reality, Modes of Thought, Adventures of Ideas, Religion in the Making,* and "The Center for Process Studies").

Appendix F
Kindness as A Trinitarian Metaphor

The purpose of this book on "Jesus' Gentle Galilean Glories" has been to gather Jesus' gentle and kind teachings found throughout the New Testament into one source with special attention to their transforming qualities. Every time I felt that I was finished, a metaphor like trinity would cry out for more attention. In this chapter I gather up the fragments of bread relating to trinity and suggest that kindness is an appropriate metaphor for a fresh interpretation of trinity.

It is important to see that the word, Trinity, is not in the Bible; it is a metaphor employed by theologians to represent how God relates to humans. Metaphor comes from two Greek words: μετα, meaning "across," and φερος, meaning "to carry." So, a metaphor "carries across" meaning from one realm to the other, meaning that is not readily accessible to our everyday experience and understanding. The very fact that we are dealing with mystery is the reason we need metaphors. It is the nature of metaphor each time it is handled to present new meanings and to invite creative thinking that is often hard to put into words. Kindness is a multifaceted metaphor.

Kindness is my process hermeneutic for interpreting the biblical message. This has been my hermeneutic in this book from Alpha to Omega, from beginning to end. Kindness has transforming energy. Here is the heartbeat of my hermeneutic:

In the closing chapters of *Process and Reality*, Whitehead sought to show how God relates to the world and how the world relates to God. In this major work among his philosophical writings, Whitehead was primarily concerned with elucidating the "primordial" nature of God. This metaphor for him gathered all the wealth of potentiality, the divine ordering of all possibilities for the world. These possibilities may be defined as God's love aims and purposes for creation. For Whitehead order was not sufficient for explaining the novelty and freshness of the new and keeping the massiveness of the order from degenerating into mere repetition. "It belongs to the goodness of the world, that its settled order

> **The kindness we show to ourselves, our family, and to all living things is the greatest healing force in the world.**

should deal tenderly with the faint discordant light of the dawn of another age" (PR, p. 339).

The satisfaction of these aims and purposes in tenderness that nothing be lost required Whitehead to present what he described as the "consequent" nature of God, i.e., God's prehension or feeling of all entities in the world. As primordial, God is unchanging in goodness and love. As consequent God is in the world and in us, feeling our sorrow and our joy, our hatred and our love. As we feel God's joy and love we are changed; and as God feels our joy and love God is changed, for this is the nature of reciprocal love.

My use of the metaphor, kindness, as a process hermeneutic for interpreting the biblical message is also useful for combining both the primordial and consequent aspects of God. As these two roles are relational concepts, they have served as guidelines for elucidating the Trinity, a doctrine that seeks to show how God relates to the people of God, first in the Scriptures and also to us. For me, kindness expresses this relationship best.[257]

Kindness as used in the Old Testament carries well the primordial aspect of God. Kindness is a key metaphor for the way the Jewish people experienced God. Exodus 33:19 defines God as kindness in this foundational "I am" saying. "I am God, and I show mercy and kindness to anyone I chose" (CEV). This verse names God as Kindness. So what the Christian belief in the Trinity names as God the Father is best conceived as "God is kind." Kindness is a gender-neutral term and does not alienate like the name, Father. The previous chapters have amply shown this reality. The faith of Israel can be stated in these three words: God is kind. The Psalms of Israel are filled with the "loving-kindness" of God. This first part of the trinity can be stated as "I believe God is kind to all living things.

Kindness is also an appropriate metaphor for expressing what is intended in the second part of the Christian Trinity: the Son. Paul expressed the birth of Jesus in these words: "When the kindness of God came, God saved us" (Titus 3:4). Jesus' self-designation was "I am kind" (See Matthew 11:28-30). Self- designations should carry more importance that titles we apply to Jesus. The second part of the trinity can be stated as "I believe Jesus is alive in the church teaching kindness."

Throughout this book I have spent a great deal of time on Trinitarian thoughts. Most of the New Testament, virtually equates the Spirit and the risen Jesus, seeing their role as one as in the Gospel of John, chapter 14. When discussing God, Jesus, and the Spirit we are talking about mystery filled relationships. Using kindness as a metaphor makes these relationships as clear as possible. Kindness certainly communicates better with children than

---

[257] See *Trinity in Process: A Relational Theology of God*. Eds. Joseph A. Bracken, S.J. and Marjorie Hewitt Suchocki)

the title, Holy Spirit, which can be a spooky title to a young child. The Spirit is best equated with the risen Jesus. The third part of the Trinity can be stated as "I believe the Spirit is the Risen Jesus continuing his kind teachings in the church."

The Bible does not teach that there are three Gods. The Old and New Testaments profess that "The Lord our God is One" (Deuteronomy 6:4; Mark 12:29). This is the one non-negotiable truth in any discussion of the Trinity. The Christian Church has not done very well in explaining the Trinity so as to maintain the oneness of God. It is time for starting over with new and fresh meanings. I believe one way of doing this is to make Kindness our new Trinity![258]

I believe God is kind to all living things.

I believe Jesus is kind and call us to be kind.

I believe the Spirit is Jesus alive in the Church teaching kindness.

Our Bible closes with the prayer: "I pray that Jesus will be kind to all of you" (Revelation 22:21, CEV).

My faith response is: I cannot give all the kindness the world needs, but the world needs all the kindness I can give.

---

[258] See my book, *A Relational Trinity of Kindness* for more on the trinity.

Bibliography

Adams, Edward. *Parallel Lives of Jesus: A Guide to the Four Gospels*. Louisville: Westminster/John Knox, 2011.

Allison, Dale C. *Constructing Jesus: Memory, Imagination, and History*. Grand Rapids: Baker, 2011.

Aslan, Reza. *Zealot*. New York: Random House. 2013.

Bauckham, Richard. *The Theology of the Book of Revelation*. New Testament Theology. Cambridge: Cambridge University Press, 1993.

Beale, G. K. *The Book of Revelation: A Commentary on the Greek Text*. The New International Greek Testament Commentary. Grand Rapids: Eerdmans, 2013.

Berry, Wendell. *The Gift of Good Land*. San Francisco: North Point Press, 1981.

Blevins, James L. *The Messianic Secret in Markan Research, 1901-1976*, Lanham: University Press of America, 1981.

Borg, Marcus J. *Jesus: A New Vision*. New York: Harper Collins, 1991.

_____. *Jesus and Buddha: The Parallel Sayings*. Berkeley, CA: Ulysses Press, 1997.

Bornkamm, Gunther. *Jesus of Nazareth*. Trans. Irene and Fraser McLuskey with James M. Robinson. New York: Harper & Row, Publishers, 1960.

Bracken, Joseph A. S.J. and Marjorie Hewitt Suchocki, ed. *Trinity in Process: A Relational Theology of God*. New York: Continuum Publishing Co., 1997.

Bultmann, Rudolph. *Jesus and the Word*. Trans. Louise Pettibone Smith and Erminie Huntress Lantero. New York: Charles Scribner's Sons, 1958.

Burrows, Millar. *Jesus in the First Three Gospels*. Nashville: Abingdon, 1977.

Carson, Rachael. *The Sense of Wonder*. New York: Harper & Row, 1987.

Charlesworth, James H. and Loren L. Johns. *Hillel and Jesus: Comparative Studies of Two Major Religious Leaders*. Minneapolis: Fortress Press, 1997.

Chilton, Bruce. *Rabbi Jesus*. New York: Image Books, 2000.

Cobb, John B. Jr. *Becoming a Thinking Christian*. Nashville: Abingdon Press, 1993.

_____. *Christ In A Pluralistic Age*. Eugene, Or: Wipf and Stock Publishers, 1998

_____. *Lay Theology*. St. Louis: Chalice Press, 1994.

_____ and David Ray Griffin. *Process Theology: An Introductory Exposition.* Philadelphia: Westminster Press, 1976.

Cole, Dwayne. *A Center That Holds: Adventures in Kindness.* Cleveland, Tennessee: Parson's Porch Books, 2015.

_____. *A Prayer of Blessing: As You Go Remember This.* Cleveland, Tennessee: Parson's Porch Books, 2015.

_____. *A Relational Trinity of Kindness.* Cleveland, Tennessee: Parson's Porch Books, 2015.

_____. *A Relational Hermeneutic of Kindness.* Cleveland, Tennessee. Parson's Porch Books, 2019.

_____. *God and Evil: An Ode to Kindness.* Cleveland, Tennessee. Parson's Porch Books, 2019.

_____. *Jesus' Transforming Beatitudes: Selected Sermons for Year A.* Cleveland, Tennessee: Parson's Porch Books, 2015.

_____. *Jesus' Transforming Love: Selected Sermons for Year B.* Cleveland, Tennessee: Parson's Porch Books, 2014.

_____. *Jesus' Transforming Gentle Teachings: Selected Sermons for Year C.* Cleveland, Tennessee: Parson's Porch Books, 2015.

_____. *The Apostles' Creed: A Living Creed for the Living Church.* Cleveland, Tennessee: Parson's Porch Books, 2014.

_____. *The Book of Revelation: Jesus' Kindness Transforms Suffering.* Cleveland, Tennessee: Parson's Porch Books, 2015.

_____. *The Serenity Prayer: A Pathway to Peace and Happiness.* Cleveland, Tennessee: Parson's Porch Books, 2015.

_____. *The Story of the Bible: Authority, Inspiration, Canonization, and Translation.* Cleveland, Tennessee: Parson's Porch Books, 2015.

_____. *Encounter: Bible Study for Adults.* Vol. 70, Number 4. Memphis: The Cumberland Presbyterian Board of Christian Education, 2003.

_____. *Encounter: Bible Study for Adults.* Vol. 78, Number 2. Memphis: The Cumberland Presbyterian Board of Christian Education, 2011.

_____. *Encounter: Bible Study for Adults.* Vol. 84, Number 4. Memphis: The Cumberland Presbyterian Board of Christian Education, 2017.

_____. "Jesus Prays for the Church: Sermon Preached at the General Assembly of the Cumberland Presbyterian Church," *The Cumberland Presbyterian Magazine*, 1998.

_____. "Taking the Pulse of the Universe," *The Cumberland Presbyterian*, January 2004.

_____. "Hermeneutical Theory in Transition as Reflected in Interpretation: A Journal of Bible and Theology." A Th. M. Thesis, The Southern Baptist Theological Seminary, Louisville, Ky., 1969.

_____. "Baptism and the Lord's Supper in the Gospel of John: A Hermeneutical Inquiry." A Ph. D. Dissertation, The Southern Baptist Theological Seminary. Louisville, Kentucky, 1973.

Cullman, Oscar. *Christology of the New Testament*. Philadelphia: Westminster Press, 1963.

Daley, B. *The Hope of the Early Church*. Cambridge: Cambridge University Press, 1991.

Darwin, Charles. *The Descent of Man*. New York: Modern Library, 1977

deSilva, David A. *Introducing the Apocalypse: Message, Context, and Significance*. Grand Rapids: Baker Academic. 2002.

Ehrman, Bart D. *Did Jesus Exist? The Historical Argument for Jesus of Nazareth*. New York: Harper One, 2012.

_____. *How Jesus Became God*. New York: Harper Collins Publishers, 2014.

Feuillet, A. *The Apocalypse*. Trans. T. E. Crane. New York: Alba House, 1965.

Ferrucci, Piero. *The Power of Kindness*. New York: Penguin Group, 2006.

Ford, Lewis S. *The Lure of God: A Biblical Background for Process Theism*.Philadelphia: Fortress Press. 1978.

_____. *Transforming Process Theism*. Albany: State University Press. 2000.

Frankl, Viktor E. *Man's Search for Meaning: An Introduction to Logotherapy*. Third Edition. New York: Simon & Schuster, 1984.

_____. *The Will to Meaning: Foundations and Applications of Logotherapy*. Expanded Edition. New York: Meridian, 1988.

Fridrichsen, Anton. *The Problem of Miracle in Primitive Christianity*. Trans. Roy A. Harrisville and John S. Hanson. Minneapolis: Augsburg Press, 1972.

Fromm, Erich. *The Art of Loving*. New York: Harper & Row, 1989.

Fuller, Reginald H. *The Foundations of New Testament Christology*. New York: Charles Scribner's Sons, 1955.

Funk, Robert W. *The Acts of Jesus: The Search for the Authentic Deeds of Jesus*. San Francisco: Harper Collins, 1998.

Funk, Robert W., Roy W. Hoover, and The Jesus Seminar, 1993. *The Five Gospels: The Search for the Authentic Words of Jesus*. New York: Macmillan, Polebridge Press.

Gibson, David and Michael McKinley. *Finding Jesus*. New York: St. Martin's Press, 2015.

Good, Deirdre J. *Jesus the Meek King*. Harrisburg: Trinity Press, 1999.

Hartshorne, Charles. *The Divine Relativity*. New Haven: Yale University Press, 1948.

Heacox, Kim. *John Muir: And the Ice That Started A Fire*. Guilford, Connecticut: Lyons Press, 2014.

Horsley, Richard, and John S. Hanson. *Galilee: History, Politics, People*. Pennsylvania: Trinity Press International, 1995.

Jacobovici, Simcha and Barrie Wilson. *The Lost Gospel*. New York: Pegasus Books, 2014.

Johnson, Elizabeth A. *She Who Is: The Mystery of God in Feminist Theological Discourse*. New York: Crossroad, 1994.

_____. *Truly Our Sister: A Theology of Mary in the Communion of Saints*. New York: Continuum, 2004.

Jones, Peter Rhea. *The Teachings of the Parables*. Nashville: Broadman Press, 1982.

Jung, C. G. *Archetypes and the Collective Unconscious*. B. F. C. Hull, translator. Bollingen Series XX. Princeton University Press, 1969.

_____. *Encountering Jung: On Evil*. Selected and Introduced by Murray Stein. Princeton: Princeton University Press. 1995.

Kaufman, Gordon D. *The Theological Imagination: Constructing the Concept of God*. Philadelphia: Westminster Press, 1981.

_____. *In Face of Mystery: A Constructive Theology*. Cambridge: Harvard University Press, 1993.

_____. *God, Mystery, Diversity*. Minneapolis: Fortress Press, 1996.

Keller, Ernst and Marie-Luise. *Miracles in Dispute*. Trans. Margaret Kohl. Philadelphia: Fortress Press, 1969.

Khalidi, Tarif. *The Muslim Jesus: Sayings and Stories in Islamic Literature*. Cambridge, MA: Harvard University Press, 1991.

Levine, Any-Jill. *The Misunderstood Jew: The Church and the Scandal of the Jewish Jesus*. San Francisco: Harper, 2006.

_____. *Short Stories by Jesus: The Enigmatic Parables of a Controversial Rabbi*. New York: Harper Collins, 2014.

Marxsen, Willi. *The Resurrection of Jesus of Nazareth*. Trans. Margaret Kohl. Philadelphia: Fortress Press, 1970.

McFague, Sallie. *Models of God*. Minneapolis: Augsburg Fortress, 1987.

_____. *The Body of God: An Ecological Theology*. Minneapolis: Augsburg Fortress, 1993.

Meier, John P. *A Marginal Jew: Rethinking the Historical Jesus*. 4 vols. New Haven: Yale University Press, 1991-2009.

King, Karen. *The Gospel of Mary of Magdala: Jesus and the First Woman Apostle*. Salem, Or: Polebridge Press, 2003.

Martin, James. *Jesus: A Pilgrimage*. New York: Harper One, 2014

Moule, C. F. D. ed. *Miracles*. New York: A. R. Mowbray & Co, LTD, 1965.

Muir, John. *The Story of My Boyhood and Youth*. San Francisco: Sierra Club Books, 1988.

Murphy, R. "An Allusion to Mary in the Apocalypse," *Theological Studies*, 2:565-73, 1949.

Nurbakhsh, Javad. *Jesus in the Eyes of the Sufis*. London: Khaniqahi Nimatullahi Publications, 1992.

Ogden, Shubert. *The Point of Christology*. San Francisco: Harper & Row, 1982.

Pagels, Elaine. Revelations: *Visions, Prophecy, & Politics in the Book of Revelation*. New York: Penguin Group. 2012.

_____. *The Gnostic Gospels*. New York: Random House, 1979.

Parini, Jay, *The Way of Jesus: Living a Spiritual and Ethical Life*. Boston: Beacon Press, 2018.

Perrin, Norman. *Rediscovering the Teaching of Jesus*. New York: Harper & Row Publishers, 1967.

_____. *The Kingdom of God in the Teaching of Jesus*. Philadelphia: Westminster Press, 1963.

Plato. *The Collected Dialogues of Plato Including the Letters*. Trans. Lane Cooper et al. Edited by Edith Hamilton and Huntington Cairns. Princeton: Princeton Press, 1961.

Pope Francis. *The Name of God Is Mercy.* Translator, Oonagh Stransky. New York: Random House, 2016.

Rohde, Joachim. *Rediscovering the Teaching of the Evangelists.* Trans. Dorothea M. Barton. Philadelphia: The Westminster Press, 1968.

Ruti, Mari. *The Summons of Love.* New York: Columbia University Press, 2011.

Schleiermacher, Friedrich. *On Religion: Speeches to Its Cultured Despisers.* New York: Harper & Row, 1958.

_____. *The Christian Faith.* Trans. H. R. MacKintosh and J. S. Stewart. 2 Vols. New York: Harper & Row, 1963.

Schmithals, Walter. *The Apocalyptic Movement.* John E. Steely, editor. Nashville: Abingdon Press, 1975.

Schurer, Emil. *A History of the Jewish People in the Time of Jesus Christ.* 3 vols. Edinburg: T & T Clark, 1890

Schweitzer, Albert. *Reverence for Life.* New York: Pilgrim Press, 1969.

_____. *The Quest for the Historical Jesus.* Trans. W. Montgomery. New York: Macmillan Publishing Co. 1968.

Selhub, Eva M. *The Love Response.* New York: Ballantine Books, 2009.

Stein, Robert H. *The Method and Message of Jesus' Teaching.* Revised Edition. Louisville: Westminster John Knox Press, 1994.

_____. *An Introduction to the Parables of Jesus.* Philadelphia: Westminster Press, 1981.

Suchocki, Marjorie Hewitt. *God Christ Church: A Practical Guide to Process Theology.* New Revised Edition. New York: The Crossroad Publishing Company, 1989.

_____. *The End of Evil: Process Eschatology in Historical Context.* Albany: State University, 1988.

_____. *in God's Presence: Theological Reflections on Prayer.* St. Louis: Chalice Press, 1996.

Tabor, James D. *The Jesus Dynasty.* New York: Simon & Schuster, 2006.

_____. *Paul and Jesus: How the Apostle Transformed Christianity.* New York: Simon & Schuster, 2012.

The Greek New Testament, Ed. Kurt Aland, Matthew Black, Carlo M. Martini, Bruce Metzger, and Allen Wikgren. Third Edition. United Bible Societies, 1975.

Thompson, Leonard L. *The Book of Revelation: Apocalypse and Empire*. New York: Oxford University Press. 1990.

Tobin, Thomas. "Logos," *The Anchor Bible Dictionary*, Vol. 4. New York: Doubleday, 1992.

Tournier, Paul. *The Violence Within*. Trans. Edwin Hudson. San Francisco: Harper & Row, 1978.

Wainwright, A. *Mysterious Apocalypse*. Nashville: Abingdon, 1993.

Whitehead, Alfred North. *Adventures of Ideas*. New York: The Free Press, 1967.

_____. *Process and Reality*. Corrected Edition, ed. David Ray Griffin and Donald W. Sherburne. New York: The Free Press, 1978.

_____. *Modes of Thought*. New York: The Free Press, 1968.

Wilson, Barrie. *How Jesus Became Christian*. New York: St. Martin's Press, 2008.

Wilson, E. O. *Biophilia*. Cambridge: Harvard University Press, 1984.

_____. The Future of Life. Vintage Books, 2002.

Weinberg, Steven. *The First Three Minutes: A Modern View of the Origin of the Universe*. Updated edition. New York: Basic Books, 1988.

Wink, Walter, *Engaging the Powers: Discernment and Resistance in a World of Domination*. Minneapolis: Fortress Press, 1992.

_____. *Naming the Powers: The Language of Power in the New Testament*. Philadelphia: Fortress Press, 1984.

_____. *Unmasking the Powers: The Invisible Forces that Determine Human Existence*. Philadelphia: Fortress Press, 1986.

Wright, N. T. *How God Became King: Getting to the Heart of the Gospels*. London: SPCK, 2011.

_____. *The Challenge of Jesus*. London: SPCK, 2000.

Zeitlin, Solomon. *Who Crucified Jesus?* New York: Bloch, 1964.

Other Books by Dwayne Cole

A Center that Holds: Adventures in Kindness.

A Prayer of Blessing: As You Go Remember This.

A Relational Hermeneutic of Kindness.

A Relational Trinity of Kindness.

God and Evil: An Ode to Kindness.

Jesus' Transforming Beatitudes: Selected Sermons from Year A.

Jesus' Transforming Love: Selected Sermons from Year B.

Jesus' Transforming Gentle Teachings: Selected Sermons from Year C.

The Apostles' Creed: A Living Creed for the Living Church.

The Book of Revelation: Jesus' Kindness Transforms Suffering.

The Serenity Prayer: A Pathway to Peace and Happiness.

The Story of the Bible: Authority, Inspiration, Canonization, and Translation.

www.ingramcontent.com/pod-product-compliance
Lightning Source LLC
Chambersburg PA
CBHW050200130526
44591CB00034B/1652